BY THEN I WAS THIRTEEN

" The great pity or shame is that though we all have a book in us, seldom does it come to fruition. Started perhaps, but not carried through to the end. So many people will relate to the times or events herein as if they were their own, or at least have an understanding of it all. Thus, you can laugh or cry or get involved to the end. Hopefully the sense of satisfaction for you in reading it is as great as it is for me having at last put it into words."

Derrick (Taffy) Rees

'By Then I was Thirteen'
First published in Australia by Lexington Avenue Pty Limited
31 Boundary Road Wahroonga, Sydney. 2076
Attention; Mr Tony Powell
Telephone 94899035 / 94896732
Email lexington@bigpond.com

National Library of Australia
Cataloguing-in-Publication data
Rees, Derrick 1924-
Autobiography
ISBN   0957739303

Printed by McPherson's Printing Group
Photographic Reproduction by Ron Jones Photography. Cammeray. Sydney

To be born Welsh

Is to be born Privileged.

Not with a silver spoon

In your mouth,

But music in your blood

And poetry in your soul.

INTRODUCTION

This is not a novel, there is no plot to take you through to a happy and well thought out conclusion. This is the story of my life. It comes from my heart. It is how it was and how it is. Truth really is stranger than fiction and so much more satisfying in the end. The whole thing may turn out to be a shambles going back and forth, repeating things and getting out of sequence till, like myself, you wonder if it is true? But read on, maybe it is.

Thirteen years old and that bad night before sailing out, a man already.

Like it or not and whatever schooling there had haphazardly been, was hardly worth the effort and thank God, [I thank him a lot without him seeming to take much notice], but thanks anyway for all the books and comics along the way as they were my main, and often only, education.

Unlike in real books where there are credits and nice words for everyone, the only ones to mention are Rhondda and Alan for giving me the outdated word processor with the sticky keys so as I could pick out, two fingered, the scribble of foolscap pages that even I have trouble reading.

I had a lousy machine with no colour and sticky keys. Then I lost a full book to Michaelangelo's virus and had to do it all again, so I hope for better luck this time, as even doing it once was traumatic. Nathan, my grandson is the one to thank or blame for this story reaching completion. With patience and great care, he nursed me through the old computer and new printer problems when I was ready to toss the whole lot, notes and all, out the bloody window.

My stack of short stories got me little or no feed back so they must be garbage. Spending so much time in my little cubbyhole at the back of the house is a worry. My good lady wife says if I don't stop and take her dancing or down to the beach swimming I'll be in serious trouble.

Just the same, thanks to all those who were part of it, good bad or like the cottage mother at No.2 Church Homes, bloody awful.

An apology; It is for any of the Welsh language I may use in my over 60 odd years recall of events. Inside my head it is true Gymraig but the spelling may have gone awry.

PROLOGUE

It was April 1938, just up from the docks at Southampton, so much happening it was all getting a bit too much and the build up of emotion and tension inside of me must have set it all off.

"Big boys don't cry."

"What a heap of shit," I thought as it finally got the better of me and bloody nearly in tears already and then in a proper stew for it happening to me. "How the hell would they know?"

Just because someone, well intentioned I suppose but without a clue how a kid really felt, pats you on the head, [don't you hate it when they do that] and says something dumb and condescending like, "There's a big man we are." On top of it all, that would make you cry and just when you thought you had it under control.
They were the right words I suppose, platitudes, but I reckon coming from half of them, as in some of the places we had been in so often it was more than likely a "Glad to be rid of you," sort of thing.

That's how it was with me then. A big boy having turned thirteen and when the reality of what you'd done, or were doing, really hits you and every thought comes rushing in as you lie on the big strange bed, in a hotel with another boy on the other side of the bed with problems of his own.
There were clean sheets and lots of pillows. There was carpet all over and no need for a pot, with a loo down the hall. Near the fancy lamp to read by and not ruin your eyes, was a big bowl of fruit and near the door the huge brown case full of more new clothes than you'd had in a lifetime. It made you wonder if the bed, the bowl of fruit and everything there was real because on the side of the case was your name, Derrick R. Rees and the address a Northcote Children's Farm School at a Bacchus Marsh place in Victoria.

You think about it all and you cry like a bloody sook.
So boys do cry, big or little.

There were 28 of us in the same boat, not in the boat yet, just in the hotel before going aboard in the morning. We were 16 boys and 12 girls, girls who are allowed to cry but just to be different, just sobbed for whoever it was they were missing. My two sisters were OK at about 8 and 10 years of age and grown up enough to go along with things. Having each other to hold in the bed big enough to hold all our family, they soon dropped off. In the boys rooms, two or three to a room instead of the big dormitory, we had our private mixed up thoughts of anticlimax after days and weeks of the excitement that had built up.

Believe me I was older and brought up rough, so if I cried, so did they and there was none of that, 'Big man' stuff. All the fun and promise of the big boat and a new land would have gone down the drain if a mum or dad or any sort of friend had showed up right then.

A funny thing about the other boy sharing a bed and whom I'd not really got to know yet. He didn't give a damn, just sat and ate half the fruit in the bowl, went to bed and played with himself as he dropped off. Funny bugger I thought and he never cried either!

Strangely enough, as we saw the littlies to bed, some only six years old or so, never having had it so good in their short forgettable lives, they only needed a reassuring pat and a smile from us as we tucked them in. They seemed to trust and accept us as family, which in the coming months and years is exactly as it was to be.

Slipping into their own little land of Nod on their last night in good old England, things were looking up as whatever happened on the morrow had to be an improvement on what had gone on before.

The events of my life to me seem fairly ordinary, surely everyone has a story of similar interest to tell.

Somehow my friends and family always listen with interest as my memory recalls my youthful days which cover so much time and space.

The fascination of the early days seems to increase over the years as further events unfold. It seems the telling is not boring, on the contrary, everybody without fail says, "Write it down".

It was my good friend and solicitor Kevin McGregor from Beecroft who, having heard about our weird family and its events, insisted I jot down little things as they come to mind.

Everyone has read or should read, 'A Fortunate Life' by A.B.Lacey. A story of an Australian boy and his fascinating tales of Aussie life.

It was an inspiration to me to make a start. I do believe, as Kevin suggests, it could be just as interesting in its way if and when completed. From the paragraphs I've already written and it being a true story, I am certain there will be many a smile and most certainly many a tear as the tale unfolds.

Fremantle, as our initial step ashore in Australia was the end of one lot and almost the beginning of another. I say almost because in the next few days through the Great Australian Bight, every man and boy wished to die in the horrific seas that scoured six weeks of gluttonous living out of us all, till it was in past Point Nepean, Port Philip Bay and into Melbourne at unbelievable last.

The past was now nothing, the old country deserved not a thought as the 120 degree heat of the greatest drought imaginable, where everything went up in smoke or blew away in red dust and we, like it or not, a part of it.
This was the new beginning! Was it? Where were the golden beaches, the beautiful birds, the Kangaroos and those little Teddy Bears even?
It was nothing like I had dreamed of or what we'd seen on those slide nights back in Treforest and for just a brief moment there was the thought I'd got it all wrong! I would wake up from one of those nightmares I sometimes had and all this would slip away like the fantasies on the hillside at the Cottage Homes used to do.

'Brown', that was the colour from Port Melbourne right out to Bacchus Marsh, then way out to Glenmore. A brown, dry and arid endless expanse with blobs packed under strange trees. The blobs were sheep, mostly dead and in the heat haze like mirage all around, the earth and all its parts seemed to move. The movement, as we soon enough discovered, was a billion skin and bone, mangy fur rabbits. Rabbits with nothing left to chew but who as their instinct dictated, bred on and on as only rabbits could.
The 'Marsh' as we were to know it, was the magic and almost mythical place I'd dreamt of for so long. Bacchus Marsh, where the whole township fed lemonade and cakes to the little pioneers who in a short time would bring fresh, new life to the district.

Dedication.

To Lady Alice. S. Northcote, D.B.E., S.I. [Star of India], Lady of Grace, Order of St John of Jerusalem. Wife of Australia's third Governor General.

Baron and Lady Northcote had no children of their own.

This is an extract of a letter to Mr Harold Luxton, later Sir Harold.

Compton Place.
Eastbourne.
May 17th 1932.

It is my intention to create a fund by my will, for the purpose of assisting the emigration of children from England to Australia and of maintaining them on arrival till employment can be found for them.

Signed, A.S. Northcote.

Lady Alice died 1st June 1934.

It Had All Begun.

Inspired by Rhodes Scholar Kingsley Fairbridge and his work at Pinjarra Western Australia, the dream Lady Alice had to assist children such as I, was becoming a reality.

The Lady Northcote Farm School, in the years to come, was to assure this gracious Lady, the love and eternal thanks of the children arriving at Glenmore, to their new home and assured bright future.

Note;

The 2850 acres at Glenmore, was donated by Sir William Angliss, himself a migrant in 1884. It was he who welcomed us to this, our and his, chosen land of opportunity.

Derrick and Dad, outside 123 Primrose Street, Tonypandy.

1

* Rhondda Boy *

'The Rhondda', the old Welsh spelling was Rhontha, or so I am told.
Well into the nineteenth century, the Rhondda was to change into the
enormous mining and industrial area the whole world associates it with.
Perhaps it's better known as my South Wales of, 'How Green Was My
Valley' countryside.

It is difficult to visualise it as it was back then. The beauty of the verdant
pastures surrounded by the splendid mountains, which the tourists are
only now rediscovering after a horrid one hundred and fifty years.

Yes! One hundred and fifty years of the living hell, the search for and the
mining of the 'Black Diamond', coal. This and the steel industry, which
logically followed, was a period to last to the 21st December 1990, a
Friday, when the last pit in the Rhondda was to close.

It was opened in 1875 and its closing was the end of an era never likely
to be seen again in man's time.

My forebears were part, I should imagine, of the sparse population in the
lower Rhondda where the farms were well scattered and the towns or
villages few and quite remote.

The census taken in 1801 showed only hundreds in each area. The
farmers and merchants were served by mills at Pandy and Dinas or Nant
Clydach, near Tonypandy.

The Glamorgan Canal from Aberayron to Cardiff via Treforest was
opened in 1794. The canal was always a favourite for the boys of
Treforest and all around. It is in the canal where the great factories
poured out gallons of hot water, where even in winter the water was
warm just down from the outlet and a favourite spot. Even with the worry
of the globules of warm tar because when a blob hit you it spread all over
turning you into a horrible mess.

The expansion of industry in the Rhondda when the folk were truly
Welsh and quite successful as farmers, tradesfolk or merchants, caused a
great social and cultural advancement. Wales was really the land of

poetry and song in those days. Chapels overflowed and the Eisteddfod a source of constant conversation and interest with its poetry and song.

The proportion of males of working age, 12 years and over and working in the mines, was 70%. It can be seen why coal dust was in our blood and how soon, every family lost their share of loved ones to the industry we grew to curse.

In the years after the riots of 1910-11 and up to World War 2, thousands of Welsh families, dads or just kids, moved out to migrate to foreign shores.

Doreen and Yvonne, Bernard and I became part of the statistics of that exodus. We left our homeland because of wretched conditions and circumstances. The story shows what a blessing the move was to become for us. We had only lost the early years, there was still time for a new start in a new country.

All of us, Pommies, Wogs, Migrants and Welshman, love Australia and no one is more proud to be an Aussie than I.

I've been called a Pommie bastard, I'm told I'm as thick as a Welsh plank. I've worked in the bush and in the 'Big Smoke'. My trip round the whole coast of Australia in a caravan, the first time for six months and then for twelve months, qualifies me to say as the popular song says, "I've been everywhere man".

It's 61 years since the 'T.S.S. Largs Bay' put me ashore in this country, the place I personally chose as my home, the home of my children and my grandchildren. I can swear it's true that I dreamt and fantasised of such a land of sunshine while up in the ferns, on a hill in Wales, desperate for warmth and security.

As an expatriate, it seems I think more of my homeland than those left behind. It is my good fortune to still have my home back there but this is the home of my choice and allegiance. We should all owe allegiance to the country from whence we derived our infant nurture. Come to think of it, there was never a lot of that around but that's the way it was!

The nationalistic way of the Welsh is more evident than other British. We have our songs and poetry, Bards and a few Saints, all important to us as we sing, 'The Land of our Fathers'. It's always with a smile we claim to be the original Britons but it is true never the less, ask any Welshman, he'll fight to prove it.

When my wife and I went back to Britain in 1972, it was to visit and re-establish family. To search out family history and hopefully to find out if we were Bastard Welsh or from good old stock there before the drastic invasion of every nationality in the century to come when coal was all that mattered. There were farmers and trades people, perhaps a minister or two for good measure.

Some of us must have been tradesmen as the family motto is, 'Spes Mellioris Aevi', which appropriately means, 'Hope for a better age.' It is on the family crest, which shows a Lion rampant, holding a Plum Bob. The 'better age' bit certainly came about, while the plumb bob is regularly used by myself, my son and my grandson, all of us plumbers, builders and shoplifters, sorry! 'Shopfitters.' Dad, of course, was also a carpenter of sorts.

Like the Irish, the Welsh are fighters, just for the fun of it, on the rugby field or in times of war when called to arms in the name of the Crown. The Scots play their bagpipes going into battle, the Welsh sing and prove to be the best of fighting men.

Most of us have seen the movie, 'Zulu' and felt goose pimples in the battle of 'Rorks Drift' when 'Men of Harlech' was sung by the men and boys from the hills and valleys of Wales as they went in to battle. In that fierce conflict, we were awarded eleven Victoria Crosses, the highest award possible. I stood proudly on my visit to Carnarvon Castle where the medals are kept to this day so that all can stop awhile and ponder. It is there of course that our Princes of Wales are invested.

As the coal fields opened up far and wide, so started the invasion of those seeking work. Hordes of Irish and their families, Spaniards, Yorkshiremen, Cornishmen and all the others.

Our heritage was soon endangered but the true Welsh still went to Chapel three times on Sunday, all dressed in their very best. Religion was at a peak and the singing helped keep it that way.

It is said, so must be true, that when Dai Morgan sang flat in the final of the big Eisteddfod and they lost, he was banished to Canada.

Welsh history is not well known but is said to have started in the early days A.D. when Osterius Scapula, a Roman General invaded Flintshire. We know it began a thousand years before and even before the days of the Celts.

St David is our patron Saint of Wales. A visit to St David's Cathedral is a must, the architecture of the Cathedral is not only beautiful but also breath taking in the thoughts of its so early conception.

The records of the early days mention the rivers Taff and Rhondda as being clean fresh streams full of trout, minnows and gudgeons for little boys to catch. So different to the black, oily looking sewers and drains they have become. As the only water supply for so many people, to drink it was almost certain disease and death. This is evident by the thousands who perished in the unsanitary conditions.

The Rhondda once flowed fresh and clear, down from Dunraven St and where Riverview was to be. The Rees clan have No.'s 6 and 7 but it was only tiny No.6 when my Dad and his many brothers and sisters were born.

At the end of Riverview, just about the bend in the river, is where the original slaughterhouse for the district was. The discharge of refuse into the river was no problem as there was no other pollution and nature managed to cope, in fact the fish were fat and plentiful round by there.

In 1917, the Earl of Dunraven sold it to Mr Stockwell and then in 1939 it was finally closed after being such an important part of Tonypandy's life. We are all pleased it was closed because by the time Cousin Angie met Mick and they had time to settle down and raise sufficient funds. It became available and today they have a lovely bungalow with landscaping down the riverbank and a beaut spot for the geese and chickens to run around.

Though the traffic on the once undreamt of new bridge may upset them, the ghosts of yesteryear must be glad to see the scene has become peaceful once more as the hills slowly turn back from pit black to the green of yore.

My youth had left little time for impressions of early days, only for survival. By reading of times around the eighteenth century, I have gained firm and positive impressions of the valleys.

The demand for coal and steel began tearing the country apart and in the 150 years to come everyone was caught up in the need and greed for wealth.

I discovered the fascinating time of Pack-muling and rafting, about barging and the flat boats on the canal. What incredible times of hardship and endurance. The canals were as busy as our roads are today with over loaded barges being pulled and manoeuvred by horse or mule, any animal available, helped of course by any family member with an ounce of strength to work.

Each poor beast strained day after day along the well-worn tow path, giving faithful service till the day it finally dropped and died. Who could show pity? Not the barge master, for him it was keep up the pressure or lose the job, and the family soon starved. It was dog eat dog, the Irish called us Welsh scum, and we called them Irish bastards. We were all on a pittance that could never feed or clothe the children for survival to teenage years.

Enough has been said about the iron masters of Tonypandy, the coal masters and the exploitation. Cheap labour was readily available. Irish in droves, tin miners from Cornwall, others from Lancashire, Yorkshire and Staffordshire, all after jobs. It was work or starve with families waiting around in hope. Relief or the Dole was unheard of and soup kitchens or food queues were years away in the future.

The coal masters capitalised on the labour situation and put them to work underground by the thousands. It was a seventy hour week @ a shilling a ton. Most children were down the mine by age ten but history shows that six and eight year olds were used in three and four foot seams of coal.

Accommodation was vital, the building boom of all time occurred as the masters built the row after row of terraces we see still being used today. These were built almost at the pithead to save time travelling but as demand grew these terraces soon extended for miles around. Though stark and bare, with little or no furnishings, these buildings were rented to the workers. With the rent and the cost of food and supplies from the master's store, the indebtedness grew week by week to only be settled at death's last call.

This was usually long before old age, as the deteriorating sanitary conditions were appalling and so sadly the kids went first. No need to further mention the Typhoid, Cholera and Smallpox epidemics of the times.

Unionism needed to come to the fore and in those early days many a martyr gave his all, meaning his life, for what he believed. It was early days but we owe thanks for the excellent conditions we whinge about, but never satisfied with today, to those who started the movement. Maybe in the demand for excessive conditions, our leaders are becoming the masters of the time.

So in the last years of the century the worst seems to be coming to an end. Not quite, but at this time, William meets Margaret, there is a courtship and a lovely Chapel marriage before they went as a couple to Riverview overlooking the river and the valley.

'Hope for a better age' the motto says and I suppose with this hope, they started the family.

2

* Getting Ready To Leave *

The 28 of us, as the second party chosen to travel to Australia as part of the mass migration of children of the time, had left Middlemore homes in Birmingham after a tedious and extended stay.

Doreen, Yvonne and I had said goodbye to Hubert from Merthyr and Rex from Cardiff, the ones we met in Wales way back before Xmas and who we came to know so well in Middlemore. God willing we would see them again in the near future when they followed us out in the next party of kids. We wanted to be together on the farm especially Hubert and I, as we had already planned to start a horse ranch.

We had said our goodbyes way back last year to Mum, to little Bernard and Myrna, plus half of King St, Treforest and all the many friends we never realised we had. The excitement in our little village was a major event, some said it was the Antipodes we were going to but where we were heading was a mythical place called Australia.

At the hotel and on the trip down to London and then Southampton we all assessed each other and quickly sorted out a pecking order essential to such a mob as we were and for the difficult time ahead on the six weeks it would take on the 'T.S.S. Largs Bay', to get to Australia.

Our parents, singular or plural if they were still around or, if neither, the cottage mothers in a home or for some kids the Father or Sister in a convent. None would have known us.

The girls were so smart, all dressed up, all looking the same but very nice and so clean. The boys you wouldn't believe in their shorts, white shirts and tie, jacket, long socks and real leather shoes. The only time I'd had it so good was in the 'Homes' when charity did us all up so we looked good in church.

Everything we now had, and all that was going on, was courtesy of the Lady Alice Northcote who we didn't as yet have a clue about but she was really something or someone if she had enough dough to pay for all this and a boat like the 'Largs Bay' to take us away in.

There was an impatient wait just hanging around anxious to get to the dockside and our first glimpse of our boat. Some of the kids were a bit of a pain with their repetitious;

Taffy was a Welshman, Taffy was a thief
Taffy came to my house and stole a leg of beef
I went to Taffy's house, Taffy was in bed
So I picked up a rolling pin and hit him on the head.

It was funny at first but got damned monotonous after a while so I sorted a few of them out. As the 'Big Kid', I sort of pulled rank and let them know who was who and that there was still someone in charge.

Those words of the song must have been written by some Englander who was jealous of we Welsh as the original Britons. As Wesley or St Tydfil had said, 'God's chosen people.'

As it was an unbelievable day, sunshine and getting hot, a good omen and we were as happy as ever we had been. Breakfast had been a miracle of eggs and bacon, sausages and toast with thick butter and lots of jams. We had real milk, as much as you could get into you and fruit to fill the pockets of the jackets for afters. The room where we ate was real posh, doilies and silver and with things in fancy glass dishes and special knives instead of digging in with a messy buttery knife and mucking it all up.

Our big cases went off in a van as we all pointed out which one was ours. We each had little in the way of private things, just a little box or parcel. I had my biscuit tin full of marbles. They were to sell to the kids over there in and around Bacchus Marsh, so I could win them back and sell them again and again.

I thought I was rich already because before we left home in Treforest there was a new coin minted. It was a twelve sided threepenny piece, ten sides round the edges and a head and tail. They looked like gold when new and everyone got the same idea and gave them to us as souvenirs or keepsakes. "Keep them", they said, "they won't have them in Australia and you can sell them and make money." Besides them, I had nearly two pounds that I had saved and hidden away from Mum and the others. I never did get the money Mum owed me from collecting the wood every night at Tonteg.

It was a long walk till, all hot and sweaty, done up in our new outfits like a lot of 'Toffs', we went up the gangplank.

Everyone made a fuss of the, 'Brave little new pioneers' and in no time at all, with all the excitement, the boat slipped away.

Just as well there was no time to think that there was never a relative or friend from either England, Scotland, Ireland or Wales. We were a mixture, none of us could understand the others accents, there was one or more of us from each of those places and we all left England behind, maybe for ever! English or whoever, who now cares?

There was one who came, a lady and she rushed up as we were going up to the boat. Not really a gangplank or she would have knocked the kid off into the water. We all stopped to look round to see who had the visitor, none of us surprised or disappointed at no one turning up for us. We didn't expect it I suppose.

She was grabbing at the other Derek in our party of 28 and it's funny I thought she looked to me like a Tart instead of a mum and as we watched, it was over real quick. She gave him a hug and a kiss and must have been a mum because she took out a hanky, spat on it and wiped the stuff off Derek's chin. I bet she even told him to be a good boy.

She gave him the big teddy bear she was holding, kissed him and was gone.

It was a stupid present for a big kid of eight and useless to cart out to a place where there were real bears and it somehow soon disappeared. Derek told me later about a little sister back in the orphanage place they had lived in. He never ever heard of her again, nor of his mum. That was it, one of the many who never showed up ever again.

We landed at Fremantle and were let off for a days outing in May of 1938. It had been six weeks and I had just one penny left and it wasn't a real one as it had, 'One Penny' on one side Australian like. All those threepenny bits with twelve sides and my two pounds, were long gone on sweets and rubbish in the six weeks of reckless spending through the Mediteranean, down through the Suez canal and Columbo and places where ice creams were a must.

With my penny, we walked up in the heat to the little shipping town to the store where I bought an icecream. There, on and in this strange land, making a new start, I was pennyless.

It didn't matter a bit and I didn't give a shit. Sorry, we had been told to act like little gentleman now and not swear. We were also told that this was 'God's own country', but by the look of Fremantle on that day, in the heat and with the flies, he'd forgotten to finish it.

22

3

* As a two year old in Tonypandy *

My Dad, William Richard, was one of thirteen born to William and Mam Rees. Our Mamgu was an angel of care and understanding, not only to hers but also to all others in and around her Tonypandy.

The only photo of any of we children up to the time we left is the one of Dad and I, he in the standard flannel shirt, waistcoat and pants and what looks like slippers. I, a fat, knobbly kneed two-year-old standing outside No.123, one of the many houses all the same in our Primose St, Tonypandy.

For me, it all started in the Llwynapia hospital across the way and along from Pandy Square itself and up from the Glamorgan pit with its history of disaster for all the valley folk.

Irrespective of everything, you love your parents as I did till the day they passed away at almost eighty years of age and within a month of each other, neither knowing the other had gone. Though 12,000 miles apart, it was a lifetime apart in a way.

They had been married at St Thomas' church in Goole Yorkshire. Later, as if in a 'damn you' or a 'bless you' frame of mind to resolve, compensate or whatever for the past, I placed an inscribed plaque for them together in my wife's family plot at the St Thomas' church at Enfield, and that's another time I cried. I also swore at them for being such stupid damn people but at the same time felt at peace I suppose you could say, because like it or not, they were together at last. "Try and separate now," was perhaps my bittersweet thought.

I never really blamed them for their shortcomings, excusing all the times that took us apart and instead generally I blamed the times and the economy for all that took place. They had both made it damned hard for we kids but now, what the hell!

What I'm going to write is not going to upset them or any other folk as they have mostly gone to the non depression times, valley in the sky.

These pages may have the nitty-gritty, just as it was at the time thing and may touch a tender spot but, as the old scribbled notes come out of the case, it will all emerge as the truth it is and now, having said that and in a bit of a stew again, the hard part is where to start.

My dad was born almost at the turn of the century, 10th May 1899, so it's easy to remember his age and birthday, not that birthdays meant much to us. Presents were a non-event too and he was seldom or rarely around to do much about them anyway. When he did turn up each time it was little things but mostly a pocket full of sweets for us and half the kids in the street. It seemed he needed to prove to everyone, he was a good Dad.

Dad's mother, Mam Rees, [Our grandmother] in Riverview St with more on her plate than anyone I knew and with kids and grandkids turning up all over the place, remembered birthdays and knew when and where each child was born. Mamgu was a toughie, it is said that she had thirteen children. There was a Garfield who died early or at birth so next year, quite undeterred, there was another Garfield. There is no Uncle by that name so he must have gone too.

While at Treforest the girls got presents from Mr Price next door. Our Dad, not being round regular like, Pricy sort of filled in for him.

As the older one and thinking I was the only one to check it out, knowing even at that stage about dirty old men, I found old Pricy to be a lovely old man who just found pleasure in having fresh young folk around, giggly and stupid as they mostly were.

So much about the early days or times in Llwynapia or Yorkshire will come out sooner or later. In Howden, even before Goole I was just somehow there after leaving my valley in Wales. Douglas and sister Betty were there, Betty was always in Yorkshire, never got to Wales with us, so strange till we got to know about the Aunt Mathews bit. We were to learn that Doug was not Welsh either having been born in Scotland, Edinburgh of all places and while Dad was in the R.A.F. there.

All that mystery stuff is to come, the Aunt Athelia Mathews involvement, the living in strange and alien counties and countries, it was a bit much for little kids to worry about. The mum and Aunt Mathews saga was going to be enough to try to comprehend in the near future but we would be back in that part of the world often enough to figure some of it out.

Howden is possibly my first memory of Dad and I can clearly remember the morning, cold, wet and miserable but as with the English, acceptable in the excitement of what was a world famous event. [We didn't realise it then.]

Dad dragged Doug and I along by the hand as we hurried at daybreak to Howden Aerodrome with everyone from miles around to see the launching of the R101 Airship. [There were two, the R101 and 2]. Our Dad, as ex Air Force, knew someone and we got to get in close. Aunt

Mathews was heavily involved with the inventor Barry Wallace, as she had been station mistress at the 'drome' for some time. It is he who was to become famous in time to come for inventing the bomb for use by the Dam Busters in W.W.2. Karl was there at the time too and he invented the Graf Zeppellin. Our Aunt was invited by him to the launch of Hindenburg in Germany, where she would have again met Amy Johnson who married Hindenburg.

I was proud of Dad at that time, a pity I was too young to appreciate it all but I do recall it was nice and cosy afterwards back at our Aunt's house having breakfast together. Mum and Dad, we three kids and our prim and proper bossy aunt for once not picking on Dad and calling him Welsh scum as she was want to do so often.

He was never in Yorkshire with us again after that time and never saw Betty again. I know that when we left London to come back here the last time, Dad went back to the pits or somewhere and was never to see Douglas again. Can you believe it, his first born and the baby he boasted about winning every beautiful baby contest Mum entered him in, yet he never saw him again. So weird and incomprehensible that neither he nor Douglas made the effort. As far as I found out, Betty, as the daughter Mum had before she and Dad met and who he loved and cared for up to the time he left Yorkshire, never saw him make the effort to see her either.

How could a parent be that way? Not see or find out if they were alright. 'God?' and the thought of it now still boggles the mind. "How could it be?"

So we went back to Tonypandy in Wales, not to Mam Rees as she had enough to manage, we were well out of Primrose St and not yet in Cambrian terrace. Doreen must have been around then but in the moving around, being in and living with different people, Dad out of the mines and also out of work, it was a rotten mixed up time thereabouts for a few forgettable years. Douglas was there a while, but not long before he was soon gone for good.

I suppose that if I was four or five by then it would make it 1928 or 9 and that would have to be about the worst time in the century for anyone, let alone the folk in the Rhondda valleys with the terrible conditions imposed by the coal and iron masters in those depression days. The book, 'Rape of a Fair Country', tells of the steel master Crawshay who built his Cyfarthfa Castle up Merthyr Tydfil way where the Glamorgan canal was and where the barges took his steel into the heart of Cardiff.

It was a time of exploitation when typhoid, cholera and smallpox were as rife as the flu today, a time when whole families were gone without a trace.

4

* Cambrian Terrace, Llwynapia *

Then somehow, we were back in South Wales and in Cambrian Terrace, Llwynapia, the last street up the hill from where Archibald Hood's statue was to stand in his honour as the philanthropic do-gooder of the time.

While he may have built the row after row of terraces for cheap housing he made a fortune from them and the cheap labour of the tenants in debt to him for life. Nothing seems to have been done since.

Our street of terraced houses was a run down hellhole of damp, smelly and unhygienic disaster and not too far removed from the cholera and such of earlier days.

From the little window at the front, could be seen a haze of fog and mist over a valley losing itself in slag heaps, choking itself in lung destroying coal dust and fumes. Out the back, our lane was just a few feet wide and would never fit a car if anyone ever got one. The doors all opened right on to the lane, across was a stone wall covered in weeds and nettles. It was just high enough to make you miss if you emptied the piss pot over it instead of dumping it in the W.C., as we ought to.

There were a couple of them, lavatories, W.C.'s, or shit houses as everyone justifiably called them, so why not we kids too. They were derelict, leaky structures, pneumonially drafty with a wooden seat fit only to stand on for big jobs over the cracked and brownstained pan.

Everyone in the terrace used the 'lavs' day and night and all the piss pots not surreptitiously tossed over the wall were tipped down the hole to seep away somewhere. The warm, sickly smell in our sometime summer or the stink on a wafty foggy morning still comes to haunt me when I dare to recall or think of the place.

At the top of the wall in a football sized area before you came to the woods, was the rubbish tip. An accumulation of rubbish and waste, sardine cans and such, broken prams and bikes, wheels with spokes to stick into kids bare feet, everything there of no further use even to us.

We played there most days and half the night in the weak sun of summer or anytime we were told to go out and play in bare feet and chilblains as there were rarely any hand me down boots at Cambrian.

Dad was there for awhile and as I think of it, it's the good times you remember best. It must have been spring as the dead trees had buds and little green leaves. Hazelnut trees were pointed out to look for later when the nuts were ripe. Up from the slagheaps there were flowers in rebellion on the hillside with a brave splash of colour.

We climbed the mountain, Dad carried Doreen as we, all together, Mum and Dad, Doreen and I did it for the first time as a family.

Dad took time to tell us stuff about the Pit and the strikes of 1910-11 when police on horse back rode down Dunraven St bashing at the strikers, some of them former workmates. The history was fascinating but not for us on such a happy day.

Up the top among the ferns after passing the early glades of bluebells, we had our picnic as Dad pointed out in the distance what he said was Barry or Cardiff or somewhere.

We never realised there and then, that except for a brief spell to come at Tonteg when Dad and I would have some time together, it was the only time we did it all together. Mum only did her walking pushing a pram or hawking the big basket of blackberries, both of those events yet to come.

Sadly Douglas wasn't there either, he was back with our Aunt. I wished he was with us then, a time I needed a big brother most.

Uncle Dai, [A real uncle] told tales of collecting the nuts from where we had been, it was up past Gelli farm on Gilfach mountain. It's where the wimberries were he used to pick for his Mam to make pies and tarts. He told of the cottage loaves of bread with the golden top crust he pulled off to smother in home made butter and jam.

We never had homemade butter, just 'drippin' and salt. I threw in the home made butter bit as it sounded so good but the jams were truly home made and put on thick, were a treat.

In Llwynapia and Tonypandy it seemed it was for a long time and with a lot of memories. Doug was missing, as was Dad half the time. The times he was back were special like the Xmas I recall most and the time when all the men on the dole dug the swimming pool.

Cambrian was where we lived with the Sparrows but I can't remember Mr Sparrow, like my Dad, he too was missing. It was a share everything place, Doreen slept with Mum, Clifford and I had the top room to share. We slept together in an old iron bed to share the shortage of blankets and mostly used old overcoats and clean coal sacks to keep out the damp as we cuddled together for the warmth and company to survive.

I started school from Cambrian, the school being only a few streets away. It may sound strange in the telling but in my confusion and at a tender age, [Tender, that's a laugh as I was never that I'm sure], the exact times are a vague blur because in those five to six year old years, I started school on three occasions. New schools were my great speciality.

It was once here, once in London and once in Howden, Yorkshire as the moves around the country came quickly, one after the other.

The start at Cambrian was the absolute worst start of all and a disaster for any little kid but worse for me as I had to get home alone, which I did to find there was no one there and I had to clean myself up with cold water from the tap outside in the lane. It is the only water supply we all had and everyone used it to fill pots, kettles or buckets or rinse out the 'poe'. I left a mess as I tried to rinse out my shitty pants and giving up in despair, tried to bury them up the back in the tip. Doreen will confirm this, as it was Mum who told her of my burying the pants.

What happened was that at school the first day and as the new kid, the poorest looking, scaredy-cat kid, I was hassled and teased till trying not to give in and cry, I shit myself.

Teachers in those days of tough times had little sympathy for such events or even the sight of it running down my leg and told me to get myself home and clean up.

Hardly five, the new, second hand shorts mucked up and the mess down as far as the elastic holding up the socks on the skinny legs as I snuck home by the back streets where no one would see me and laugh as I got to Cambrian terrace.

Nothing was locked, nothing worth pinching in those days, but nobody home anyway. Mum was off somewhere, probably at a ladies get-together reading teacups and it was Clifford, home off shift at the pit who came and fixed me up. He was just up from digging coal, miles down under and was as black the coal itself. Only the eyes were clear but he fixed me up first before himself, as he was my special friend.

5

* Clifford Sparrow *

Clifford Sparrow was only a kid but by valley and pit standards, old enough to start work down the mine. There was years between us, we both missed our dads and though just a boy he had to be old enough to become the breadwinner so it was 'ready or not' and down in the cage for him.

In the history of the mines in the valleys it really is true that children much younger, even eight year olds, went down to spend the full shift in the pitch black for the few pence that was vital for a family to survive. Often Mum and Dad had shifts of their own and with no one at home to care for the little ones, so it was perhaps the only way to go!

I used to get up, even in the dark to see him off. In our musty but cold little room I would watch in silence as he pulled on his stiff old pants and grey flannel vest, everything was the traditional miner's dress of the day. Cast off suit coat with one button or tied around with string, a once white silk or other scarf in shades of grey tied round the neck with the pride of being a miner and the real, second hand or good boots, a priority.

Even at five o'clock the fire would be lit by his mam and there was tea and toast. His box was ready with its bread and cheese for the long shift ahead and we would see him off with the all others stepping out from doorways, looking up at the sky to perhaps see what they were going to miss all day and then stoically setting off in the freezing cold.

It was like that on his first day and I missed him like all hell.

Then there was the last day, almost too difficult even now to bring back to mind and write down on paper because down at the Glamorgan mine, where the cages had gone down and the workers had spread out, there was the explosion that all valley folk fear and dread by night and by day. It was all a blur and a befuddlement of events, not for such as I to report on or try to describe, but Clifford never came home.

I had the empty room to myself, all the blankets and coats, all the rotten stinking bed, just to myself. Even the comic books we read over and over till we knew each one by heart. I left them there to fade with no one around to share the stupid adventures.

All of it just left and it was somehow a relief that we soon moved out of there for happier places.

This poem was not written for my Clifford, it is by Anonymous but it is surely meant for just such as he.

A YOUNG LADS FIRST DAY IN THE MINE.

It's a quarter to five, my mother would say,
I wish I could stay here for the rest of the day.

So it's down to the table for toast and jam,
The fire is lit, thank God for Mam.

I slip on my coat and get ready to freeze,
While Mam fills my box with my bread and my cheese.

The miners go by with their hob nailed boots,
The hooter blows with three short, sharp hoots.

Into the lamproon I go, with knees all a tremble,
While old men and boys, by the cage they assemble.

As we get to the bottom from the light of the day,
An old man shouts out; "Hey son come this way."

"Pass me the mandrill," the old man would say,
"There's nowhere to go, your here for the day."

The old man works on with his sad old eyes,
With lungs filled with dust and a throat that's so dry.

He knows where he'll be in a twelve months time,
On a bench on a hill on a road nearby.

The shift has ended, we're back in the cage,
I'm thinking of cawl with its onions and sage.

We walk up the hill now, oh so slow,
Old Tom walks behind us, he's sixty you know.

As I walk up the hill, I think of my grub,

And the welcoming water that waits in the tub.

As I walk up the stairs, with sleep in my eyes,
I jump into bed and give one little sigh.

If I must work there from a young small lad,
I hope God don't take me like Grandsha and Dad.

A Rhondda Boy.

6

* Early Days In The Rhondda Valley *

There was always something going on to entertain kids, especially ones on the loose who could do as they pleased, sort of back lane kids. Voting or Election Day was fun, we wished it was on every day. Cars! Not many of them around normally but on election day they were there to take folk to the voting booths. The cars had those running boards and luggage racks on the back, it was easy at the last minute to grab on and ride in to Pandy Square where everyone was nice to even grubby kids like us so as not to offend potential voters. We made the most of getting into the sandwiches and cakes. Some kids with dads in the know, got jobs carrying round sandwich boards and singing songs.

I forget the start but it was, Vote, vote for-----------------etc
and the end was;

> **If I had a wooden leg**
> **I would hit him on the head**
> **and he won't go voting anymore.**

There was Guy Faulkes night, a sort of cracker and bonfire night the kids today will never know but for we kids in the thirties era it was the 'most bestest' time. There were fireworks collected for weeks ahead and an enormous bonfire where every man, women and child had the chance to lose a finger or an eye but we all sang and shouted to forget the blues and the poverty. For the night at least.

Drinking was OK, it was mostly done in the pubs so it was home brew out there and everyone who could afford a packet of Wild Woodbines, smoked endlessly so as to be able to light the crackers off the red fag end.

Of course, at Pandy, Llwynapia, Trealaw, Pennygraig or any village or town, Chapel was a must and the heart of the community. Like it or not, you went to listen to the Hell and Damnation preachers, so rife at the time, whether in English or Welsh. You went to sing, everyone sang, in choirs or at Eisteddfods or just to be a part of it and the singing is probably what saved most folks sanity in those days. The worse the conditions or the more hellish they were, the better they sang. By the wonder and pure magic of a male voice choir, they must have had it real bad because they all sang like angels.

From a very early age kids realised that if you attended Chapel regular like, you were in line to be chosen for the Charabanc trip to Barry or Porthcawl about July each year when you got a bucket and spade and a shiny shilling to spend. Some kids reckoned it was a long time to be good or to get cleaned up in 'going to meeting clothes' each week for just one day at the seaside, but it was sheer hell to be the one to miss out. So we all went.

By 1931 times in the valley were worse than desperate, more men out of work than had a job to go to. Ones own families even, were hard put to help each other as most had less than nothing themselves.

Food, anything at all got together by the women, was somedays available in the Square. A mum could get a pot of it for her little ones or you could turn up with a dish and spoon for a bowl of such a thing as "Faggots and Peas." On a cold day, what a joy! The Faggots were any bits of meat or fat, especially pork scraps, made into little balls or pieces and all boiled up in a great black cauldron. You had them with a dollop of mushy peas or all mixed together. I forget exactly but not the lovely warm reek of it which comes back to me even now as I write.

Bread was the thing, with anything at all on it or just as it was, bread with milk, if there was enough after the littlies had their share or just with sugar and water. 'Pobs' we called it and most kids were reared on Pobs and or bread and 'drippin'. A slab of bread and drippin with plenty of salt, was an absolute joy. In one of the homes when the drippin ran out, they gave us lard. I hated them and the stuff, the humiliation of feeding it to us and it makes me sick to my stomach to even mention it.

The Rees' were never rich but Mam Rees always managed. Maybe when Uncle Dai joined the navy, Uncle Arthur the army and Uncle Stan off somewhere making his imaginary fortune, there was sufficient coming in so that in the time we were around Tonypandy, there was bread as a staple and often only diet. Our Dad with a family to provide for came home from the mythical jobs with not much more than the regular bag of sweets.

My lovely Aunty Beryl, Dad's baby sister and actually only a few years older than I, told me things on a visit back to Pandy, only a short while before we left Treforest for good. She told how Mam Rees would make wines, elderberry, parsnip, apple and even parsley. Elderberry, [Gwyn Ysgaw] was the best seller and if you were not Rechabite or teetotal it could be made with sufficient kick to make you forget all your troubles.

Beryl said her Mam would make a batch on Thursday to sell at the weekend. It sold for the princely sum of one penny for a small bottle or tuppence a flagon. Then on a Monday Mam would iron a dozen shirts for two shillings, for the so-called rich as she called them.

Her Will, William Richard, my Dadchi or grandfather from whom Dad and I got our name Richard, spent almost two decades in the parlour made into his bedroom, the front room of No.6. The cough, the coal dust on the lungs or just the damp, took him as it did so very many.

I think Dadchi lived on Mam's 'Pwden Rees Mamgu'. Grandmothers rice pudding, there was also Pwden pwmpen made from pumpkins from the Gower at Swansea. Hers were the 'original' pumpkin scones and pies as far as we were concerned.

Our grandad was a sort of sacred mystery to we kids, his room was a sort of sanctum sanctorum. [I read that in a Masonic book I once found.] No one with possible germs was allowed in there but on the occasion of a visit from Treforest to my Aunties, I was allowed to go in and say, 'Bore dachi,' [Good morning].

We were left alone to chat and I answered his few questions. After he had looked me over, he paused and said, "So you're Will's boy," it was as if he was pleased to see me. Then when Mam come in and said I should go now, he held my hand and quietly said, "Good luck," looked at me and said, "Everything is going to be alright."

None of the other kids got to meet or to know him but I thank that God person, or whoever, that I did.

Christmas wasn't much and in my early days in Tonypandy I didn't care if there never was one again as there was a disaster and more of those stupid tears. It was the one time the kids seemed to understand it was not quite right and so they never gave me hurry up and called me a sook. I think they knew how I felt and what a rotten thing it was to happen to a kid at Xmas.

It was not anyone's fault, just a simple but never to be forgotten, stuff up!

What happened was that with such things as presents being out of most families reach, the men and women organising the Xmas party and also needing to fill in tedious times of ought to do, spent their time making toys. Wooden toys, rag toys, Welsh dolls, Jap dolls and every sort of doll dressed in cut up scarves and dresses. There were spinning tops and all those things enough for a parcel for each child on Xmas day.

The whole effort, the community get-together and the build up to it made the morning in the big hall a great time for almost everyone.

The names were read out and you went up to get sweets, a tangerine and some got a sugar pig, a real treat and popular at the time. Then you got the present and as I waited the pile got smaller. There were only a few left, just dolls and then there was none.

All gone, everyone down the front and me at the back left alone and damn it all, I was crying!

What does a kid think? Why wasn't my name called, why wasn't my name even put in and how could they miss just one kid?

I sort of toughened up but as I did, 'Evans the Shoe' saw me and must have seen or jerried to what went on. He came and asked me what present I'd got and damn it all, I was starting to blubber away and as if I couldn't care less, I whispered, ------ 'Nothing.'

It took only a few minutes for him and a committee man to find a cricket bat. A real nice bat and a lovingly made bat which they said was really meant for me and that was that, though in my heart I knew I was just an oversight.

It was almost worth missing out as I got heaps of sweets and stuff, a pocket full of tangerines instead of the one to a child each year and a bag of sticky Barry rock left over from last July's seaside trip.

Like all kids, we had our little ditties.
We sang;

> **My father is a funny un**
> **a head like a pickled onion**
> **a face like a squashed tomato**
> **and a nose like a cheese.**

The head like a pickled onion bit was more to do with 'Williams the Sweep' and his shiny bald head but my Dad was the funny un. He could make all the other kids laugh and was a favourite when off the train at Pandy station after being away heaven knows where. He'd hand out sweets like he owned a factory, then arrive at our place with hardly a one. I thought it was funny too in a way, how he got in and out of work regular like.

Just the same, we were proud of him the time he organised the men to bring the picks and shovels going rusty from no use and to all meet where it was decided to dig a swimming pool.

What a joke! Really a big laugh, it always rained enough to fill an ocean down by there, but swim! You'd have to be mad. That was OK, it was home made fun and as they say about us, "As thick as a Welsh plank".

Never the less Dad and the gang did it, a dirty big, huge massive hole in the ground. A heap of mud and clay as big as Pen Rhys for the hordes of kids to slide down and with mud for miles around as it rained or drizzled the whole time.

Though it took some time it was like a picnic with something to do and all having fun. The women brought tea, jam and chip butties, Welsh cakes and any other nationalities cake so long as it was food. It was for once a happy time. Even the old ones staggered up on rickety knees smoking the white, [brown] clay pipes and seeming to enjoy the laughs of the kids. Most of the poor old buggers had little to laugh about but were always cheery.

My Mum always boasted in her Yorkshire brogue and said we were all, "Sooch bootiful babies" and after days in the mudpack, washed clean under the cold water tap 'outer back', we were white as snow and just as she had said.

It was done, ready for a big opening day but nowhere in miles to stand without slipping on your bottom, [I could say arse but that's rude]. The whole area was a slippery slide but worse was to come as a band of men in suits and white celluloid collars, watch chains across fat waisted guts, sorry, bellies, standing back pompous like to announce;

"This hole is closed, definitely no swimming" and went on to say it was unhealthy, a breeding place for disease and all that! And "Go home".

We all did, disappeared with picks and shovels, tea kettles and such and left it just as it was.

A rare and happy time with our Dad and he as a leader for once. I often wish I knew what happened to our swimming hole but as was often the way, we soon found ourselves elsewhere. Never thinking too much then but wondering now, how the devil we got from one place to another, mostly pennyless, yet travelling so far.

7

* Londoners For a While *

This time it was to a strange English world, not like Yorkshire where we were sort of accepted because of Mum, here we were 'furriners' and people seemed to look on Taffs or Welsh as Heathens who spoke funny and sang all the bloody time, even if not in Church or Chapel.

We were somehow, almost established in a new house, a brand new house and not a pokey terrace. It was an experience, never before and never again.

Douglas was there with us and for the life of me I can't recall going back to Howden that time, as we must have for him to be with us again.

We were in a new estate, council houses maybe, on a new road with a new grocer's shop next to us on the corner. It was new everything and so strange after our million year old slag heap of a valley full of terraced houses.

Though I never really knew for years where it was, it was Hayes, Middlesex and we were to be Londoners this time with the Tower, St Paul's, the King and Queen at the palace and all that, not far away. Can't remember ever getting in to see any of it.

All that Kings and Queens of England stuff was going to be crammed into us in the school just up the road.

I can't remember much about London itself or how we got to it and it was to be 1937-38 before London became a reality for a short moment while we stopped there and visited Australia House before it too was left behind and gone, seemingly forever!

Dad was a miner for just a few years, as was each man and boy but in his sojourns away he managed to work on houses and buildings till, with the cheek of necessity, he called himself a carpenter and that is why we were here in the new house in Hayes.

It was a job, work regular like, not just for a while and then move on but for good and the house to rent came as part of the deal.

There was Dad and Mum, Doug and I with Doreen too but she was only a baby and didn't go mad with excitement over our little fenced in kingdom, all ours. There was dirt and no garden yet but it was new dirt that washed off easily in the nice kitchen with new taps. There was even a proper place out the back to wash clothes.

The furniture was a bit of a giggle, tables and sideboard Dad made from packing cases, the rest picked up on tick, so much a week and with a good job it would hopefully soon be paid for. Mum and Dad had a bed that squeaked and shuffled all over the bare boards as they made love to catch up for lost time, happy times together with room to breathe.

We had mattresses on the floor donated by a St Vincent's man who took us for Irish, that was OK as St Patrick was really Welsh. His bones are actually at rest in an English Church yard.

There wasn't a flea in sight and never a need for the small toothcomb to get out nits to squash between finger and thumb nail. No 'Black Pats', those monstrous cockroaches found all through the coalfields.

It's funny about nits, shaved heads were a way of life and every weird mixture the old women used to mix up to slather over our skulls failed dismally and time with a small tooth comb was the only way. Mum was never a great one to notice what was going on with us, never did much about it but each time Dad was home or just on a visit, one of the things he did was de-nit us all, give us a bath and find clean clothes to put on.

We started a new school at Hayes, right up the road to the old part of town, strange to us and unfamiliar and where they gave us Taffys hell. Not only the other kids but the teachers too who took out their spite or temper on new kids, especially 'furriners' like us. Doug soon sorted out most of them fighting like a thrashing machine for himself and me but copped heaps of the cane for being a rabble-rouser. He never cried once even with his cold hand swollen from the caning.

Being London and it being the late twenties when coal and wood smoke poured from a million chimneys to mix with constant fog and mist, we had what was called a pea soup fog and you really couldn't see your hand in front of your face. It was like night all day and you could only recognise someone by their cough. Coughs almost as bad as those full of coal dust back in the valleys.

Then there were the nice days with sunshine when we could play outside and watch the road makers and navvies at work. Just for a moment I wondered where our Betty was, why she wasn't here with us as Douglas somehow was. She was never with us, always back in Yorkshire with our Aunt who kept her and eventually Doug too, away from we Welsh scum.

But, back at play, there would be the devil to pay when we got tar on us or our clothes. If there was no paraffin handy, Mum would try to soften the spots with butter so she could scrub us off. More often than not the tar would spread and we looked like little black boys. If we cried and put on a show, there would be spare change available for the first time ever and we were given money for an ice cream at the shop next door. For a farthing we got a full ice cream cornet with little bits of ice in it. The farthing, long since gone as worthless, was a quarter of a penny, an amount easy to cadge from almost anyone.

On such nice days, especially 'no school' days or days when Doug and I hooked it, as we often did, we could go down the road to the fields and orchards. Not tiny allotments or little garden plots like back home but real farm places. Some of the people in the new houses used to go down after tea to collect manure, we never called it that, only shit but that's rude I suppose but it was good for the new gardens.

We were only interested in the apples and pears, a shirt full at a time to race home, get into trouble for doing it before everyone got stuck into enjoying them.

Sometimes we had to hide in the wood till nearly dark, down where the rabbits played and hedgehogs [I think they were] dug up little dirt heaps. We pulled up bluebells to see who got the longest stem, played and fantasized till late home to cop it for not doing our jobs. There was always a job for kids to do, stupid jobs that really didn't need bothering about to our way of thinking.

Douglas and I used to watch in wonder in our back yard at the sight of our Dad stripped to the waist in the weak sunshine, a sight for us together, the special and only times as he shadow boxed and exercised. Together as we were there, he told us of the good old days in Pandy in the gymnasium the men built next to the biscuit factory where you could get a big bag of broken biscuits for a penny. Tommy Farr and Dad trained there. Tommy went on to fight Joe Louis for the heavy weight crown and only lost on a Yankee hometown decision. Dad, we discovered, won a title in boxing while in the Air force. A cock sparrow, my Mum said about him and I can smile at that and a bit embarrassed for him too as we had listened to them carrying on as they did on the rare happy occasions together.

Much later in Treforest, hunched in front of the fire with the coal all gone, Uncle had been telling us of the romance of the past and Mum and I listened with interest as he said there was the first King Rees. There was our own hero, Owen Glyn Dwr and mixed up in his ramblings there was even King Arthur and the bloke doing his magic stuff named Merlin. Uncle Davy told us, Rees or Ris meant ardent in Welsh, [I had to ask what ardent meant]. "That's understandable," Mum said, "They are all such sexy beggars the Welsh."

As I later came to know and understand more fully about the sex thing, other than the games all kids play, I can think to myself, "Now who is the sexy one?"

8

* The Walk from London to Yorkshire *

My mind is a blank over what went on next, it was just a mixed up mystery as neither Mum or Dad talked about it, in a way it happened so unexpected that we kids had to go along with whatever was going on.
It was, or had been too good to last anyway, the school was nothing, never did get us anywhere. The things in the house which the men in the van came and took away were never ours long enough to care about and a funny thing to think of at the time was that the trees in the orchard had no more fruit to nick off with.

Dad was gone during the night to Cardiff, to see a man about a job. God, you could ask, what went wrong with this really good one?
Mum spent the night sorting out what to take, what would fit in the pram in fact because that was where Doreen was going to ride and that's how we were going to travel, each with a hand hanging onto the pram.
There must have been a mix up over the buildings, unions or something and Dad was told it was no use hanging around, just to move out and in a hurry would be best.

So there we were, on our way, Mum pushing the pram stacked with bundles and Doreen in the middle somewhere. Doug and I had our good boots on and dressed up proper as if going somewhere as we really were this time.
It was all a bit of fun to us at the start and when we were told we were going to Yorkshire and Aunt Mathews we cried "Hooray!" and thought of her hot baked potatoes with salt and butter or of the apple barrel at the back door, or the chestnuts from amongst the leaves in the Cathedral grounds to take home and roast on the griddle over Aunt's roaring fire. Nothing could have been better! It was just day one.

Mum walking back to Yorkshire wasn't a big deal to Doug and I. Just because there was no money left and it was the only way to go meant little to us, just a bit of a different way to go. The carriage or pram was one of those old fashioned, high sprung things you associate with nannies in prim blue and white striped outfits and stupid little hats. Prim and snooty, they pushed them around the parks with their noses in the air as if they owned the whole outfit instead being just a lackey of their posh bosses.

Our pram was a bit of a wreck and it would be a wonder if it made the distance! We'll see along the way if it does!

Looking back on it all in later years to think and wonder where we went, it was a miracle we ever got out of London proper but it must have been up through Luton, maybe up to Bedford. Market Harborough seems to ring a bell and there were lots of them, bells I mean, church bells in so many towns as we headed for Leicester. Bells ringing in the late evening told us it was time to look and find a place to stay.

I know we played Robin Hood with bows and arrows we had made going along, there were Oak trees like his merry men hid in, to play while having a rest or wait till Mum came back with some grub. It looks like we went through Nottingham and I like to think it had been Sherwood Forest.

One thing I remember from always seeing 'It' there with us, was when she went off with 'It', carrying 'It', not wearing 'It'. We were almost there, only a few days to go it seemed and 'It', Mum's most prized possession was missing. It was what she threw over us to keep us warm and what covered up her travel worn and grubby look. With a scarf and her little hat she looked like the Queen and posh enough for folk to think, "Poor thing," as she pitched her tale of woe.

The lovely fur coat from Aunt Mathews' days of former grandeur was gone. Not till much later did I find she had hocked it, with never a chance to ever get it back, but the money from it did get us back to Howden.

Leaving London it was in a pea souper, London's notorious fog and we couldn't see a thing, our feet and clothes were wet before we even got out of Hayes. If there were signposts worth mentioning, we couldn't read them so until it cleared a little, we just kept heading out that way! Mum pushing the pram, Doreen not big enough to walk but heavy with parcels packed round and we five and six year olds clinging one each side.

It was an adventure to us at first as we were allowed to run ahead but by the afternoon we didn't understand why we weren't going back for tea.

That first night, getting awfully late and not deciding where to stay, the fun was long gone and as we stopped at a railway crossing to let a train pass through, we could see the people inside cosy and warm sitting down behind the glass having what our empty tums said was dinner. I think we all felt hungry and bewildered, each with one's own thoughts.

We waited and watched till it was gone into the distance before crossing the rails to find somewhere along the way to spend the night.

One thing about our Mum was, for all her shortcomings, she was good at cadging food, a drink of water or anything. She used to tell us she was born a lady but they, as she put it, "Never seemed to need me."

So we cadged our way along, mostly stale bread. Mum got cups of tea and if there was time, read the tea leaves and got a few extras. Milk was a worry but at farms we got some to scoff down in a hurry. In the poorest looking places they shared their bowl of soup with us and gave us a shed or pointed out an empty house to stay in and dry out. Doreen would get her bum washed and a change of pants and we had our lick and a promise before cuddling up for the night.

Most of the men and women along the way were nice to us, some smarty-pants kids called us names and some toffee nosed ladies just wanted us out of their places as if we were making it look untidy. We got used to standing pathetic like because it often led to a feed and a shed for the night. Mum, never much good with her own, but a genius at beguiling other people and everyone said in sympathy, "What a dear and lovely lady."

Being only five-foot nothing, she must have had the heart of an Ox because she got us there, put cardboard in our shoes and picked stuff up along the way. We ached and snuffled with runny noses, got hot and cold but mainly freezing cold. We got those rotten nits again, we missed Dad for the first time and wished he were there to clean us up but God knows where he was or if and when we'd see him next.

We walked and walked, sometimes in the early morning to get warm when it was too cold to sit around any longer and in the hope the next farm or house would share their breakfast. The thought of a soft-boiled Googy egg with toast fingers to dunk was a dream that lasted for miles as we chewed on Hips and Haws from the hedgerows.

It wasn't much fun anymore unless the sun came out to steam our shirt and shorts dry or make the puddles dry out and the pram easier to push.

The wheels had got all wobbly and the black canvas stuff hood sagged and let things fall out till one day in a bigger town Mum left us in a bus shed and went off with the old pram.

Doug and I must have looked at each other right then and thought, "This is it, she has left us," but then again she will have to come back for Doreen.

'Don't move,' she told us, 'not a step from right here till I get back and look after your sister.'

One boy gave us his apple core, a lady who shuffled away from us a bit, gave us an orange and told us to eat it over there, pointing outside. A man who came along asked where we were from and when we said "Tonypandy," he said, "Good God," and opened his lunch box and gave us half his cheese sandwich. We grabbed it and he looked pleased when I said, "Diolch yn fawr," instead of, "Ta very mooch," as they all did up here in the north.

We ate it and the orange and the apple core, peel, pips and all.

Then our mum came back, new pram and all, not really brand new but the wheels were straight with all the spokes in and it was so easy to push. The hood didn't stay up but it got us to Howden, in a proper mess all round in fact but that's enough of that trip.

9

* In Yorkshire *

Our Aunt managed or even owned a hotel. She managed clubs, such as the Royal Hunt Club and the 'Station' at the Howden aerodrome. She was used to Royalty and rode to hounds looking most elegant and regal herself on the black stallion in the photo we have of her. Mum grew up amongst all this stuff and was taught piano which she played beautifully in our time whenever a piano was available and that was rare after we left Yorkshire.

I think Mum was spoilt by all the men in the clubs and hotels. Not a life suited for what was ahead for her. She learned all about pubs and how to handle men and women or how to get the best out of them without even trying.

Hopeless at house work and hopeless with money, whenever there was any, and though she loved her children as she told everyone, raved about how they were all 'Loovly babies,' she was worse than hopeless with us.

Connie, as Mum was known by everyone in and around Athelia's or Aunt Mathews as we knew her, was considered a bit of a lady, almost upper crust but not snooty. A bit down at heel at times but with her fur coat, little cloque hat and paisley scarf, she always looked quite posh.

As such in poor old Goole with the war almost over she was to be a bit of a character, an identity and considered a bit of a catch still.

There was actually another bit of a catch, a very nasty one about adoption and quite upsetting to me and all that may hopefully come out later.

In Wales she was a bit of an enigma when she went there with her Will. His protective sisters really checked her out and she needed all her charm being from England, [Irish or Scot was bad enough]. Looking so bleeding posh and from strange unheard of Goole and Howden, it was touch and go. Living in Wales on and off and in so many places, having and presenting more new family, sharing the desperate times as she did, she was accepted as one of them but still spoke 'foony.'

Right from the early days I can recall the cups of tea and someone hunched over the table listening intently. She was really 'Fey'. I think that's the funny word for eerie or weird, or a bit you know what and she could really tell the future. Till the day I left King St, she was always at it, reading the tea leaves in a real china cup or anything that would hold a brew. It was OK because she would go off looking like the Queen in her good togs and come back with a bit of money or at least some extras for supper.

All ladies want to know about the future, anything to get a lift out of the humdrum. I could do it myself I reckon having watched the guyver they go on with so often.

"There is a tall dark man, ... "You will get a letter,"..... "Whose name is it starting with?" and so on. The funny thing is she got it right most of the time.

There was for a time a crystal ball and that was really a big production till it got lost or stolen. It was to the pawnshop I'm sure and never enough money to get it out of hock, but with it Mum was brilliant and we should have been rich. Never did of course, she was too religious and nice, didn't like giving out bad news.

Religion was big with Mum, always went to Church, though in Wales she had me down as Church of England and to please her I was confirmed and all that stuff. We had to go 'regular like' to Chapel and were always at practice for one thing or the other. Mum knew good songs other than hymns and could play the piano, so that always went down well. Very serious about her Church but Mum was mug cunning too. I think the message we got in those early days was, go along with religion and you'll be better off than those dumb non believers who missed out on the trips and little benefits. I still don't know what to believe to this day because whoever it is up there running the show is certainly ballsing it up down here.

Everyone in Goole went to Church and at the time we arrived back there in pretty rotten condition, ragged and like the scarecrows we had passed in the fields. Our aunt, not wishing the neighbours to see us as such, reluctantly clothed us and put shoes on our feet just as Mum knew she would if we could just manage to get back there.

Our Betty was excited and for once showed emotion. She was the one who was always so neat and tidily dressed but so quiet. Meek and mild I thought. I often thought a lot about her and us before some of the truth of the story came out. She really enjoyed us being back there, it gave her a break from severe old Aunt Mathews. She played and had fun with us but always with the reservation or fear, as if not really one of us, and like as if we'd soon be gone again and she would be left alone. Doug was kind of hers in a way and she was jealous, I feel, of Doreen and his special care of her. We others had a sort of silent understanding.

Little did she know how soon she would have our Douglas all to herself again and that the whole situation would, in later years, cause her also to rebel and give Athelia strife.

St Thomas' Church was where Mum was married and being back and attending again, she was made a fuss of. We all went to Church looking like rich kids in our outfits courtesy of our Aunt and sitting in the pews everything smelt of carbolic soap and old prayer books plus the fancy soaps and perfumes of the ladies in their 'go to meeting' outfits, with a touch of camphor ball cupboard smell.

Coming out we learnt not to push and rush but to shake hands and look sweet, then as a sort of reward we all went along to the sweet shop, open specially at coming out time for those such as we, going on the ritual after Church walk.

In Goole after Church, everyone walked, paraded in fact, all dressed up like sore toes. I remember the big day when the new bridge was opened to be marvelled at as we crossed over high above the river. We ran ahead and played, continuously being told not to scuff the toes of our shoes. The young men, Swains they called them [Sounds like pigs] and their coy lady friends did their courting hand in clammy hand and so much in love, I suppose!

That was a very nice time.

It was a nice time too in 20 Richard Cooper St, next to Mrs English, [a time soon to be interrupted]. It may have been she who had the old piano and it was maybe the only time we all sang together with our Mum. She sang her funny little songs, songs I was to learn word for word over the years but Doug and Betty probably forgot, not being full Welsh. Being born in Scotland, seemingly with more anger than music in his blood or poetry in his soul, Doug was not quite like we mad Welsh.

Mum sang and both Doreen and I never forget the pussycat song, silly as it may be but it went like this;

My old friend Mrs Johnson made a cake all on her own
it came out of the oven like a slab of portland stone
she hit it with the hammer but it would not break apart
she gave it to the cat to eat but I said have a heart.

Don't do that to the poor puss cat, oh, no, no, no no
don't do that to the poor puss cat, do nor treat it so
do not drive your cat away, you may be a pussycat yourself some day
so don't do that to the poor puss cat, oh, no, no, no.

It may have been a short period but it was a nice time, still with never much money, just a handout here and there but we soon had meat on our bones and looked a bit more bonny.

Hot baked potato, brown skin and broken open, with butter and salt, to hold in your cold hands to warm them as the steam rises in the mist. For just a short time in Howden, that's what we had to go home to from school. Who did them for us I'll never know but it was heaven.

There was always, as it was everywhere, the snotty noses, scabby knees and festered scabs from scratching fleas that were as bad as ever, but we played in the streets and managed until!!..............

It was a big until, ominous even, because coming home from school, round our place was our Aunt, Mrs England, and half the street sticky beaking at the bit of excitement that was going on and our Mum for once almost in tears and then we were off again.

Going back to the Rhondda. It seemed Dad had been in touch, he had a job, a share of another terraced house to live in with relatives and he wanted us back.

In the short time here we had got used to the different world, how quickly the London and coalfields lives were forgotten but it all came back in a rush and I suddenly felt I wanted to go home.

Betty never ever came with us so there was no thought of it this time either, though I wished she were by the way our Aunt was going on and giving Mum hell about that 'Lazy Welsh rubbish.'

Also, frighteningly dominant and aloof, "You're not taking that boy," pointing at Douglas and it was obvious who was boss. I didn't matter, I was too much like Dad I suppose. I spoke Welsh and was not what you would call her favourite. Mum, who could handle anyone in most situations, had no chance with Athelia, haughty and strong, immovable and pig headed too I reckon. So, Doug was to stay and that was that.

Going out of sequence again I'm afraid but it's a fact and so very sad to report, that in 1993 when I was in Yorkshire, I located and found an untidy mound in a lonely, remote Church yard. It was where our Aunt had been dumped and forgotten, never a soul ever to visit or pause and think of what she had been or had done. For what it is worth, I said a silent prayer and a farewell with no one else to know or even care. What would Doug's thoughts now have been of this person, this lady who could be grandmother or whoever? Athelia, who once modelled for the painting in the dome of the Church in Hull, the enigma who mixed with nobility and folk of fame, our Aunt Mathews, the influence on all our lives, but now at rest without even a name on a stone.

After the way we got here to Yorkshire, I wondered how the devil we would get back now but it must have been a money order from the money Dad borrowed that got us there but once again it's very vague from the time we left the others on the platform.

Many of the times and events in Yorkshire were to remain a mystery for years. Our Aunt's real story? What did Betty and Doug do? He rebelled and swore to be with us again, what did happen to him? In later years correspondence there were enquiries about Dulcia and David, about the lamplighters boy and the boy who got the bonus of adoption by the rich shipping mob but not ever to know of us, the real family. There is no mention of the twins, vaguely mentioned in Mum's vague forgettery, and possibly lost at birth.

Only time has a possible answer.

Doug was only six or seven and told me things about Dr Dooley and catching him in the front room. There was the merry-go-round man, Morley. It was the mystery of the man that comes around and all of it confirmed by the letter Doreen introduced. It mentioned Athelia's things, not mentioning the silver or the paintings, even a little Constable and there was a collection of Strode worth a fortune.

There was only Betty or Douglas to leave it to and they got nothing and know nothing. Mum probably went back after we left and there's no knowing what went on but it was all gone and that was once again that!

10

* The Sad Leaving of Yorkshire *

It will seem I'm saying it for affect but the day we left was miserable, rain, fog, mist, the works and it was miserable. It was bad enough that we were going to leave Doug and Betty. The awful premonition too was that we were never coming back because our Mum and our Aunt had words 'we've never heard so-called ladies use before. In all fairness to Mum she didn't say anything really awful but what she learnt in pubs and clubs came out from her alter ego to surprise even I.

We were at the station early and got an empty carriage with window seats to look out. No big cases like other travellers but big bundles that Mum had put together as she had taken everything she could to tie in blankets and rugs. We were first in our carriage and filled the racks.

We let all the windows down on the wide leather strap with holes to suit where you wanted it and we talked out to Doug and Betty. There wasn't much to say, just a build up inside, look around and fidget. There was just us there after most of the others had left due to the drizzle.

The blast or toot gave us all a fright and we started to move. Mum just sat and as she looked out the window, they were gone. Doreen and I waved and shouted as they ran alongside the carriage with us. Betty was in despair or whatever and had gone back to being quiet again while Doug was still shouting something in anger and only stopped at the end of the platform. Nowhere else to go and -- they were gone.

Bloody hell and damn, God and Jesus. In the frustration like any kid would have had, or thought about, it was spiteful and angry. 'Holy shit,' what was it or life all about?

I didn't understand why we were so different, why us?

All in silence, Mum with nothing she could say. Doreen was in no time playing with her golliwog doll and me there stewing over everything, planning dire plans and going to raise merry hell when I grew up.

I soon did that of course out of necessity, grew up I mean and as the clickity clack and the tootly toot of the railway crossings, the clang, clang, clang as we whizzed along soon put me to sleep it was soon OK again. Just another mixed up phase over and soon be home?

Looking out at kids climbing on the crossing gate, I nearly lost it again thinking of Doug and I doing just that such a short while ago from London to Yorkshire.

We sat looking out as cities went by, we changed trains and tootled along till signs changed and we could hear people on the station speaking proper, not the slangy lingo round London, or so differently from county to county up to Yorkshire where it got worse. You know what they sound like, 'Out er back,' 'Oop ter poob,' and stuff like that. It was supposed to be the 'Kings' English, as she are spoke.

Again! Where we first went I don't remember, but it was a little train, a bus and one of those long walks. Tonypandy, Treforest, Pontypridd were all mixed in and we lived in most of them at some time.

The job Dad had found was only good for a short time, they never seemed to last long and it was always the dole or the workhouse or with relatives that could fit us in.

In Tonypandy, all Dad's sisters were fascinated by their brothers choice of partner. They were never to know the circumstances or how it was thought by some that he had been hoodwinked into marriage and with Mum having her two daughters already.

He was maybe dumb or just love struck but at least to his credit, he was honourable. He stood up to Athelia for once and as he said, made an honest woman of his Connie.

They were in love, really loved each other as perhaps only I can tell or know, even to my hearing and feeling them together in early times as I supposedly slept at the bottom of the bed as quiet as a dormouse. My Mum was a great lover and Dad had by all reports been besotted from the start. I think besotted covers it. Yet and even so, they were eventually to go their own ways, stuffing up all we kids lives sufficient to almost hate them. At times? Not really. We never did, not one of us, though at one time in the future I could have killed for the stupid adoption event not necessary to tell in detail here.

In Pandy the sisters were reservedly kind to Mum, never failing with a handout at the regular tales of woe. They silently blamed her for their pet brother's crazy coming and goings, [Never really his fault sort of thing] and though nothing was said, they, she and we, could read that the thought was there.

Without exception, all the families we stayed or lived with liked Connie. They always forgave and forgot the damned awful mess she brought Will's kids back in, each time we turned up.

11

* A Time in the Workhouse *

The workhouse, the old men's home and there were lots of them in South Wales then. They are usually attached or near the Cottage hospital, if there was one and ours was at Pontypridd, up from the station I think and a good long walk from Treforest.

I don't know where Doreen was, she was not with me or with Mum at the time. I was only in there myself because of my poisoned thumb which got all festery and putrid from no one doing anything about it. They nearly took it off but Mum was at the hospital, they fixed me up in there and I was allowed to stay as long as I kept out of the way.

Mum right then was in the workhouse, not really the workhouse but working in the hospital while expecting another baby. She was known to have babies like shelling peas but this one was a bit of bother. I think it was actually quite easy but she wanted a bit of a rest, a chance of free board and lodging in fact and she offered to work there till it came along.

Kids were not allowed in the old men's section but as my thumb was real bad with puss and blood and stinking rotten under the rag, I was allowed to stay in Mum's little closet and spend the day keeping out of sight in and around the workhouse.

Mum of course was soon a favourite, put on her act, singing and entertaining at the piano and reading teacups more often than scrubbing and polishing floors. One thing she was good at was knowing how to use people.

To me it was wonderful, everyone nice to me and giving me the fruit and sweets of little interest to them now, sick as they were. As is the case, people always take grapes to hospitals and most of those there, too sick in bed to eat them. So I was their boy, there to help them out.

The Ponty workhouse or poor house was full of old men or at least they all looked old. In there it was that sickly, smelly old smell and everyone coughed and rasped, those with their teeth in chattered away trying to keep them in and I laughed at them for being funny but they didn't mind.

To me the smell, the phlegm and spit all over the place instead of in the pot, the coughing till they cried and nearly died as every now and then one did, never worried me. To me they were all nice men, they just sat around, lay around, listening to me twittering around doing things, their eyes watching slobbery mouthed and taking it all in.

They kept little things for me as I did the jobs the nurses asked me to help with, their eyes followed me around as I whistled and sang, they tried to join in the Chapel hymns they too had learnt when once a boy like me.

Even the strict, bossy starched nurses were nice to me, made a sort of pet of me. Imagine me a pet! Who would believe it but I lapped it all up for as long as it lasted which it didn't. Last long I mean.

The men may have missed me and the nurses too I suppose but I missed them in a way by my being made special by them. I was in a way, sorry to leave. It had been a different world for a while.

It's probably a dumb story but when a little bird came and sat on the windowsill at the end of the long dormitory I tried to catch it, they left crumbs there so it kept coming back. One old chap told me that to catch a Dickybird, you had to put salt on its tail, so I put some salt out.

Next morning when I got there, everyone must have been waiting for the dumb little kid I was and it had worked because there on the sill was a Dicky bird, yellow and fluffy, not a real one but one of those off the big Easter eggs. To me it was real enough, real enough for the whole dormitory to clap and smile. That was very nice too.

It had been nice, horrible mostly but nice and it seemed like ages there but really only a few months I suppose and then I was a brother again. Mum had the next little Rees kid and called her Yvonne Arnold. Yvonne because everyone at that time yearned for the glamour and excitement of anything French and Arnold, I think, from some dumb French stage actor. Mum just loved anyone on or off the stage.

A pram turned up, we were good at prams and this one was a pretty good one they dug up from the charity lot in Pontypridd.

It was strange to be out again, no one had thought to come and visit or take me out and I'd been inside, seemingly forever. So out the gates and onto the footpath. I'd forgotten what outside was all about and for just a fleeting moment I expected to see Doug and sister Betty, then the flash was gone.

It was just Mum and I, Mum happily pushing the pram with the new baby as we headed out for the terraced house still looking and smelling the same, a family to each room and after the almost already forgotten, clean and spotless hospital, we were back home!

12

* We Drifted About for a While *

I don't know why it took so long and on the hottest of days. We had to call in for drinks of water and for Mum to give Yvonne the breast. She sucked and dribbled, punched with little fists as I watched. Entranced is the word because as a kid I knew how good it was because Mum always fed us till we were walking, or time to move over for the next one. The only other thing we had at home to suck on were the corners off the square loaf of bread dipped in sugar. There were no rusks or fancy stuff then.

As we walked it was a bit like the journey from London but without Doug and with the new bub instead of Doreen. I lagged behind and missed him, not much fun on your own.

Why we went right out to Rhydfelin I don't know because Treforest was just up the road but we did go there for the night and the next day. Waking up in the morning, there was Doreen and lots of people to make a fuss of Yvonne. Mum was settling in as if to stay.

The time after the workhouse is pretty vague, different people and places, all a mixed up time till we went into the Church village homes, [That's a time I won't forget.] Mum was away sometime and Dad was around on and off. It was from Treforest I think that he took us up through Tonteg to Church village that day.

We went to school, I hated it in London where they called us mongrels and in Howden where they didn't know whether we were posh or poor and it was hard to get into a gang to play. At Treforest we went a couple of times, separate times and it wasn't much. School was never important except for the silent reading class where they left us alone to read. We read everything, Doreen and I, we would sneak books out to read in bed. Most places in the schools out of Wales, they just let us read. I suppose because we were foreign rubbish and just passing through so we read adventure stories, comic books and books about other lands with bears and Kangaroos while the other poor kids swotted up on Kings and Queens or nine times tables. It was all a waste of time because in all the places in England we had been, they spoke a different and stupid sort of

English, half of them not understanding the other half, not like us speaking the same sensible way all over Wales.

Uncle Davy read us history books and told us about everything. He said that Gymraig [Welsh], was once spoken right up to Scotland and all over England. In Parliament the Lords and Ministers tried for years to ban Welsh in schools and even at work or home. He told us we were the original Britons and the first King was a Rees.

With a straight face he told us kids that Jesus Christ was Welsh. We know that St Patrick was, to be sure to be sure.

There wasn't much to laugh about those days but our Davy Jones was a funny man, I think!

13

* Dad Took Us Off to the Homes *

Whatever it was that set it off, it looked like the end for us, we'd lost Betty and Doug, never expected to see them again because Dad told Mum she wasn't taking his children back to that 'Bitch'. He never ever spoke like that before.

They never ever fought and never swore at each other, never took it out on us or each other in all the times we were poor or with nowhere to live. This time nasty things were said and they ranted and raved to let it all out.

I hated to see them argue even more than Doreen and Yvonne who just sat quietly. It hurt more than my broken leg or busted face. It hurt deep inside and I wished they would stop and we could be back in Hayes, Middlesex in the nice new house where they made love in their own room and we, on our own mattresses, felt so good and secure.

This time it was Dad who did the dirty work as Mum was poorly, sick and under the doctor, not with the usual nasty pull of coughing but like never before as she went on about her 'Loovly babies.'

He bundled us up, just as we were and not taking a thing with us he seemed to know what he was doing. Treforest station was handy so we walked, always walking somewhere but this time no wobbly, squeaky pram and we caught the train.

The little railway station at Church Village which we were to get to know so well, was so pretty down in the woods with trees all around. Between Tonteg and there we saw rabbits half in and half out of the yellow gorse, the brambles had green berries ready for summer and even the goose gogs [gooseberries] could be seen in the hedge rows and lane leading to the signal box and platform. That was the last we were going to see of the countryside for as long as they were to keep us in.

We walked up the lane to the village, to the corner but not really to see the shops because we went left to the gates of the drive and that first time is still confused and hazy but we tried to understand what was happening. Doreen, Yvonne and I, Dad hunched up and had nothing much to say.

Dad, this time of the muck up, had been too embarrassed to go to Mam Rees or any of the family in Pandy. Mum was forbidden to make the usual trek to our Aunt, so with great trepidation, here we were being delivered to the Principal's office, where our particulars were taken down. Dad just stood around till they said he could leave and he did, looking as forlorn and lonely as hell, none of us knowing then if we would see him again.

The girls were led away to a cottage just for girls where I was to seldom see them except under a cottage mother's eagle eye or just in the distance at times.

I was taken to a huge brick building, two storey and to me, like a gaol. It was the No.2 cottage, second on the left passed the bootmaker's shop where I was to find my only real friend in all the days to come.

Church Village was the name of the little township or district with the Cottage Homes, I thought it was Church Homes. They were in a big, walled and separate section from the town and across from the shops, there was a Church just up a bit.

Outside the homes, like all villages, religion was important. Inside, with a captive audience or congregation, it was a priority and uppermost in all the grownups minds. Constantly so, till it hurt as it did with a whack or a twisted ear if caught not paying full attention. In our carers or so called guardians mind, hypocritical as all hell most of us thought, Church or Chapel, morning, evening prayer and grace was most important. A lot of kids lost religion there, they felt God the Father and his Holy Ghost or Spirit had deserted us and the whole damn thing not worth thinking about.

We did love the singing, joining the choir was great and as well as putting you in the good books, at times it had you thinking there may be someone up there! Some of the boys, and girls too I suppose, out of necessity some times, were good at using religion to survive. At the same time they could take or pinch some things without any fear of all that hell and damnation stuff they bashed into us.

I pinched fruit off the cart of the man who came around on a Saturday afternoon. Kids who may have had visitors and had a penny to spend could buy fruit, not sweets, bad for the teeth, but they did buy sweets.

For whatever reason, all the kids who left Britain, all the ones at Northcote at least, then and to this day are sweet eaters. Mushy cream cakes too.

The regulations, from whoever started the homes, said that each child should have pocket money, so we got a penny a week and it bought practically nothing so, while a kid at the front bought illegal sweets, we snitched stuff from the back. It wasn't a sin to us then, only if you were caught.

It was mostly a Protestant home and not many Tyke kids, as they were called. Being Catholic was different, they could pinch anything as long as they went and said a heap of 'Hail Mary' and Church stuff. They then got off scot free to do it again next Saturday.

We were like a little village of our own, strictly segregated from outside. There were about a dozen cottages, some workshops, the Principal's office and right out the back, the sheds and produce, gardens for vegetables and playing fields.

Some cottages had nice ladies as cottage mothers who made life bearable but others with an apparent hatred of kids made their life hell, especially for boys, as they referred to us, who were dirty minded, smelly and abhorrent little brats.

We knew but couldn't tell anyone because who would listen, that the pocket money, fruit and or sweets or such that a visitor may have brought, seldom got back to us. In No.2, it made us hate the one in charge and that was a worry because hate was a worse sin than missing Church or playing with yourself. Some of us thought of going Catholic so we could confess with the other kids but we didn't know what to do in the box next to where the Father sat.

Roses remind me of the homes, gardens of them. Strangely beautiful in such a drab place. Doreen in later years said to me, and she never swears, "What a bloody awful place, but I remember the roses." It all could have been bearable except for being in No.2 with the cottage mother a real Tarter and making life hell. I never really hated anyone but went close with her discipline and regulations and disgust for little boys.

Our dormitory in No.2, as in all the cottages, is hard to describe. It was a great long, cold room just to sleep in. To laugh or even giggle would have Miss up in a second and anyone, innocent or not, could cop it. Even the goody-goody ones, always sucking up to her to get the good jobs or extra bits on their plate at meal times.

There weren't many sunny days, it seemed always wet and cold and the whacks she handed out hurt like hell on the cold bum or back of the legs and that was another thing! To pee the bed was a sin beyond belief and one poor little bugger could never help himself. Each day we all stood quiet as mice as she checked each bed.

It was rotten and hard for the poor sod to strip the bed, cart it to the bathroom on his skinny legs to wash and ring it out.

It's funny how you forget names but he was 'Pee-the-Bed' to all of us who, without knowing it, helped make his life more miserable.

'Pee-the-Bed' disappeared one day, probably gave up and pined away we reckoned as it really wasn't worth the effort. You can't dwell on those things much as lots of friends and family just came and went.

It's easy to see how so many of us got cunning pretty quick, got to know how to use people or sometimes just mix in and not be noticed at times when an unsuspecting kid could cop the blame for whatever had gone wrong.

Everyone got new clothes, a full outfit, even a new suit which was essential for attending Church on which occasions we looked like posh little grammar school boys. The boots were made on the premises, it was nice to be dressed up with leather boots. The bootmaker would measure the feet and from the sheets of leather with the special smell, Hey presto! a perfect pair of boots. He and I were good friends, he let me sit and watch him with his awl and thread and we would talk all hours till I got into trouble for being missing but he was my bright spot and friend among the otherwise over strict guardians.

In one way at least I was like my Dad, he was always wanting to get his shirt off even in the weakest watery sun. We were both dreamers, he only wanted to go to someplace like the south of France for the warm sun. He may have done that too, he had the time. In those early days I never knew where it was I wished to go but as long as it was warm, with the sun on my face, it would do me.

He must have been on my mind, I hated him, I missed him and even had bad thoughts such as, 'Silly old sod, where are you?'

Then, there next morning, even before school there he was and it caused a real stir of excitement as it always did when any kid left and went out.

The girls were sent for and together we met at the office. Doreen and Yvonne went crazy and wouldn't let go of him as it all sank in that we were going home, to wherever it was this time.

There was nothing personal to pack but we were allowed to keep the school clothes we wore and some others quickly put into a bundle for us. The best thing was the boots, otherwise we came in with nowt and left much the same.

You remember funny things and though it sounds dumb, it was Friday, the day we all had to line up for the glass of Epsom salts or senna tea pod brew. Often a dose big enough to have the little kids mucking their pants by Saturday morning. It was good we just got out of that week's horrible lot just in time.

Just to walk out, down the drive and along past the shops to Tonteg was wonderful. Tonteg is, or was, a quiet little village before Treforest, about three or four miles I suppose and to us, used to walking trips, it was easy. Dad carried Yvonne piggyback part of the way and for the next short while, maybe it was the best time he had with his girls. He'd seen a bit of Doreen but Yvonne was new to him, as he had missed getting to know her.

14

* To Tonteg and the Times There *

Our Mum and Dad were reconciled, that means they were back together again. Dad had got the job in Cardiff which he could easily get to each day from our neat little Tontag station a few minutes walk away.

Tonteg was country, better than Hayes in London and with nicer trees and fields, no stinking thick fog and even orchards to get free apples and pears. Our house was the remains of a terrace, it was run down with stairs broken and plaster needing scraping and painting. No one could afford the luxury of paint so it just stayed patchy. It was just another narrow house, one up, one down but 'out er back', [Not, out the back]. We could see Devils Bend, [or was it Elbow?] and the Treforest untouched countryside this side of the steel works, where factories and housing estates hadn't yet reached or been thought of.

After Tonypandy and the valleys of coal, slag and steel with not a tree left standing anywhere in sight from the need of pit props and wood to burn in furnaces, where the hills around were smoked and black as the slag heaps around every which way. It was nice there.

Tonteg was one of the many lovely villages scattered through Glamorgan. We had running streams of tinkling water collecting in ponds to swim in. Minnows and Gudgeons there aplenty and easy to catch to put in a jam jar to take home and keep. They all seemed to die. The walks were different, down along hedge rows with blackberries and little sweet strawberries. The goosegogs when ripe, were as big as your thumb and everything there was a different Wales to what we knew. Perhaps a new start and being so clean with new clothes to wear and everyone happy, it made all the difference.

I was soon allowed to roam and find the best hazelnut trees and mushrooms by the basketful, and nobody but us to bother picking them. Being big enough it was great to roam freely where I liked. There were rabbits and I quietly sat and watched them, their whiskers twitching, hopping in and out of the brambles. It was as though I was in the book myself with bad Brer Fox watching and wishing a Brer Rabbit for his tea but the fairies and friendly elves gave due and timely notice and nothing bad happened in the book or there near the magic rings.

Along the railway bank were primroses in yellow abundance and at the bottom in the dells, the sea of blue bells paused as the train choofed passed, it was all so peaceful. The foxgloves as tall as I, waved to one side in the gush of the breeze or as if to miss the shovel of coal the Stoker from our old valley town threw out knowing I'd mark the spot to collect it later.

Coal was everyone's fuel, if you could afford it or if , as an ex colliery worker you got an allowance. Wood was scarce and away from the valleys not many got the free coal, but we did.

It was free, and cheap because Dad and I would take our sacks in the late evenings to go along the railway line and collect the coal that fell from the tender behind the engine. We were told it was illegal but I think that only meant if you were caught and I didn't know what illegal meant anyway.

Sundays at our Tonteg were special with Dad home for the day and Mum nowhere to run off to. Like the time we walked up the hill from Cambrian at Llwynapia, we walked together again. We went along the road collecting coloured toffee papers and bits of silver or gold paper, then back at home, using cotton wool and stuff, Dad used to make beautiful pictures to hang on the walls all over the house. It was perhaps the only time such a thing as 'Decor' came into our lives.

Dad was the first, in fact, to have a set of three ducks in flight, on a wall up a stairway. An idea for the future?!!

The neighbours on one side were sort of hermits and we never saw much of them. They kept chickens and they laid their eggs everywhere except in the nests so we looked round the rubbish at the back and always had free fresh eggs.

On the other side were two old gentlemen, not really old, but both nice to us as they liked to chat or watch us as we ran around and played. They were crippled with that arthritis thing and could hardly get around without taking long rests.

They gave us wines and jams they made and we gave them the mushrooms and berries we collected. Being good Chapel folk, they never asked where all the apples and pears came from and they didn't really want to know.

Soon to become a Rechabite myself, it's strange in our community or society if you could call it that, my Dad never took to drink or went regular for a pint or six. It was just the home made wines for him. Then again, maybe the old fellows next door did something special with their brew, as it often seemed a good time there for he and Mum, even better than in London before it all fell apart, because here we were sometimes bundled into an early bed.

I can recall the noise and the laughter, the parent's fun and games as I listened, fascinated, but somehow happy that they were happy. The groans and moans went on into the night I suppose but with everything all right at last, I had soon gone to sleep.

Living as we did in a myriad of places, sometimes a single room or with relatives, often a rented room where we kids must have been a nuisance, the noises of shagging and carrying on was often painful to me when it was not my Mum and Dad.

The job Dad had as a carpenter must have been pretty bad as he never got much pay and we were still as poor as ever. The mushrooms, free coal, free borrowed fruit and the eggs from the secret nests next door were a great help but our regular food supply was cold chips. Still half warm when we got them late at night, but by breakfast… stone cold.

We lived on them when we could get them from the fish and chip shop across over the other corner. Eggs and chips with bread fried in the fat was the best ever dinner. Mum was never big on doing vegetables and I only recall spuds and some packet peas or such.

The fish shop thing and the free chips was Dad's doing, he got friendly with the lady who owned the shop and did little jobs or something! She liked him too so when he suggested we could use the chips left over each night it started the bonanza of cold chips to last us our time in Tonteg. A chip Butty may be an English tradition but more often than not it was our school lunch too.

I keep saying it's a funny world and for me it was funny, funny peculiar. Strange to go from Tonteg to start my new school at Church Village, the one just across from the big wall surrounding the homes we had just left. Looking over at them, we all felt we had escaped or something as we could hear the kids inside, the ones we were playing and doing jobs with only days before. I wondered if they could see me now, what they would think or say at me being out here.

From Tonteg it was a long walk there and back and especially for the girls. I didn't mind, I was always walking somewhere, day dreaming walking and wasting time.

My special friend was the street sweeper who with his big heavy broom swept the kerb endlessly and with his shovel popped it into his handcart. He was 'Evans the Road', or the sweeper to everyone but out of respect Dad said to call him Mr Evans. We never knew his full name, it wasn't Evan, that was his surname, a nice name I thought.

For whatever the reason, all the marbles and glassies, steelies or tors he found along the way in the pits or gutters, he kept for us. Marbles were big and the game everyone played all along the three miles to school. Tonteg kids were always late playing follow on and got more cane than the others. We were late, and grubby too, with shoes a mess from rustling around under the huge beech trees just before the shops, for nuts. The shops were on the way home. Mal, the rich kid, always bought sweets and if you got on well with him, he shared them.

Beechnuts are special, a sort of three cornered nut, sweet with a taste you never forget. A pocket full can last for ages in class as long as you were sneaky and only chewed when Sir wasn't looking, otherwise you got a clip on the ear.

The nuts and apples were good, there was no canteen or such those days and if you didn't take playtime or big lunch you either stared at kids with food to get a share or it was nuts and an apple. Beechnuts were like chewing gum but that was an American fad and would never be allowed here!

On the way to school, little snow apples were a penny a double handful but on the way home after playing gangsters in the long, wide hawthorn hedge till almost dark, you could get a shirt full cheap if you were sneaky and quick. The orchards were near the cemetery and one evening we saw ghosts in the evening fog, we ran like hell dropping apples along the way. Next night quietly sneaking a look we saw a new heap of dirt and lots of flowers. Our ghosts were just the gravediggers.

I was always late getting home but it was OK, no one worried. I would go the long way round past the Isolation Hospital, all closed in with hedges and trees. The Conker trees were best there, not real chestnut trees but horse chestnuts, the ones we used to play Conkers with. You drilled a hole through with a nail and put a string through with a knot on the end. The idea was it hung down on the string and each took turns with each other's till one broke. The winner became Conker No.1 and so on. The old man told me to heat my Conker in the hot ashes to make it hard and I beat them all till they found me out.

Sounds pretty dumb but like marbles, it was the best game in town.

Colds were bad, we used to get soaked among the trees and it was cold most mornings and evenings so it could have been summer or winter, and with respect to a Welsh summer, as they say, "Summer this year is on a Thursday."

Until something put a stop to it, I was always early to school and helped with the boilers or to do things round the place. The caretaker who looked after the boiler cleaned up too, he was nice to me and it was great in the warmth of the boiler room after we shovelled the coal and swept up. The others outside were cold and frosted but inside it was snug.

Somehow, being only about eight by then, there was a funny feeling, you'd call it intuition or instinct now but then I was just a kid. When later, or pretty soon in fact, we were taken away from there to go across the road again, I was attending Church and there were rumours about it!

Maybe rotten luck took me away, even good fortune, but leaving may have saved me from becoming a poofter or something as they say.

You get to know about things in institutions and homes, even religious places, more so in religious places where you were told you went to hell or that limbo place for doing bad things. Celibacy and even the word makes you think. They say in Convents and Abbeys that celibacy is practised. Sounds stupid practising doing nothing.

Kids soon got an awareness of what was going on, they could use it to advantage to get things, right or wrong, and do bad things in defiance of everything.

I don't know about in the girls cottages but boys cottage mothers were obsessed that we were all smelly and filthy minded beasts and needed a lot of time on our bony knees. The more Churchy or spinstery the carers, the more depraved we boys seemed to be.

It is a sin but one could easily get to hate them and though in Mam Rees' family women were most respected and those from Bethel Chapel or such got us through bad times. I was tempted to call one woman, 'Bitch', as Dad had done that once about Athelia.

In South Wales a fever, diphtheria or some awful plague was not unusual in those bad years. Consumption was part of a miner's or his family's life but it was a terrible shock to us all, just as we were really getting together as a family to find Yvonne being awfully sick. It was Scarlet Fever. I think kids died from it and I can remember her with her head shaved, sick and like a ghost and we others thought she was going to die, another one was going to leave us and this time she'd be dead.

She went up to the Isolation near the Conker trees where we still played and we thought we saw her in the window way up looking down. We were never allowed to see her and thought it was another goodbye, little knowing that when she did come home, Tonteg soon was to be almost a thing of the past.

No one much today remembers him, Guy Faulkes, who ages ago tried to burn or blow up Parliament House or something on the 5th November. He became a hero and an excuse to have the bonfire and fireworks night held all over Britain. A night you got covered in soot and ashes, smoke covered the Island for days and those with bad lungs coughed and carked it all up.

We made 'Guys' out of straw and paper, dressed them in old clothes, button eyes, a big bunger nose and an Easter bonnet hat or something funny. He was paraded round town after school in an old pram to the incessant singing out of "Help the Guy" to collect money for fireworks. Tough as times were, people couldn't resist digging in, probably thinking of doing the same themselves as kids and giving pennies or halfpennies enough for a bang up night.

There were good times and Christmas was one, a chance for poor kids to collect handouts of cakes or sweets, money too but not a lot of that. Tonteg was pretty good with some nice old homes and at least one newer and modern street where Malcolm lived. Groups of us would sing Xmas carols, singing came natural and we knew all the words from our regular Church and Chapel. We loved singing and the best part of being Welsh was you forgot bad times and remember things like singing carols.

We did have other words to carols other than those in the hymn books, such as;

> **While shepherds watched their kidney beans**
> **all boiling in a pot.**
> **A lump of soot came tumbling down**
> **and spoilt the bloody lot.**

The other thing in Tonteg was the 'Yodelling'. We never knew about it as such and people think of it as little men in leather pants and a funny hat, on a freezing hill in Austria or Switzerland calling out, "Your old ladyooo."

In our gang you had to be able to yodel to get in. Even Doreen could yodel and better than most but she was a girl. No way of getting into our gang.

Yvonne missed a lot, she liked to tag along with us, along the road to Treforest to a spot where we could look out across the Rumney Valley, across Taff Vale to where we could watch the whole fox hunt. We could see in the distance as the horses and riders dressed like Lords and Ladies galloped into view after the brown and white horde of baying hounds. Once we even saw poor old Brer Fox go down in a heap of dogs. They chased them off and cut off his tail. I think we pretended it was just a make believe world of rich folk in fancy dress.

The turnip field, [Swede turnip, not those awful white ones] was across the road and a couple of us would go one way to get the farmers attention. Others would snitch a heap of turnips to eat like an apple as we went on to play in the old South Wales steel works which was miles of enormous rusty buildings and massive derelict machinery. There were fences and 'Keep Out' or 'Danger' notices but not a soul in sight so we could play there all day. It was almost as good as the tip but not as pongy, though our clothes and pants got rusty and worn from sliding down massive rusty girders.

Though Von missed a lot of things it was probably only a few months but we missed her.

It was a time about the mid thirties when the depression we heard about but never understood, must have been coming to an end because empty shops were reopening and people seemed to have a bit of money to spend and to go to the pictures. We liked the new sweet shops with mountains of cheap sugary everything. Hard-boiled humbugs and sticks of Barry or Porthcawl type rock. A penny got enough in a big bag to work at ruining teeth all day.

Mal's father, who was Malcolm too, had always been in work right through, in Cardiff council or such, so Mal always got pocket money. He was my friend and I helped him each day coming from the shop at Church Village, to eat through his bag of sweets. "You'll ruin your teeth" and the funny or strange thing about it is none of us had bad teeth then or ever. We never had stomach trouble either and at Tonteg for instance, our diet was chips, bread and drippin and lots of salt. One place we were in we got a piece of fruit cake on Sunday and as I may have mentioned, when the drippin ran out, we got lard and it still makes me sick to think of trying to stuff it down without throwing up.

As the eldest and a boy with Doug gone and it seemed for good, I had the best time with Dad. I got to know him as we went out to do the coal gathering, the early morning mushrooming and in his burst of getting fit, a bit of running and exercising. He would start to tell me about his boxing days but at the time I was more interested in going for a swim or looking for birds nests. I used to take an egg, put a hole in each end and blow out the middle. We got the rare ones to put in cotton wool in a box to sell to collectors who were too fat to climb trees and get them themselves.

We were always collecting wood along the way to light the fire as wood or sticks were scarce. It was my job to get enough sticks each day to light and get the coal going. Mum told me that if I did she would give me a penny a day. So I gathered sticks, wood, broken boxes, anything to make up a bundle to use every day from then on.

I never got a penny, not one and I felt cheated and thought about it a bit as a kid right up to the time I left Wales. It was a contract and I felt Mum had let me down, but she never had any money to spare I suppose. By my reckoning she owed me about a pound.

Down near the bus station where we used to hang around to get a stamp on our hand from the boss conductor, there were a row of derelict houses and a bonanza of wood. I could get in through the 'Keep Out' sign on the fence and bash out the plaster of the walls and ceilings to get to the lathes or pieces of real good wood for kindling. It was good till some officious, stuck up man in a suit came along all bossy like and said, "Piss off kid, you'll get yourself killed."

Just up from there, and it's funny now but not then, I got the mother of a hiding from Dad's thick miners strap. The first and only time I think that he whacked me and it was for smoking. His guilt for being so dumb himself maybe because he smoked two packets a day all his life when and if he could get them.

Fags were too dear for kids to buy, even those horse dung Whitings, three in a packet for a penny. So we tried everything as a smoke, any dry leaves rolled in paper and even those stalks of cane plants from where the chickens nested. They were soft in the middle and made the eyes water and your head go fuzzy.

Then we saw the cigarette rolling machine in the shop at Church Village, you know the thing you put in a cigarette paper, then the tobacco and rolled it till out came a nice, neat, almost shop bought cigarette. Almost! Mal paid for it, it was for his dad he said.

I'd watched the miners back in Pandy rolling enough fags the night before to put in a Capstan or Wild Woodbines tin so they would last through the long shift down under.

What we did was go round the streets all over the village collecting bumpers till we had a bucket full. There were Players, Wild Woodbines, Gold Flake and every other brand, mostly the cheapies but some with cork tip. Lots of 'rollies' and they were the soggiest and yellowiest. God knows who had puffed away at them but with the soggy bits cut off they all went into the bucket.

We took our bucket of bumpers up the back of the bus depot and into the ferns where we thought it was safe and we set to work making cigarettes enough for a shift of miners for a week. With only nicotine left on the bottom of the bucket, after all our work we had one each. Lit up in style and puffed away to get as sick as dogs and maybe it was just as well we sent up the clouds of smoke because we could have died feeling so bad.

The Constable riding by the bus depot saw the inspector waving and asked what he thought the smoke was up in the woods. He left his bike at the depot and came up to investigate.

He took us, our fags, the machine which had cost a whole shilling and he called our Dads. That's when I got the belting I mentioned. You couldn't help thinking afterwards, what did he do with the hundreds of cigarettes? Did he realise the probability they had every disease in Wales in them, T.B. the lot?

They looked good enough and I bet he smoked every one. I never smoked again and not only because of the belting or the ever increasing cost of fags but because it seemed a dumb thing to have one always stuck in your face.

T.B. was something that meant little to kids though tuberculosis was what everyone got with the phlegm and horrible stuff constantly coughing up. I'd seen enough of it in the piss pots at the workhouse mixed up with the smelly shit of the poor old fellows who couldn't make it to the W.C. way down the other end.

Mam Rees used to say casual like when someone coughed till the eyes watered and they nearly choked, "There's a nasty pull of coughin for you."

Our Dadchi had the worst pull of coughin and as I think about it, it was a blessing when he gave up and slipped away.

Thinking about Tonteg later on while at high school at Treforest, I wrote an essay about Dad at Tonteg. I put in bits about our walks, collecting coal and making those pictures for the stairway and walls.

I said about the time he leant over me before going to school one day and explained how, "Pull this one tight, keep the laces flat," then how to tie them once and then double to stop them coming undone. It had been a special and rare time and I called the essay, "My father taught me to tie shoe laces."

Teachers are damned funny, it was the only time our English teacher, our Welsh English teacher, cranky old Craddock Evans, was ever nice to me.

He even said, "Da iown Rees bach", a bit of Welsh I never forgot as it said, "Well done young Rees."

Tonteg was very quickly becoming our town and after school we were allowed to go out and play till it was dark or we were dying for our tea.
One by one the other kids disappeared into the newer and nicer homes that looked unlikely to collapse like ours. They had lights on in every room and smells of real food would come out from each one as we said, "Nos da chi." I was the last one on the street kicking a tin along and dreaming that one day I'd have a house with all the lights on, with the food too, as well as just the smell.
The friends there at Tonteg and all our gang, seemed to come and were gone so quickly I forget the names except for Malcolm, long for Mal. He was special as was the chip lady and perhaps best of all, Mr Evans, the street sweeper who gave us all the marbles. For a while I thought the school cleaner was my friend but I'll never be sure of that.

By now it must appear that our dad was always on the go and that was the case again. The good safe job in Cardiff didn't last long, he soon only went days 'irregular' and then it may have been for relief or the dole. But to add to it all, the terrace with our house in it, was to be condemned as unfit and dangerous.
Both Mum and Dad, who had been so happy for just a few months, had to figure it out and decide what was best to do. It must have been as hard as hell for them but with Church Village just down the road and nowhere else to go, and as they told us, "It's only till we find a place" and we were back into those Cottage homes.

15

* The World Falls Apart. Into the Homes Again *

It was up to the Principal's office we went again, looking a lot less neat and tidy than when we came out which seemed like only yesterday.

No one can describe my feelings or the girls too I'm sure but being back there must be like a life sentence to a prisoner.

There was a new man in charge and a different secretary so on finding we had been there before, inmates she called us, she arranged a cottage for the girls and they were soon taken away quiet as mice.

The man then asked me, "Who was your mother?" and God, whoever it was, St David or even the good Lord Jesus, was up there taking pity and watching over me because, scared stiff and apprehensive of going back to No.2 cottage, I said, "Mrs Rees," which of course is my own Mum's name.

The gentleman looked up his book and said, "Good, Mrs Rees has a place, you can go to her in No.6 cottage."

The wonderful part was that this Mrs Rees was a kind and caring lady, a real Christian and one who kept her cottage full of disciplined but happy kids, as content as any kid in a home could expect to be.

In a way, most of us you could say, got to love her.

Maybe it's a childish way of thinking but I felt like sticking my finger out in a coarse gesture and saying, "-----------" or something rude because when my old cottage mother in awful No.2 found out I was back, she was really annoyed not to have me again.

I can tell you, I would have often run away as some kids did. It wasn't worth it as they were back in hours or days to really cop it hard in every way.

Conditions seemed better but maybe we were experienced now, knew what to do and were treated as oldies and not new kids to be picked on. I wasn't quite as skinny either and boasting my Dad fought and trained with Tommy Farr seemed to help a bit.

Pocket money had now doubled to tuppence and the same man with his cart was around on Saturday. Same old story, not quite, I felt a bit sorry for him and gave pinching fruit a miss. I got picked for the daily vegetable run more often because the workers there were from outside in the village and some of their kids had gone to school with me so I was given the most and best fruit and vegetables. All that sort of stuff and the old routine went on.

School was a bit better and I think I learned a bit there. Geography was good as it took in other parts of the world especially the Empire, even to Australia, down the bottom of the map or the other side of the atlas. We had books about it from a teacher whose brother had gone there and wrote and raved about beaches and swimming most of the year. It was called South Wales too, but the new one.

In our country we've always had a Prince of Wales, usually the next King and a sort of compensation to us in Wales for what the rotten England of long ago did to us. We had Edward as our prince and we all loved him. He understood our troubles and was a good man.

There was a short break for us all one morning when he was due to come and drive past our gate in his car. We were all let out of school to stand down the road and wave or cheer as he passed, but he surprised everyone when he told the driver to stop, then he got out and walked along. Even to me he looked sad and sort of sorry but he smiled, shook hands and talked to some of us and I felt very proud.

Later on when he abdicated and went off to live with Mrs Simpson, all the Welsh folk were disappointed because, as our King, he would have done so much and we'd have got a fair go for a change.

As far as I'm concerned, if he was really in love and I could see he was, then good luck to them both and stuff the stupid system.

I have not told anyone but, in Nov 1998 after writing all this, feeling quite strongly about then and now, I wrote to Prince Charles as our now Prince of Wales. I expressed my sentiments in a personal manner using almost the same last two lines of my thoughts, [as above,] as I had for Prince Edward.

The envelope with the E-ii-2 and Buckingham Palace stamp came soon after. It was with warmest thanks and good wishes and from His Royal Highness. I thought that was nice.

Never expecting ever to see the two old men, our neighbours from next door in Tonteg with the arthritis trouble that kept them from taking long walks and especially such as the one from Tonteg to Church Village and the homes. So it was a real shock one day to be taken out and told I had a visitor or a friend and there was one of the brothers to visit us.

Just coming to see us was the greatest gift ever and as Corinthians 13 says of charity or love, "And the greatest of these is love." That's what it was, as was the penny bar of Cadbury's chocolate, one for each of us. It was all they could afford and even now as I write it all down I still cry.

There was a feeling, not really anger or hate, but of a not understanding why all those who should or could have come but never did, yet a man like that could make the effort.

Makes you bloody well think doesn't it?

So we were back in for the second time and for a nice lot of new clothes too as well as boots and all. Footwear and especially boots or shoes were a thing in my life. Having been a boy of the district outside the walls and they, trying in a way I suppose to be nice to me, I was allowed to go out and attend the Church on Sunday. It was weird and funny being out of the place, there were lots of my school pals all with questions and I had to make up stories about my Dad. For once I was the best dressed kid and it was sort of all wrong being out and then a relief to go back inside, which I did and stayed there till I was to get out for real and go some place and start all over again.

Up the back, on the hill over looking the playing fields, it was still cold and as before the feeble sun just snuck through for a while and was gone. As was the habit in those days, the thoughts were about that place where the sun shone every day and everyone in the pictures was brown all over, not glum but smiling and happy.
I must have been a dreamer, just happy to watch the others playing with a football with a flat inner tube they called a pigs bladder. There was never a bicycle pump or a patch outfit to get it up hard again.
Kids called me names like Sissy for not playing or teacher's pet when only I was let out for Church. I could have shut them up with what Dad taught me but it was nice up in the ferns to just think about things like where was my Mum or Dad, what was Doug like now? I even thought about when we would get the next brother or sister. Some mornings, the stupid kids on the field had their shirts off as the weak sun poked through and they looked obscene and indecent with their skinny white bodies to match the patch of white frost still on the green tufts the miserable sun couldn't thaw out.
When we got a real cricket ball, shiny and red, the only one we'd ever had, it was a bad time for one kid. He got hit under the arm missing a catch. He got sick and died. None of us could believe it and wanted to know what happened. He was dead and gone to Heaven we were told.

Heaven must be full of kids because even in my time lots have gone from here and the valleys.

Cricket was a good game and I used to have a cricket bat, that one I got that Xmas at Tonypandy, made by the men on the dole. Funny it was never used and then somehow lost along the way, I guess I sort of hated it.

Collecting cricket cards was better or any of the sets of cigarette cards, sports, soldiers, animals, everything. The animals were ones we knew plus strange ones from foreign countries but Hobbs' and Hutton's cricket cards were special and as everyone in England and Wales smoked, there were trillions of cigarette cards to collect and swap.

One kid none of us really liked or got on with, not because he was pimply and skinny with sties in both eyes but because he didn't want to mix much. He had visitors and had one who brought him a big box of every sort of card so we made up to him to share them. He also got a big bag of nearly green bananas from the man who was a sailor, not his old man, but one of those Uncles. Though the bananas were hard and pithy we all helped out and ate them to later all get the scours. There was also a bag of Barry type rock, it looked as if it had been half sucked but who cared as it was a treat and we were nice to him till it was all gone.

No one brought books or anything to read but I must have ruined my eyes reading under the blankets when there was something, any old rubbish such as old copies of Punch. Books like Robinson Crusoe or Gulliver's Travels went round the whole place and you had to wait your turn. There was the Bible and kids would look for naughty bits to giggle at and there was lots of begetting in one part. There is still a lot of that going round.

There were books on the war with pages on U-Boats and Kaiser Bills pointy helmeted Germans or Huns. It seems England was always fighting a war or getting into foreign countries, saving heathens and sending missionaries. That's something I know, because there was always a job for someone from the Churches to go off to China or some bleeding place as a missionary. I bet that some of them, like our No.2 cottage mother, gave the poor sods hell and hurry up.

A lot of the war stories were about my Dad's war, who, as he was a bit young, missed going away.

I liked the older wars best and can still recall one of the best, it was in a poem, 'The Burial of Sir John Moore at Corunna.'

> **Not a drum was heard, not a funeral note**
> **as his corpse to the ramparts we carried**
> **not a soldier discharged his farewell shot**
> **o'er the grave where our hero we buried.**

Lying on my back on my hill amongst the ferns, I could see the whole picture as I recited it all to the imaginary shapes in the clouds above.

We read hymn books and knew all the words of Xmas carols and in my time, I read the bible cover to cover as a bit of a challenge. Though all our Wesleyan, Baptist and Methodist preachers preached like mad and told us what to believe, it's hard for kids to know what God is really on about when we were getting the arse end of everything all the time and the 'Have faith' bit getting us nowhere in places like this.

The Welsh Irish are happier with God. They've got Mary and I don't understand the full Jesus bit, but there's the Pope, Francis of Assisi who is good because he loves birds, St Christopher who, if you wear his medal, will save you from something. All the Fathers and Mother Superiors, Sisters and whoever, know what is going on. If you go along with it all and don't eat meat on Friday its all OK. Sausages are OK because as Cousin Mick says, "they're not meat."

16

* Out Again. Hallelujah! *

We made it, got through it all. Doreen, Yvonne and I had drifted apart in our separate cottages in different worlds where boys and girls were never allowed to mix in case of learning evil habits of sin and temptation but, we made it. Mostly hated it there not seeing each other and Doreen's, "Bloody awful place," summed it up. It was a place to go when there was nowhere else and for a while we grew up on the good food we seldom saw outside in the not yet improved economy of coalfield and steel conditions.

We knew we had made it when once again, like when Dad came before, it looked like we were leaving.

It was not Mum or Dad and we wondered what was going on till we found out Dad was away up north. Our mum had been to see the charity workers at the hospital next to my workhouse. She was now in Treforest, back with Dad and I think having a baby. No wonder we never remembered when Bernard came on the scene but Mum had arranged for the people to come and pick us up and take us home.

The man had a letter saying it was OK to release us to him and he had to wait while we were taken from class with hardly time for a goodbye or to pick up our things. I don't know who we said goodbye to after the good, bad or indifferent times but it was a dream to be put in a car and be taken out, not believing it was at last actually happening.

Down the drive, out passed the village and then looking back, I knew and swore they were never getting me back in there again.

17

* To King Street Treforest and Life Therein *

We were out for good and we left Church Village behind, the homes and all the memories. In the disbelief of being free I shut it all out for many years with a simple, "Good riddance."
Going passed the Beech trees and along the road where we had so often walked, I saw and frantically waved to Evans but he never saw me or was ever to know I loved him and did say goodbye.
Our house at Tonteg was empty, they were all empty, tired and sad looking with slates slipping off the roof and doors and windows all gone.
Our friends were gone too, another time for a 'God knows where' with so many friends that came and went. We were quiet for a time as we passed the turnip field and the steel works, no kids there playing and making noisy echoes of laughter. Then we turned up past Treforest station and along the street backing onto the field with the Druid stones, then round into King St, to No.49 where Uncle Davy and Aunty Gwen lived.
How long we'd be there, 'He' only knew. It was as Mum said, 'just for a while till the weather broke.' [Why did they always say something dumb like that?] But it was to be more than just a short while. We shared there with them till eventually God did take a hand. Not only he, because actually it was I who decided it as no one else was doing a damn thing about anything.
I'll tell about God's intervention and my reading that paper later on in the peregrinations. [Nice word, hope it fits in here all right]

King St, Queen St, all the streets were the same, row after row of terraced houses one after the other. Built and owned again I presume by the iron and coal masters as housing for the hordes. They were now, at this depressed time, mostly all let go to become run down dumps. I reckon the sons or grandsons who had inherited the millions, were now living on a sunny island by the sea or in the south of France away from the embarrassing mess back here-abouts.
There were no repairs or fixing of lavatories and nothing left for tenants after paying the rent to afford curtains or furniture. In fact finding a coin for the gas meter was worry enough as was paraffin for the lamps when the lights went out.

But it was nice and it was home again with neighbours to chat to instead of the same unfriendly old homes routine and severity. The doors all opened up right on to the footpath of the street, no awning or porches there but it was friendly and no one missed anything that went on. Most of the houses had lanes out the back where rubbish was dumped and where men and ladies could sneak back and forth to each other's places. A lot of that went on but it was safe for anyone to walk about.

Some folk had little gardens and waited patiently for the spring to grow spring onions and stuff. Pigeon coops were big as a hobby and men with pipes stuck in their mouths spent hours and days looking at the birds with their endless strutting and cooing.

I was given a pair of white fantails by an uncle. I think we ate them!

At No.49 we set up house again, Mum, Doreen, Bernard and I. Dad was in and out for a while till the visits got longer in between and till eventually he had been gone so long we lost touch. Whether he sent money, I'm not sure but it was never regular like and more likely very seldom if I recall.

We Rees' had one big bedroom, the front bedroom, it was considered big and up the front upstairs but it was really only about ten feet by ten feet as in all the houses exactly the same in all dimensions.

All of us slept in the one bed, head to foot and whenever Dad was there, it was stacks on the mill but otherwise it was mum, the baby and one of the girls at the top and the other one and I one each side at the bottom. All grabbing for a share of the blankets or overcoats. Everything usually went on the bed, as there was never a heater.

When Mum or some others got up, those with colds and snotty noses could stay in bed with all the covers, sometimes all day to just play or read. I once got into trouble the time I broke my knee and was in bed for weeks. I unravelled all the bindings round the edges of the blankets to make a ball to play with. It made the holey blankets look more ragged and horrible, and to make things worse the ball I made lobbed in the chamber pot under the bed, still not emptied and half full of you know what to go to the W.C. out the back and be tipped out.

All that work and the stupid ball was useless.

Sharing the house with Uncle Davy and Aunty Gwen and family was hard. The one room down stairs was both lounge and dining room with the old sofa, a sort of table and quite a few rickety chairs. The big wide-open fireplace was a great hole in the side wall with a stove or fire in the middle. There were the black pots and the kettle always on for tea, tea that was often weak but milky and sweet from condensed milk and lots of sugar. That is 'til the milk and sugar ran out and it was then black only again 'til relief or payday.

Uncle Davy's chair was a rocker, out of the Ark I think and it sat on the left side close enough for him to reach the old vase of rolled up newspaper quills I used to make for him to light his pipe from. He always had a clay pipe stuck in his gob and the quills were to continually light and relight it. He gave me a penny sometimes and I reckon his going rate was about a penny a thousand.

In all the houses we lived in, not counting Athelia's in Yorkshire, I can't remember any real treasures, any special little things like a special gold rimmed cup and saucer set like people have or fancy little boxes covered in shells with beads or broken jewellery inside, or tortoiseshell hair combs and stuff like that. Not even a Cupee doll on a cane or a prize off the stall of a shooting gallery at a fair.

There was never a sideboard or dresser with lace doilies and nick-nacks and strangest of all, never a photo in sight and as a matter of fact, the only photo ever to eventuate was the one of Dad and I taken outside 123 Primrose St. Otherwise it somehow seems none of our family ever existed.

As well as that and not being Catholic, there were no religious pictures and Baby Jesus statues like those of the black Irish, as they were called. It seems they had done as the Bible had said and gone forth, [and fifth and sixth] and multiplied. It was after the potato famine time, to take our jobs, but most were as Welsh as us by now.

Wherever it was, our Mum seemed to be happy round the house. Happy and oblivious of a lot too, so she sang. When the people next door in the house on the corner of the lane went out, she would go in and play the piano and sing to us and to the mob that usually gathered. She knew lots of posh songs and classics as well as the hymns, but also all the funny little songs I loved.

For Mum and I, the kids too if they were still up, Friday was special. The day I got paid for my grocery run and other jobs. We would sit around with hot cocoa, all of us jam packed round the fireplace and with Uncle Davy in his chair, to share cheese and pickled onions.

It was a joy in many ways and even as a kid, I felt good to be a sort of breadwinner.

Davy Jones wasn't really an uncle, he just happened to be married to Aunty Gwen who was a sister or someone on Mam Rees' husband's brother's side. Families were difficult for me to sort out. It seemed that Mam had asked Gwen to take us in temporarily and so for us, here we were for a while.

Anyway, he puffed away on his pipe those nights and seemed to enjoy our company and our carrying on. I could listen to him and look at him in wonder. He had the pallor of the pits on his pock marked cheeks, the tattoo of coal in scars of old injuries and the coal dust on his lungs made him cough up bricks.

He really shouldn't be smoking that old, once white, now yellow, full of nicotine old pipe, but I liked him. Every so often he would grunt in his dozing, pat me on the head with a 'Bachgen da' as if I was a good boy, and it was then I would remind him of the penny he promised me and he'd fumble around and give it to me.

As we sat around Mum would sing her songs and the one I liked was her "Pat on the back" one where it said, " I've had a good day today."

It's strangely philosophical that I think of it but our Mum didn't have many good days by my reckoning, in fact the whole 12 years of my life as it was, you could say to prove the point, was "pretty shit house!" All a bit of a shambles in fact but right there and then as she sang, it was all very lovely for all of us.

The words of her song were;

Give yourself a pat on the back, a pat on the back, a pat on the back
And say to yourself a jolly good health, I've had a good day today.
Yesterday was full of trouble and sorrow
nobody knows what's going to happen tomorrow
So give yourself a pat on the back a pat on the back a pat on the back
And say to yourself here's a jolly good health, I've had a good day
        today.

Another thing was she seldom smacked us and in her funny, Ostrich like head in the sand sort of way, she really loved us. You wouldn't believe the things she did and perhaps only I know of the time she sat in our dingy little bedroom and cried. That cry, I saw and heard. Whether it was from the frustration of the day or from the wish for the good old days as a girl of quality with Aunt Athelia Mathews. Whatever it was she was never to tell or let on what her true relationship was with our so-called Aunt.

That cry was the only bad moment or time things got to her and sent her out of control. Otherwise she went along her merry way to see out the depression. The bad times, later referred to as 'The good old Days.'

18

* Still at Uncle Davey's Place *

It's not a thing you tell a sister but I do love my sister Doreen, though at times she was a pain in the neck having to share things as I was made to do. I was miserable to her by not sharing the comic books I got from Alfie Philips or magazines and books I picked up on my stick or grocery runs. I couldn't see why she couldn't look after the other kids instead of me when Mum made me take them with me. I was, after all, the worker!

I was jealous of her and Yvonne's relationship with old Mr Price next door but I knew inside that the affection he gave them was only what they missed getting from our Dad never being around long enough to do much about it.

Thinking I was the man about the house, a bit big headed I suppose and a bit of a smart arse too I'm sorry to say. Knowing what I did of the goings on of old men and little kids, I didn't like it much but, it was really quite OK as he was a nice man and the little things they got from him along the way were just what they missed most.

Old Pricy used to feed them more good food and fruit than they got at home, so it was more of what there was for us at teatime and that was good.

Then there was the damp, one of the worst things about our house in King St, as in all the streets, was the damp. The coal fire going all the time could have helped but it was kept going only when there was coal, so it was never really warm and dry, only dark and coal dust dirty.

'They' loved the damp and the dark and they blended into every corner and cranny, waiting to emerge, hordes of them! Cockroaches as big as Uncle Davey's pipe packing thumb. 'Black Pats' we called them, black monsters with twitching feelers that scurried for cover when you turned on the light at night going to the outside W.C. 'Squish' they would go and another squashy splat all over the floor. White guts and black skin that has a smell that has never gone away even as I write this.

While Bernard was only a little fellow and Myrna was the baby, there was always something for Doreen and I to do. Yvonne too after she got better from the time the Alsatian ripped off her scalp and we thought she was a 'goner' again. It was a pain and a damned nuisance when I had to take a kid with me but the idea was for each to look after the one next down the line. Wipe their bum, or wipe the snotty nose which, when nothing else was readily available, was on the sleeve of the cardigan or jumper which we always seemed to wear to keep out the cold that gave us those snotty noses, but that's how it was.

Being old enough to want to be on my own by now, it was a bit rough having a kid to cart around on my stick round or doing messages. It was almost the end but that was it.

One of the worst times was with our Bernard who was the happiest little grub and never complained and got special attention from Doreen and Yvonne. What happened as we later found out, was that while in hospital, at Bridgend I think, he was put on the 'poe' or pot and left for hours. We wondered what he was doing there in Bridgend so long but his little botty or bowel would pop down and needed to be popped back up. That was the worst part because we all had do it without hurting him as we wiped his bum, Yvonne too and she herself just a little kid.

I think it was a miracle in the end, [I think I just made a joke] but it all turned out all right.

Bernard was actually almost a 'goner' to us, not due to anything about that but to the fact that Nurse Llewellyn wanted to adopt him, but that part comes along later.

For a time there Aunty Gwen must have wondered what she had let herself in for with us kids squabbling and fighting. The house always full and no sign now of us ever leaving. She must have thought often enough it would be nice to see the end of us.

Myrna was still in the pram when last we saw Dad, he may have popped in, as he did over all the times, but he was soon off to London again, to Shepherds Bush I think and he and Mum were finished for sure this time. Whether they got back together after we left wasn't for us to worry or care about.

The other kids, Doug and Betty too I suppose though in different circumstances, were too young to appreciate our Dad. They never saw enough of him to feel as I do. As the boy he may have liked to be like him, I was the only one to get to know him before he was gone, and for good. It was not 'good,' I meant for always but I loved him, silly old bugger, even with his always coming and going and ballsing up things. You've got to love your Dad and so I forgave him, never held anything against him, even for putting us in that home and he did that twice at Church Village when he set off to God knows where each time. He was really like the man in the comic song, 'There's a man that comes to our house,' but we missed him when he didn't turn up.

Mum, in her funny way always loved him as she did when she conned him that time looking so handsome in his Air Force uniform. She loved him well enough for him to marry her and even with the two children already there. I was to find out that she loved her Will till the day she died.

For Doreen and Yvonne the best time was at Treforest when he set us up after getting out of the homes. He made a fuss and was as happy as Larry taking over from Mum and doing the cleaning and his checking for the nits thing. Mum was hopeless at cooking except for her famous Yorkshire pudding and gravy, so Dad cooked. His baked dinner with vegetables, mostly potatoes and tinned peas, was a treat. One of us would run up to the Richard's place for a bottle of Elderberry and a ginger beer and it was wonderful.

Then he was off, gone.

19

* About my Dad *

I have mentioned about Dad and never really knowing about the early days. Mum never mentioned it and to Aunt Athelia Mathews, the subject was strictly taboo. Sister Betty was as tight as a clam and to my brother Doug too, it was all confusion and he didn't care much anyway. That's what he said but his story tells it so differently.

The mysterious looking long white envelope came to me years later and only after what was a miracle of determined destiny, that I should receive the contents whether or not I needed or wanted to know them.

The accompanying note in pencil on what looked like the lined pages of a school book, as much of it as I could read, simply said that the sealed envelope had been discovered after we had all left King St. Lost by Dad, out of his pocket and into the stuffing of the sofa on one of his last visits back in 1936-37. Gwen perhaps, or the unsigned, whoever it was who remembered the story in the 'The People' paper or who still had the address at Bacchus Marsh where we went that eventful day in May 1938.
The letter was forwarded on to me from the caretaker still in charge of the Farm School at Glenmore, Bacchus Marsh.
The six close written pages, without an inch of space wasted, were in small scribbly writing, difficult, yet as I read, possible to follow in a way, not to fully comprehend or understand but to give incredible food for thought.

It was difficult to read and hard to digest that this was my Dad's writing and thank God I was on my own as it took for ages stopping and thinking, comparing what I thought I knew or had surmised.
The six pages of his life finished half way into the sixth page and that was that. I wonder if he ever started again and told the whole story, for it to turn up and shock or amaze the hordes of children and grandchildren that surely would follow when the better times of the future allowed.

Here is the writing exactly as I received it. Simply at the top was
'Page 1';

"This is my life."

I was a corporal in the Military Police in the Royal Airforce stationed at an Airship base in Howden, East Yorkshire. I had enlisted in May 1919 for four years in the colours and twelve in the reserve. Having served in the First World War I was promoted corporal the first month of my enlistment. I was I believe a good disciplinarian not respected by a lot of the men. Being on the short side, one or two of the men thought they could take the mickey until they found I could use my hands. I volunteered to fight as a bantamweight for the station. I did win a few good fights after which I was respected while on patrol in town. I have mentioned the fighting because it had a bearing on my meeting people, which led to marriage. I had a lot of girl friends who I respected, on my off duty nights I would go dancing. One of those nights I danced with a very pretty girl who I had seen before, working in a public house. She always addressed me as Will when others called me Taffy. I was surprised when she let me take her home or at least take me for a walk through the cemetery before going home. I found she was very experienced with men giving me a lot of satisfaction When I got back to my hut I related my experience to Paddy who was also on the force, he'd been with Ros and done the same. I told him we'd be all right next week at the dance. I made the excuse of going into the public house just to see her. She had a ton of personality and above that she played the piano and sang. I told her what Paddy was up to and she said, just like men.
The news got around that I was seeing Connie a lot. One of the girls made it their business to speak to me concerning a dance we were holding in camp. It was an excuse to tell me about Connie and her two children. I had seen the children on the doorstep as I was in the town on duty. Never did I think the children were her own. She had been brought up by an Aunt who I found out later had ridden to hounds and was the manageress of the main Hotel before her husband had been killed in the war. This man, Connie's uncle may have made love to Connie unwillingly, she didn't say he was the father of the children.
When the Aunt found her niece was carrying on with a common airman, she immediately sent her away on a job to Withernsea, receptionist at a hotel. I was going to forget about her but she was not going to forget me. She wrote, I answered her letters, it was nice for me having letters so romantic, I couldn't forget her.

There was a great disaster in Hull, one of our airships had crashed into the sea with loss of many lives including General Maitland. Feeling the loss so very much I volunteered for the firing party to attend the funeral in Hull. We, the firing party were standing at ease outside the church while the service was going on. [I had written about this party to Connie] I was surprised on turning my head to see Connie walking at the back of the party. The boys giving a few whistles. She was dressed all in white, white knee boots, white hat, white gloves, she managed to tell me she would wait outside the York Hotel to see me when the funeral was over. After the funeral, which was very touching, we were loading ourselves onto a ferry when I saw Connie I asked Paddy to look after my rifle and equipment to run off before the sergeant could see me. I was off duty the next day so I would not be missed. Taking Connie to have something to eat at the York Hotel she persuaded me to stay the night. I asked where could we stay, she replied where we are, I've been here a few times during the war. I booked two single rooms, when I told her she said you didn't want to do that. I didn't sleep with her but did creep into her room and spend a couple of hours with her. In the morning we had breakfast then onto the station for her to make her journey back to Withernsea. She had told her employers she was going to see her Aunt. Fate stepped in, we were seen together by her employers who had come to Hull this very day. We parted, I left for the camp at Howden. All was well at the camp, Paddy kidded me a bit saying, you lucky bastard. About 7 P.M the same night I received a telegram. Come at once, urgent, Connie. This was from the Tower! I went to the town, called at the house, found Connie and the children crying, the Aunt going on about not having more babies. Feeling sorry for them I said to the Aunt, don't bother I will marry Connie. The situation changed immediately, supper was laid for me. The children were put to bed after I had sat them on my knees. Connie and I were left while the Aunt went out to spread the news I imagine. Connie promised me the world and I never realised what I had done. The next morning I made an application to see the camp adjutant regarding permission to get married. When I told Paddy, he said I was mad to get married on corporal's pay, besides Connie has two children. I felt I had to go through with it now I had promised the Aunt. When I went before the adjutant asking for permission to get married, he asked the sergeant if he knew anything about the woman I wanted to marry. He said she was a barmaid in a public house, turning to me the adjutant asked me if she was pregnant and if this was so, was I sure I was the father. I was asked to leave the room for a few minutes, when I was called in, he looked at me straight in the eye and asked me if I was sure about what I was doing, I replied, yes Sir. Alright Rees, permission granted but I think you are bloody fool. He must have spoken to the Sergeant Major who knew everybody in the village. The following Sunday I was off so I went with Connie to the church to have the banns read out. I wrote to my mother to ask for 10 pounds to help me pay for different items, I never got a reply because my mother knew the allowance I was making would stop. The marriage license cost 7/6, the following three weeks when I was off duty I was at the house daily and helped bath the children and put them to bed. They had taken to me straight away, not having a father in the house I suppose I was strange to them. Connie must have told them I was their father and they were to call me Dad. It was a nice feeling having two innocent children calling me Dad. The day came, Paddy was my best man, I had 14 days for this huge step I was taking. I had no money for a party so we arranged to go to grandmother's house straight from the church. The Aunt looking after the children we were happy for a few days, Yorkshire people are very friendly and not afraid to speak their minds. At a gathering of grandmothers, drinks supplied by her, I was told by one woman that I was a bloody fool to get married into this mad crowd. I passed it off as a joke. I was pleased to get back to camp for a rest. It had been sex, sex, two and three times a day. I learnt a lot from Connie, about the Airforce man, it was an Australian who was the father of the first child. My mind was corrupted. The first chance I had I was going to get away from it all, get posted overseas if possible. My sleeping out pass was granted. One night about three months after I was married we were in the house alone, the children had been put to bed and Aunt had gone for a drink. I asked Connie to play a tune on the piano and sing a song. She could sing very well. She said she didn't feel like it so I didn't press it. The Aunt returned with a man friend asking Connie to play and sing. Connie went to the piano and played feeling very lively. Me being a Welshman was mad and walked upstairs to bed. When Connie came to bed there was one hell of a row, I called her all the bastards under the sun. The row brought her Aunt upstairs. When I had finished speaking my mind the Aunt left us calling me nasty names. I thought this was the end. To make things worse Connie told me she was pregnant. I was quiet for a few weeks, then I sprung the news to Connie, I had applied for a transfer to another camp. Seeing the adjutant, my transfer was granted immediately. I was going to Scotland, a place called Invercathy near R----th, I arranged an allowance out of my pay, nearly all my pay. I had been away for about a month when I received a letter to tell me Eileen had died. I felt heart broken thinking of Connie being pregnant and now the loss of her second child. I was concerned about my unborn child. Making application for special leave the adjutant was abrupt saying what was I worrying about, it was not my child. I told him I was worrying about my unborn child and she was my wife. Leave was granted and I travelled from Scotland to Howden to bury little Eileen. A lot of people in the village came to shake my hand, I had come to bury someone else's child. Connie though not saying a lot thought I had done a wonderful thing. I believe she genuinely loved me as she proved later. I was writing letters regularly, I was trying to find a place for her to be with me for the birth. I tried but I failed. About a month before the baby was due I received a telegram. Arriving at Inverkeething at sometime in the morning. I was in a hell of a mess being on duty and afraid to ask permission for leave. When I finished my duty at 4-30 p.m. I walked to the town meeting my wife coming towards the camp.

She had found a room with some Scottish fisher folk. I got a sleeping out pass when the facts were known. The Scottish folk were the most wonderful people. The baby was born, I didn't know whether to laugh or cry, he was a boy weighing 9 lbs. Connie had made friends with everyone, her personality was penetrating, she was a good looker too. We didn't have a lot of money but we were very happy. I had been detailed to duty each day with a Squadron leader away in a special house at a sea side resort at Aberdour, not going to camp at all. The tips I received helped in the housekeeping. I couldn't afford cigarettes or any drink. Everything went very well other than it was hard to make ends meet. The baby was about two months old, a fine boy, so people remarked. There was one woman who gave us a pram to take the baby out. I wasn't ashamed to wheel the pram. A woman walking near us looking at the baby said what a fine baby, why didn't we enter the bairn for the best baby prize, it will only cost you sixpence. My wife, after the woman had gone, persuaded me to look for the tent. We found it . I left it to my wife. She was afraid of no one. I waited outside sitting on the grass, it being a glorious sunny day. It seemed hours till my wife found me, she was all smiles, then showing me three half crowns she said we had won a first prize for the up to six months section. I was very excited and proud. We had fish and chips, fish fried as only scotch folk can fry it. Though not having much money, this was one of my happy days.

Some weeks later I was called back to camp to be informed the camp was closing down, I would remain with a skeleton staff to clear and store equipment. Seeing I had my wife in town it would give me more time to find accommodation for her at Leuchors where I, would be later posted.

The only mention I will make about the clearing of the camp is that the Officers had a lot of stuff taken to their own places, in fact lorry loads, I myself helped myself to a few small things. Eventually I was posted to the R.A.F station at Leuchars. I was in the officers mess as Batman waiter in *charge of the men under a sergeant. My wife followed me in a couple of days.*

Once more she found a room near the camp and I was given my sleeping out pass. We were able as married airmen to get our groceries from the canteen at cost price. I got on well with the men. Being a strict disciplinarian some of the men hated my guts especially seeing I was a Welshman. One incident made me sick. Having to walk through a short corridor to the kitchen I saw one of the men, a bit of a scoundrel, spit into a plate of soup then place it before a Major Doctor who had a vile name at the camp, one of those old timers who wore a monocle, one who treated the ranks as dirt. I couldn't report the man knowing he would be severely punished or perhaps discharged with ignominy. The man who was not a clean person himself had the cleanest quarters of us all, his officer swore by him because he would wash his socks, press his clothes and cup of tea were always ready. After dinner I spoke to Jock about what he had done, Well, he said in broad Scotch, "The Bastards nae a mon at aw."

My wife and I were happy with ourselves, she had made friends with the airmen's wives, one was the officer's wife who lived next door. I couldn't mix with officers though on a couple of occasions I was invited to their house, my wife played the piano and sang for them. I was in strict training for the R.A.F boxing championships to be held at Henlow. I was going to represent the station as a bantamweight. I had a friend who in fact joined up with me. He was going to represent as a welterweight. The officers took an interest in me seeing I was working in their mess.

That was all, half through the page and just as I was really getting the picture of those early, simple but so involved days. So much to think of, so much comes to light that I must have read before but never taking proper note in reading the scribble at a time when I had bigger problems of my own. The six pages were only a minute abandoned attempt of what could have been six hundred pages, if only. If only?

Mum had walked him through the cemetery, was it the St Thomas' I knew and in the end so relevant to the St Thomas' at Enfield where I put them together at last.

When he mentioned going to grandmother's house it becomes a Pandora's Box, as I've never heard about that. Grandmother who? What side of what family?

I found out for the first time it was an Australian who fathered the first child. How strange, I have already mentioned we had relations in New Zealand and now this!

I find out at last where Douglas was born, Invercathy it seems and also when little Eileen actually died and when Dad was in Scotland.

In Dad's pages it mentions receiving the pram. I can't help but laugh as I realise that my, or our, pram collecting and pushing episodes all started back then. So much to rethink, it may need a rewrite but then again maybe for sanity sake I should just continue as before.

Mum herself told me the story about the cooking. It was on the occasion of the first dinner she cooked for Dad at Aunt Mathews when they were just married.
Everything, all of Athelia's finery was laid out, serviette rings and dinner napkins, all the silver that went missing in years to come. A spread fit for a King but also enough to scare the life out of a valley boy in case he spilled something or broke a Spode dish.
Mum said she served everything, the roast beef, baked potatoes, the carrots, peas and head of cabbage from the garden. It was a disaster that ruined the meal and possibly her urge to ever cook again because under the cabbage leaf was the biggest, fattest caterpillar grub. The meal and the magic of the moment were ruined. Perhaps in a strange way, even from there the relationship was ill destined.

As I thought about it later, so many disasters. Did he marry again, did he get a good cook and were there more kids like us out there and would we ever know?

20

* Times in Treforest *

Primary school at Treforest wasn't much and just far enough away so that by the time you got there in the rain you'd be as wet as a shag. [I didn't understand that saying because a shag to me then was what went on in bedrooms or up in the ferns.] People also said, "Great weather for frogs," and we knew all about them because when it warmed up there were tadpoles in every boggy hole and millions in the puddles or any container of water at the tip. Some kids were sissy and said they would tell Sir what we did but we all tried it. It was to stick a straw up a frog's bum and blow it up like a balloon. It didn't hurt them as they just went phut and hopped away.

Until high school I can't say we had much in the way of clothes. Hardly any kids there posh enough or with dads in work regular, to have proper pants and jackets. Miss called us a disgrace looking over her stupid little glasses sitting on the end of her pointy nose. Shoes were mostly sand shoes, only new with nice white laces for a day. We wore them winter and summer unless Mum got a bonus from her tea cup reading and then one of us got shoes, real ones. It was usually, "No shoes this week," and we took our turn to get a new pair that usually lasted about six weeks.

We were lucky kids as we had the field to play in. It was there that the ring of Druid Stones, like a smaller Stonehenge, stood. It had the huge sacrificial stone in the middle with the stained channel to the scooped out bit to catch the blood. We played games and fantasised weird games there.

Anybody with nothing to do on a fine day, or any old day in fact, sat around and smoked and coughed, and spat. They talked football or kicked a ball or whacked away with a splintered bat at a tennis ball. Except for dole day, when most spent the day and half the night at the pub, but there was always someone sitting around and watching.

In our tent made of old bean poles and covered in opened up coal sacks and worn out curtains, safe and out of sight, we played our games and Mavis as usual wanted to do naughty things. On a warm day we would come out for air and to breathe. The Dolies or shift workers would heckle us with, "We can see you through those curtains." Guilty as hell, we thought they could. The boys, almost old enough, but not quite knowing all about it, got red blushing faces when they said it, "Pulling your pud will send you blind," as they all laughed like mad and we'd run for it as fast as we could in embarrassment.

We knew the big boys were at it all the time and most found out later, if not pretty soon, that masturbation was sheer hell and an uncontrollable compulsion for most boys. One can't blame the kids, what with sex going on in the same room when you were pretending or trying to sleep.You just got to ignore it as no one really cared. You just had the first thought of it. Something set you off having intended never to do it again and 'Bingo,' it was done. All that hell and damnation thing they taught in church or in the homes was stupid stuff and left kids with scars of guilt that often could never go away.

A few doors down from us was Alfie Philips' place. His Dad was rich, in our street anyway and a bit above us round by there. Alfie got regular pocket money and was my friend. They kept pigs in sties up the hill at the back and everyone took their scraps to the Philips and got a penny, a halfpenny or if only a miserable bit of scrap at the bottom of the bucket, hard boiled sweets to suit the amount.

Most kids pandied or sucked up to Alfie for his favours. He was a rotten kid with his yellow teeth and he smelt worse than his hungry bleeding pigs but I used to talk him into taking me with him to the pictures, as he was the only one with money. He liked Doreen and though she thought he was horrible and not nice like Eric and Billy Tarr across the road, I told him I'd help him get on with her.

Radios or a wireless were rare out our way, a wireless to us was what some kids at high school made out of a matchbox and a crystal or cats whiskers or something. Alfie had a real one and we would listen outside his front window when some news came on about some scandal or murder. Things like the abdication of our Prince of Wales, all the stuff about Mrs Simpson, the new King and Queen, the coming Coronation and things that hopefully gave us a day off school.

There were newspapers to read of course. I think there was the 'News of the World', 'The People', the 'Pontypridd Observer' and the 'South Wales Echo'. Some English papers too, slipped in with their rubbish and running we Welsh down. Kids sold newspapers but seldom read them. It's just as well there were lots of newspapers because under the bridge at Ponty or any such place like park seats, plenty of unfolded papers were as good as some of the thin blankets for warmth.

On the radio we were getting the songs of the twenties and thirties coming out from America. In the pictures were gangsters and girls in coloured costumes and feathers. We also got the funny things that the English were good at, such as words to popular songs, ditties about big events.

At the time there was a Dr Buck Ruxton who had killed a lady, his 'misses' actually. It was on the radio and everyone was talking about it. The song everyone was singing was, "Red sails in the sunset, red sails in the night" etc so the words the comics wrote were to that tune and went;

Red stains on the carpet, red stains on the knife,
for Dr Buck Ruxton has murdered his wife.
The maid saw him do it, he thought she would tell
so Dr Buck Ruxton, killed her as well.
The judge found him guilty, he put him in a cell
now Dr Buck Ruxton is on his way to hell.

It's funny you remember dumb things like that but can't remember what day it is.

About 1935-36, the rifle fire in the range back up in the hills seemed to increase. It was a place we knew well and it was getting busier with men setting up new targets up to a mile or two apart. I think the Hitler talk over in Germany had a lot to do with it.

We used to play all through there and still did, never lost a kid even with all the live bullets now whizzing just over our heads. It mucked up the birds nesting and egg collecting but the hazelnuts and best blackberries were in there still and we collected them and played just the same as ever.

The hills and the woods in our Wales were wonderful, trees and ferns to play and hide in. In the bracken ferns we made houses to play Mummies and Daddies or better still, Doctors and Nurses. Mavis, my cousin was the ringleader and got us into all the naughty but nice things. It's funny, or perhaps strange, that none of it made a bad impression on us, no bad influence or evil effect. In fact, I believe that kids from that era were to be more sensible in becoming the best of partners and family people.

For all that we had pervs and queers even in those days and one was our famous or notorious, 'Tosser Evans', not my Mr 'Evans the Sweep' from Tonteg, or Craddock Evans but 'Evans the Back Lane' and everybody poked fun at him. He would offer money to any kid that looked game to go down his lane to toss him off. It didn't matter if they didn't because while he was talking he'd do it himself. We used to run passed and laugh at him and try to get him to chase us and we all reckoned he was a harmless old sod.

21

* King Street in Normal Times *

I was going to write about Mavis my cousin, how much she meant to me, what she did to me and for me but it is really too private to relate. They are lovely private thoughts so I'll just leave them be.

So back to reality and to Mrs Simpson who got her teeth into our Prince. It finally happened so quickly and then it was Coronation Day when King George and his Queen were to be crowned. George, even to my young mind, didn't look up to it but she was so lovely and a beautiful Queen as we all thought.
With her coat and hat, gloves, the smile and elegant wave, our Mum was so much like the Queen that when she walked out, most folk commented on it.

Mrs Simpson was on everyone's lips, some for her and Edward to be happy and stuff the crown but most Welsh were sad to see him go and not become our King. Having seen and shaken hands at Church village, even I knew he was unhappy with the whole bloody set up and I thought to myself, "Good luck Sir."
We sang the song;

> **Who's that walking down the street?**
> **Mrs Simpson ain't she sweet**
> **She's been married twice before**
> **now she's knocking at Edward's door**

Then the Coronation and the best holiday ever. Every street with tables and trestles down the middle for food and sweets and those tangerines that appeared only at festive times. Not a car in sight and we had no trams, the bus drivers were off for the day like everyone else. Hats and crackers, or bon-bons as they were called if you were posh. God knows where it all came from but the home made wines and ginger beers came out from every secret still and bottle in town.
It was a time when everyone got stuck into the spirit of things and made decorations, flowers, paper roses and streamers from paper mache in every colour.

Our No.49 was covered in red, white and blue roses made by our Mum and voted the best display in the whole street. It was a special, happy and rare day. Rare because men with that rare day off work said, "What happened to the rain?" It always rained but for this once it was warm and sunny.

The house on the corner with the piano, where the men used to sing coming off shift waiting for the water to heat for their tub, was a big hit with the windows flung wide open. We all sang, 'God save the King', Mrs Simpson's song, 'The Isle of Capri', 'Cwm Rhondda' and 'Calon Lan' till we were hoarse and the street looked a mess but it was all a day not to forget.

There was always singing, choir practice in the Chapel in Queen St opposite the grocer shop, Band of Hope on Mondays, Rechabites for kids and some meeting or other going on all the time, and it kept the throats and lungs busy.

Band of Hope was OK, some sissy stuff and lots of games. We played spin the bottle up the far end so we could go up behind the stage when we got a forfeit. It was when you lost and had to pick a girl and go behind the stage and kiss her. Some of the bigger and bolder boys came out smirking out the side of their face and bragging they had their hand up her knickers. There was the one girl who got picked a lot but I didn't fancy all that kissing stuff with her.

Another funny thing, this time about Rechabites and most of you won't know what they did or were. They were against the 'Demon' drink. Preachers went on a treat and gave the men merry hell all the time. I took the oath, as we all did. It was not to touch drink till your majority, that means till your 21 and can vote. I actually never did touch the stuff till I was 22 but then worked on catching up for the rest of my life. The best part of all the meetings was the singing and the build up to the Eisteddfod, so choir practice was a time to belt it out to be chosen.

There's nothing in the whole world as bad as practicing all year on a poem or a song, saying it backwards and sideways till on the day, in your clean white shirt, pants and borrowed jacket, hair slicked down at the last minute by mum's spit and you stand before the adjudicator and go blank.

In some schools in Wales it was suggested and pushed real hard by those in England that only the 'King's English' was to be used and Welsh was out. Down our way we still said 'Bore da' instead of good morning and 'Diolch yn fawr', which is, thank you very big and it hurt to be told not to be Welsh, or even speak it. Having been in Wales such a short part of life and having the Welsh knocked out of us in Hayes, Middlesex and in our Aunt's Howden and Goole, we never fully learned our language and forgot it till later in life. All that was left were things such as, 'Mynd i gwelly'--go to bed, 'Cair yr drws', shut the door or, 'Dymer fyn havod yn fyn hen' which is, this is my tongue in my head. I'm sorry but that's the way it is' even though I still sing in Welsh if I find a St David's Day meeting to attend such as our St David's at Avoca on the Central Coast.

We had Gypsies in Wales, supposedly the purest Romanies anywhere and when they called, Mum bought the wooden clothes pegs they used to make and sell. Mum got on well with them as she was psychic and a bit of a Gypsy herself and in fact told a better fortune than any of them. You had to watch them as they were said to snitch anything lying around, even to taking babies. It's part of their tradition and something about their God or Devil, whoever, saying it's OK and for them, not a sin.
On a wet day or when I stayed home to mind the kids while Mum went out we used to play trains with the kids using the chairs all lined up in a row. With the Gypsies pegs I used to put two together across each other and stand them up to look like a man on horseback and they could play galloping to the hounds games and I made up horsey stories. Marbles were still big, always marbles over the floor and cigarette cards in hundreds were still the rage. I had a train set of them almost complete from W.D. & H.O. Wills' Wild Woodbines.Trains still fascinated me from the time we saw the Flying Scotsman on its way to Edinburgh that time Doug and I swung on the gate and watched it fly through.

Stuck in Treforest wasn't that bad when something like harvest festival at Chapel was on, and that was a time! Like a Fair for the day or a week really. Every one took in fruit and vegetables, flowers, jams and bottles of everything, heaps of it all round the organ, the altar and every which way. God's bounteous favours and more especially for us afterwards when most of it was sold for Chapel funds. The left overs were there for the taking and we took it by the pram full, enough to last us for ages.

'Furriners' came round some days, as well as the regulars such as the Italian called Bracchi, the Chinaman and the Cockney rag bone man. Some called him a Wop or other names but Brachi was the happiest man on his tricycle bike with the big ice cream box and wide handlebars that matched his big sticking out moustache. The Tarr boys always got an ice cream as did Alfie, he always had the dough and if we hung around and were in good with him he may shout us one too. On a real hot day of big demand, Brachi would return after making a second batch with little bits of ice still in it.

The Chinaman with his yolk or wide bit of wood across his shoulders and bundles of brown Spanish onions hanging each side would jog down each street, we called him, 'Who Flung Dung'. Then there was the rag and bone man and he was fun and spoke like some of the Londoners we had met. He pushed his cart along and called out, "Rag bone, Rag bone," and you could hear him coming for a mile.

He bought anything, mostly rags, old clothes, jam jars and bottles. I don't remember the bone bit and what anyone would do with a lot of old bones but never having old clothes except a heap of rags from the tip. Sometimes, we found enough jam jars to get a penny or two. Some kids took a gold fish instead of the penny and put it in a jar to take home as a pet. It was usually dead by the time the man called again. The little jar would be half full of soggy bread and the fish bug eyed and all squashy.

22

* So Much of Interest to Tell *

As I was getting older, like most kids, I wanted to get a job, it was the thing to do and the chance of a bit of spending money. Paperboy was what most kids wanted to be, but it was hard to get into it unless your Mum or Dad knew someone or was regular in the shop and bought lots of stuff. Never letting up, I kept going down and asking till the day they brought out a special edition like they did for that earthquake in America or something really big. So to shut me up they gave me a bundle to sell up and down the streets singing out, "Extra, extra, read all about it," like they did in the movies. I walked to Pontypridd because I knew they bought them around the park and swimming pool area to read or lie on the damp grass in the sometimes sun. After that I got papers on a Saturday morning to flog around and it felt good calling out "South Wales Echo",--- "Pontypridd Observer", to earn my few pence as pay. I never gave up and pestered someone or everyone till the last one was sold.

It was then that I started saving and got cunning. I never handed all the loot over to Mum, some of it I put away in one of Aunty Gwen's old handbags, which I kept in the pigeon coop. A bit smelly now since we ate the pigeons. Not all of it because if I got done in time I could afford to go to the matinee at the Flicks. We got the newsreel with the Big Lion roaring, then we had a comic cartoon and before the big picture, the next part of the serial we had waited all week for. Shows like, 'The Thunder Riders', a science fiction and cowboy mixed up thriller with Tim McCoy and Frankie Darrow. We had the first, real Tarzan with things like where the girl was left hanging over the cliff all week till the hero came along next Saturday with that monkey on his back, swinging from tree to tree to save her so she could get stuck in the quick sand at the end and stay there with us in suspense for another week.

Something was happening at our flicks, more new pictures coming out all the time and people finding money to go regular. It was Shirley Temple time, every little girl was growing curls and there were 'singing cowboy kids' riding off into sunsets after all the shoot'em ups. Gangsters were a big thing in cars called Jalopies, with big cigars in their gobs and with

Tommy guns blasting away. Every kid was out pow, pow, powing and getting into the Hollywood way of life.

We were all gob smacked to see the first of what they called the extravaganza movies, the Broadway Melodies of 1930 something and a new one every year. There were dancing girls and dresses you couldn't believe and stuff for boys to boggle and fantasize over as America poured out the unbelievability of it all. The picture, 'San Francisco' was the most amazing thing we'd ever seen and never knew it was a real event till years later.

Then there was winter when it's supposed to snow, hopefully on Xmas day but it didn't always, more likely it was the usual slush and sleet or freezing winds. I hated it and even way back at the cottage homes dreamt of the sunshine and warmth to be able to swim, anywhere, as long as it was like the place we saw on the slide night where everyone was brown and only in shorts. Not like here looking all pale like a skinned rabbit.

It was winter and we made the most of it with lots of snow to play the regular kids games. We always had a go in with the old folk, we would throw buckets of water out front on the footpath at night so it would freeze and make great slippery slides. They were awake up and would be up early to clean the grates and toss the ashes on the ice or use salt and they mucked it up a treat. Every twisted ankle or crash, head over turkey, [Jenkins would say, 'Arse over collar stud'] was blamed on us.

Someone actually broke his knee! and went to bed for ages. I got lots of "I told you so's", and not much sympathy either.

We were rotten little buggers and I missed our gang when I had to go to work more and more often. It was considered fun to fill a jar or tin with water, lean it against the door, knock and run like hell. We terrorised the houses in other streets as all the doors right on the street opened inwards, it was knock and run. We never got caught, too slippery and fast and being scruffier than Oliver Twist himself, we all looked the same and couldn't be picked out in a gang.

Days when we hooked it from school and so the truant officer sneaking round the lanes couldn't find us, we would take our jam tin hanging on a string handle with a candle stub waxed on the bottom and go down into the drains. We knew every outlet and could move the rusty grills, if they were still there and we'd crawl for miles under the town. Rats and a few dead cats, rusty bike bits and stuff for old Rag-Bone. The scum and yuck was often knee deep but it was an adventure, even when the holy candles we got from the church bin dropped off in the water and the matches were wet. It didn't matter, we could listen under a manhole and figure our way out. There were lots of cuts and bruises but they didn't hurt that much, or go too festered either, but the whacks we got from being in a mess did. As did the cane next day at school without a note from Mum.

Mr Jenkins was his name, he owned the corner grocer shop in Queen St. I worked for him for awhile till he gave me the 'heave ho' in favour of a rotten kid whose Mum he was on with. By the look of her and the useless kid, he was welcome to what he got!

I could see early on that he was a flirt and very nice to all the ladies. Mum had got me the job of delivery boy from being nice to him and giving him the come on. He wasn't in her class for conning people and I like to believe or think he didn't do much good. While working there, Mum had me listen to all the gossip so as to relate the juicy bits to her over our cocoa at night. Maybe it was grist for the mill and some good bits to use for the tea cup readings.

My job was deliveries before school and after school. On some days I had to race from school to do a midday run and to most always cop a caning for being late back to class.

Mucking about the shop, tidying up and taking it all in, it was fascinating to see 'Jenkins the Shop', as he was known, operate. He was so good, he could cut up a block of butter into exact 1/2 or 1lb blocks and wrap them in grease proof paper without a scrap to spare and each weight exact. The same with sugar from a big white bag, every lot measured into brown paper bags, bumped down and sealed to the very last grain.

Jenkins was a naughty man, of clean habits in the shop but a dirty old man, but always nice to everyone, even to the old waxed moustached regimental looking war blokes who came in to try the cheese board. They tasted them all, wasted good time and then just took a bit of cheddar or our own Cairphilly, but Jenkins was still nice to them.

He told me confidently one night while closing up and looking up to the full moon scudding by up in the clouds, "It is cheese,--------- Cairphilly."

The job was worth more but I only got five bob a week. Not very often I got a tip, sometimes a sweet, a date or two or a grape, accidentally dropped on the floor on purpose. Or sometimes on a delivery, a Welsh cake or home made biscuit made with stale 'drippin'. They usually went into the pocket and then into Alfie Philip's pig bucket as I was getting a bit picky. The five bob was for five days plus Saturday morning, that was the big special run I did. The money was welcome to Mum's budget. Budget! That's a laugh, there's no such word in our place or Mum's vocabulary.

The big bike with the massive top heavy wire basket on the front was too heavy for me to ride so I pushed it everywhere, then I stood on one pedal and scudded it back home hanging on for grim death.

Saturday was special as I wheeled a full basket to our best customer up past Pontypridd and up the worst hill. The lady was very nice and lived in a posh place with lace curtains and with doilies under all the nick-nacks scattered all around. I was usually puffed out and hot by the time I got there and managed to carry the basket in. She always gave me lemonade or some drink with biscuits and cake. She told me how nice mannered I was and that I spoke better than those other nasty coarse boys, all that stuff and she patted me some times and liked to touch. In the end I got a bit worried, she was quite excited and going a bit funny. I panicked and raced out all stupid like, got on the bike and free wheeled down the hill like a bat out of hell. Pretty dumb I guess! I never told anyone in case they'd laugh.

Jenkins was OK, never mentioned the lady again and I missed the sixpence tip she always gave me for being nice as she said. I soon lost the job to a snotty nosed stuck-up kid from up town. His mother looked like a bit of a tart and Jenkins was going for her. Good luck to the lot of them I thought. The kid would never get the bike up the hill and if he did, the nice lady would have him for breakfast.

There were other jobs but not as good as my wood or 'Stick Run' as Uncle Joe used to call his business. In the depression in our Rhondda, after being layed off at the pit, he stayed off the dole or relief by collecting, cutting up and bagging wood of any kind. As all the trees for miles around had long ago finished up as pit props, anything that burned was used with, or to kindle the coal, if and when they had it that is.

My wood run was what "Boyo", the man in the back lane used to cut up and tie into little bundles. He was an old soldier, talked anyone blind who'd listen, and he just sat there on the three-legged stool all day long doing his work. I was his salesman and took the old pram to fill with bundles and hawk around for miles at a penny each or four for threepence. I tried to always go back empty after calling and knocking on endless doors and mostly did, though some nights I was the last one in the street on my run before I got home for supper.

The commission was lousy and miserable, I always had a cold with a runny nose and watering eyes. I wore out good sandshoes too so I chucked it all in as not worth the effort.

And then there was Xmas, it was holly time, a time to really cash in. I knew the woods backwards, all in and out the rifle range and no one else was going there now. The best holly with the rich clusters of red berries was in there. I collected it, carted it back and tied it in bundles and it was damned hard trudging back down. I felt a bit like the, 'Hither Page and stand by me,' and the 'Good King Wenceslas' bit in the carol when he told the poor Page to bring the pine logs hither. I sang all of those carols over and over to forget the freezing cold.

Doreen helped me with the bundles and then I took them down to the fashionable shops now opening up, to the dress shops and hair do shops and soon sold them. They were used for decorations, my holly was better than anyone else's, with more red berries and they couldn't get enough of it.

I made lots of money and being Xmas, everyone was nice to a busy kid and gave me lots of tips. Things were looking up, there should be more Xmas' I thought and it set me off to saving and thinking how to make more money.

Mum got rid of most of it pretty smartly. The money I mean, not the holly, but for a while there we were like the rich ones in King St.

The good times came in bursts, like on a rare visit by Dad when he brought little things and stayed long enough to cook his baked dinner special and do his clean up and de-nit thing. It was good too the time on Sundays when Mum went and sold blackberries to the rich folk who wouldn't get their hands all red and their fancy boots dirty picking them themselves. I still can't remember Dad sending money or even having any when he did turn up. What did he do with it? Did he blow it on the trips to France, to the sunny south he once mentioned. Come to think of it, he did often use Froggy bits like, 'Voul a vou promenade' or something like that. Makes me think about what he was up to.

Mum used to go by train, lugging the heavy basket to other villages or towns as she felt she would have been embarrassed if caught by people she knew. We kids picked the basket full of berries back up on the hill, Wimberries too but they are only as big as a pea, it took too long and we ate more than went in to the basket.

Another time was when Uncle? was around, he was good for a few extras. I don't know to what side of the family he belonged as there were Aunties and Uncles all round. We had that Uncle over by Rhydfellin way where we went after coming out of the workhouse. That was a good time, he was nice to Mum and good to us. What happened to him?

The good times were when we ate up big, when there were new shoes for the next in line or a hand out, just in time with Mum in a real dither about the new shirt, trousers and jacket for me to start school at Treforest High. What a waste of money and effort that was because after initiation day, the shirt and pants were torn and it was the end of wearing a ruined jacket to school.

At Treforest High, the boys had the lower playground and the girls had the top with the stone wall where they could lean over and watch the boys and especially the mayhem of the so-called fun of initiation day of the new boys at the school.

It happened at first break when the big and older boys went wild and the teachers and headmaster stood behind the shelter shed to be out of sight, not miss anything but to let it all happen. The stupid tradition of it all, as the new little kids, scared stiff and nowhere to escape, had coats and shirts, pants and everything, ripped off. Pants especially and we ran around to get away but there was nowhere to escape.

Some cried, some toughies cursed the bullies and fought tooth and nail, using language learned along a hard way of brunging up. Up on the wall, the girls cheered and jeered. They called out to those they knew, pointing to miserable shrivelled dicks and skinny arses and humiliating us as we huddled under the wall till the ringing of the bell saved us.

Most of us never got around to a new outfit, hardly even game to go home that night for an earful. Parents and old ones never understand what kids went through and Doreen and Yvonne, after hearing of those girls up on the wall, both acted like silly twits. They giggled and went on a treat when they heard what happened.

It was Craddock Evans that finally broke the initiation mess up. I hated his guts but was glad to see him that day. He, for some untold reason, always took a dislike to me and gave me hell till the day I told him I was going to Australia and he looked shocked. It was to be a heaven sent release for me. I beat him and he knew it because I never cried or said I was sorry when he bullied and bashed me. When I did leave I said stupid things boys shouldn't say but it was truly a case of, "balls to you and your cane old chap."

It's funny I should say that because it was about then that Mum got her ball, her crystal ball. It may only have been borrowed, we had it for a while but it disappeared again later. It was just a lump of glass to me but as they say in the classics, "Holy Mackerel", because it was true that when she went into her vision or trance thing in a dark room and put her hands on the crystal she was a marvel and better than any of your Romany Gypsies or Psychics [whatever they are]. For a while it had the ladies and women lined up for Mum to go into her trances. Most times it was somewhere else other than at our place and Mum went out always poshed up. You wouldn't know what was under the coat, scarf and gloves, any old frock would do but in decent shoes and she always had nice stockings on her legs, Mum looked presentable.

With the bit extra, that was a good time too and things were sort of looking up.

Growing up was a worry, the fun and games up in the woods got more involved and girls were now not as dumb and uninteresting. The big boys may have given the other kids ideas when they sneaked behind the gorse and bracken to peek at the girls doing a pee. We all knew what the big boys did and what the young ones tried to copy with useless little dicks and no one thought it was wrong. From the examples of the times, it was just another game.

Seeing some other kids happy and as horny as ever after mass and confession on a Sunday, there was the thought to turn Catholic. There was that no meat on a Friday thing but everyone had fish and chips anyway so what's the big deal? I've already mentioned about Mick saying sausages aren't meat.

It would have been OK to go Catholic but we'd never remember all the Saints they were always burning candles to and we would have to confess to our pinching those stub ends of candles to use in our jam tins when we did the sewer and drains bit. They were the good ones that never blew out in the breeze and as the kid said, the Holy Smoke or Spirit was with us.

Thank God in Wales we only had Dewi Sant, our Saint David, a real Saint with his own place just across from Ireland and it's called St David's. He truly and really lived and preached there and we mostly knew what was going on till the Wesleyans, the Baptists and hordes of others like Methodists and other religions came along to confuse and scare the daylights out of innocent folk till they didn't know which way was up. In the bad times, the times when the chance of free soup and a crust of bread got you to attend Chapel such as Moriah where our Mam Rees did the flowers and cleaning year after year. They were the real Christians, the ones who fed us the lovely faggots and peas I have already mentioned.

Wales, like everywhere else in the world had Irish, especially in the south and down around by us. They came at the slightest whisper of work, for work and pay enough to buy the pint they enjoyed even if it was not

Guiness. They really could work, could drink and between times bear kids. The kids were the same as us but different and spoke funny like. They worshipped different to us and had their Brothers and Sisters to run the convents they had in the cities.

Some of the kids thought they were tougher than us but old Craddock Evans soon sorted them out till they could leave and go to their own school and learn catechism and the Hail Mary stuff. They had a Saint for every day of the year and I reckon you could ask for a miracle any time but most of the Irish were as poor and in worse condition than us and with all that, could never ever rake up a decent miracle. Even though we picked each other, we were both sort of Celts and could get along together and could and did blame the English for half our troubles.

In the early days when the coal and iron masters worked their people to death for a pittance, more starved than survived and we fought each other for a job. The Irish called us Welsh scum and we called them Irish bastards yet, we both had a sense of humour and could sing and that is why we, both lots, survived.

At Treforest, our Bernard was a worry because he had that potty trouble when his little bum popped down, though that was OK and better now. He still got the first hot water for his bath. Bath time was mostly a lick and a promise with cold water and a flannel. If the big kettle had been emptied and not put back on the hob, it was cold water anyway and the flannel, come to think of it, was a grubby rag. In my mind, I can only associate a flannel as being red, as in my memory back at Mam Rees' there was a neat, stitched red flannel. Also in my imagination I see it as a piece of the red flannel shirt essential for bad backs.

Bath time at Riverview was a major production and Mam Rees did it proper with kettles coming off the fire for each in turn in and in the correct pecking order till all the coal dust and grime was settled in the bottom of the tub.

I was maybe the only one of we kids to watch and share the wonder of the fun and games of bath time of my Mam's family in front of the fire at No.6.

That was a very, very nice time.

At 49 King St., our bath time was in front of the fire too but there was no coal allowance and the fire was more half out than burning bright. For us it was little ones first up to Doreen and then me at the end with hardly any water from all the splashing and playing, and there was only yucky stuff at the bottom. When I used to throw the black water out into the white snow 'out er back', it made strange and fancy patterns to fantasise and dream over till it was, "Shut the bleeding door," or more nicely, "Put the wood in the hole."

Bernard was there and then he was gone. We didn't know where, but it was to Bridgend, I later found out, to the hospital there. A time went by and we went along with things and seemed to accept the fact he was gone. Yvonne missed him most and though little herself she was like a little mother to Bernard Oswald. It was a bad time for her too, because about then was when the Alsatian attacked her and ripped off half her scalp. It was awful and half of King St gathered around as they do, to give advice, sympathise a bit and then gossip. She lost her lovely blonde hair for the second time and Mum raved and went on as was her want with the, "My loovly baby," thing. She really was and the happiest kid to entertain, to push around in the pram or carry around on the hip as a bleeding pest! She never whinged or went on when her tatty old nappies were changed and when the cold water flannel slapped her little bum.

It all comes back how Beryl told of Mam Rees and her belief that Mum was lazy in the earlier Llwynapia days, she didn't wash the clothes or us. It is a 'not to be told history', but Mum cut up the curtains for nappies when I was born. To cover my 'Looovly Boom', I suppose.

We weren't talking about her I know but being so good with Bernard, it comes to mind how Yvonne missed him. At the hospital the Nurse Llewellyn, who cared for and looked after him, knowing Mum as she did from being a local and almost a relative herself, fell in love with our Bernard and wanted to adopt him. In retrospect and knowing now how the pattern of adoption went and was to later go, it could really have happened and there was talk. Doreen and I sensing something was going on, must have let it be known it was a definite No-No. For the time being then at least and just as it was for our Myrna too, as only time was to tell.

23

* Working, Growing Up and Going to Camp *

I was working now, bringing in the money and thinking I was the breadwinner. I reckoned it was a bit rough having to look after the others so much. I did miss school a lot as I was left with them pretty often. We played games and I showed them such things as keeping the stones from prunes we ate. We would sit on the kerb outside and rub the stones or seeds half way down on the rough stone or cement. Then with chewing gum, you could stick matches across like a native boat, stick in a little flag and sail them down the gutter where there was always a flow of something going by.

The time must have been what they were to call bonding and we needed a bit of that as the near future was soon to tell.

One time, rather than go to the field to watch the men and boys sit around the Druid Stones puffing endless fags and day dreaming, whatever dole folk dreamt about, I put them in the pram and pushed off past 'Jenkins the Shop', passed the pictures and around to where the vegetable allotments were.

It was where the lucky folk with little plots of council ground were able to grow vegetables and herbs, have a rabbit hutch and tin sheds full of garden stuff. Sadly to me it was all almost vacant now, most of it gone except for left over crops of miserable carrots or dead cabbages with grubby heads and beanstalks that were truly has-beens.

Up past there quite a way was my once favourite place, the most famous Glamorgan canal where the factory poured out hot water waste into the freezing canal water. Our gang on a Sunday or a day hooking it from school used to spend all day swimming and jumping off the, 'No jumping off bridge' Bridge and the water was great except that the specks of tar in the output would hit your skin and spread all over.

The kids were too young to appreciate or ever know why we went there or why I tried to share the fun times. They probably got hungry too as they kept asking, "can we go now?" So it was down to the allotments to grab some measly carrots to chew on and keep them quiet and I quietly pushed off for home.

To Yvonne, Bernard or Myrna the canal is nothing and though I never saw it again it was a part of my time. In years to come and not too far off either, the canal was filled in and forgotten. The allotments became an almost instant village of houses. Looking back on it, it was perhaps just a nice day for a walk with the kids.

Walking was always a big thing in our family, never a car and I don't recall such a thing as a taxi or cab in those days, so we walked. Mum had done the London bit, the one from the workhouse and many others. There was a pram to push as I had just done and we did walks to Trehafod, Cylfynedd and the one I liked to Rhydfelin. We visited relations, made up ones or real! God only knows, as some were hard to relate to, the Uncle on which side? But at each place as times improved, we got sandwiches or cake to fill up on, then told to go out and play. It was mostly dark and quite late when we got home, luckily having had a feed and being worn out, the others went up the wooden hill to the lumpy old bed and were gone in a minute.

Sometimes I wished I was a kid because there was nothing worse than getting home in the dark, so cold outside everyone had gone to bed. The fire just a warm ash and no paraffin in the lamp. Finding a coin for the meter was a curse. Mum never had one and I hated letting anyone know about my secret money place because they would talk me into using it, so I would have to use my coin sneakily. Mum would say, "I'll pay you back Derrick." Like, I thought, "What about the pound you still owe me for the sticks back at Tonteg."

The holiday Mum gave me was the best one ever and the one I suppose may have set me off to writing. She didn't actually give it to me, just used her charm and pushy Yorkshire way. I'm sure it was with a bit of acting and a tear or two, but she got me in to go.

It was when a group of so called under privileged kids were to be chosen, those run down and in need of a charitable pick me up. Mum told them I was her little breadwinner, working oh so hard, very poorly and in need of just this holiday.

"Never had a holiday," she told them and knowing my Mum, with all of them in tears, they probably said let the little beggar go and get this woman out of here.

As a result I got to go to Ogmore by the Sea, two whole weeks on the beach and in the sea and even real sunshine. There was food regular for every meal and pieces of fruit or an apple for every kid.

Chapel had done a collection and every child got pocket money and we went berserk the first day in spending it at the tuck shop. Mrs Griffiths got into trouble for allowing us to guts ourselves and sick up all night but she explained, "They all looked the same, just so many heads over the counter top." Someone sent a message back home and we each got a postal note for two shillings to spin out a penny at a time for the next two weeks.

Things fell into place for me there away on my own for once and I grew up a bit. I wrote the first story or essay of any interest to anyone. We had been playing in the sand hills with a boat I made like the prune seed ones only big, made of wood and with an outrigger like in the native books.

The essay was about sailing away to foreign lands with real sunshine and with strange animals.

Ogmore was a wonderful camp and experience, a sort of growing up time, as if I was on the move or something. We had the camp song, which I still recall;

"We are the boys who live on stew
porridge, beef and plum duff too
up the old Ogmorians, Zimbo, Zimbo Za"

Lots and lots of verses sung with Gusto over and over.

At the end of the camp was a prize giving day and while fidgeting around up the back, not paying attention as usual, my name was called! I had to rush down and read out my essay which, with the Eisteddfod or Chapel training I had, was quite easy to do. The story was, 'A day at the beach' and everyone was quiet. I was in shock when I got first prize. It was a shilling and such a surprise and for just playing in the sea, in the sun and then just writing it all down. It may have been the start.

Ogmore was like Barry or Porthcawl, not as many people and more free space. Barry Island was where the Chapels took the kids in Charabancs in July each year with the hope that summer was on that day of that year.

Each got the obligatory shilling, a bucket and a spade and were let loose to pester people, have donkey rides, go on the dodgem cars and put balls into clowns mouths to win a cupee doll on a stick for a girl or a dumb toy for themselves.

As it only happened once a year we were meant to have the fun of stuffing ourselves with hot chips, ice creams, Barry [Teeth destroying, sugary] Rock and battered fatty everything. It was wind and sun burn to go like lobsters and get sand all up our bums till we sat in the bus going back in pain. In our minds, next years outing would be no great priority, that was till about next May when we'd start being good again to qualify to do it all again.

The great Tonteg disaster had been when chosen for my first Barry excursion. The night before we had all gathered for instructions and were issued with our bucket and spade. Each received the shiny shilling and told to take it straight home. I didn't, I played and dawdled passed the orchards and I lost my shilling. Though I looked for ages it was gone and at home I got a terrible telling off but everyone went back and looked till dark. Never found it of course but I was still allowed to go. Where another shilling came from, I really didn't care but it was tied in the corner of my hankie for safety.

The weird thing about kids from round our way was that so many could swim. What with the weather cold one day and freezing the next we crazily did use any pond or stream, water tanks for filling engines and the river Taff which looked great before plastic and styrene, soon to be invented. A favourite place to cool down, or freeze up if you like, was the big steel water tank on the railway side where the engines pulled up and used the canvas hose to fill the water tender. There was a hole in the top of the tank, about boy size and big enough to drop in one at a time and we used to swim there. It was so cold it would freeze the balls off a billiard table [I heard 'Jenkins the Shop' say that] and we often had to stay in there for ages till the train left.

I'll never forget the first day of swimming lessons. It was spring and time to start lessons so we were marched to the baths in Pontypridd gardens where I sold papers. There was crunchy ice on the grass here and the sun still shining over in Africa or Australia, but not here.

The teacher wasn't going in so the lesson had to go on and as we stood around each in a thin towel, the goose pimples were as big as blackberries till the front row were told to 'Go!'

As we were going to die anyway, in we went and the thin starry patterned ice all over the pool got churned up in the mad panic to the end and out.

So much against nature's odds, we kids really could swim.

Treforest was getting smaller and with no job on Sunday we went off and walked for miles but always spent hours at the rubbish tip. It seemed to get bigger and bigger and spread for miles with mountains of stuff to play in, hills to slide down on pieces of tin, in a card board box or on a coal sack. When the berries, black, raspberry or whatever, were on we ate them but there was always good stuff in the boxes from the shops. The bad bits and dirt could be rubbed off with that soft packing paper which was real nice as well when you had to go and do big jobs among the brambles. We took some home to use instead of the squares of Echo or Observer on the string in the W.C. Jenkins said the Echo or Observer spread more than they wiped and he only used apple-wrapping paper he saved for himself. Mick Hanny later told me that the only good things in the newspapers were fish and chips.

24

* Things were Really Happening *

Things were happening making me older, sooner than should have been but it couldn't be helped, it just went on. Like the time cousin Gwen got permission from her mum to go on a picnic with the boyfriend. Knowing it was touchy, she was smart enough to suggest it would be nice for us kids to have a day in the country and that they would take us.

We caught the little Welsh train at Treforest, went through our old Tonteg looking so removed and in the past, through Church Village where no one but I seemed to care or mention that we had been there and then it was along to Taffs Well, where we got out with our parcels of lunch and walked up into the woods. It was through lanes with wild raspberries and the hedge with the leaves we ate and called 'bread and butter' and then up into the ferns.

For us it was an adventure. For Gwen and her boy friend, by the look of them, oblivious and holding hands, it was just heaven and even I knew it was perfect with not a soul but us for miles.

I could go on about the little bunnies the girls saw or the birds nests where I could have got some great eggs to pinch but it was fun and exciting to be sent off to play. Which we did, but we, or at least I, sensed what was going on and watched them. The big boy, who was a man, and our Gwen, snuggling up on his spread out 'Mac' coat. He thrashed around and she held onto him like adults do but I think they'd never done it before and we stared in silence hidden behind the bushes. Each, I suppose, with our own private thoughts.

I felt funny, holding my breath, somehow happy for Gwen in what was to me then, real love. I was sweating and hanging onto myself so the girls wouldn't see and be embarrassed and think I was awful.

Gwen was always nice and I was glad for her to be so happy. She was the one who seemed to understand what boys my age were going through. She never knew what I knew but from then on the bond from the special day out was what came through.

Cousin Mavis was a different kettle of fish with her constant obsession and willingness to let someone play or touch it, she is partly to blame for a lot of the kids in our streets forward ways, but it was all just the age I suppose.

As the start of this says, "By then I was thirteen" and my little thing as it was called, was starting to take over my life. It was a shock to meet the strange boy, or I should say the stranger, the boy who was to travel on our six-week adventure and who wanted to do funny things. He laughed when he heard my name was Derrick.

When we had our bath together in the biggest bath of hot water I'd ever seen since the Cottage homes, he showed me his stiff dick and said, "This is my Derrick." I hated that Frenchman actor who Mum was so besotted with at the time I was born and when she needed some romance in her messed up life, I became Derrick. I never did like it but that was the end of it.

Mum was a frustrated actress herself and about that time or just before all our leaving thing came up, she was in a play and the group needed a youth for an extra part.

It was fun with all the men and women and I learnt my part the first night and must have been alright as they made a nice fuss of me, but I up and left and was never to know if there was any talent in the boy from the Rhondda.

There were others to come such as Burton and Hopkins and even our happy Harry Secombe. Did I miss out somewhere?

25

* My Two Loves *

That love thing is a pain. I knew by now it just got you into trouble and it's funny how boys fall for older women, maybe an affection starved boy to an older women, [and they can tell] is an irresistible challenge.

My love was for a lady so beautiful, I went all stupid and dumb. Dumb struck too but she understood, took it all in and knew exactly what to do.

It was while playing across the river up towards the canal that I cut my finger nasty like, it was on a rusty tin, all jagged and it bled like mad.

Her place was the bungalow up the end of the old gardens and she must have wondered what was going on when this smelly horrid looking kid with blood down to his scabby knees knocked at the door.

In her blue and white striped 'ready to go to work' uniform, she cleaned me up a bit then bathed and bandaged my finger nice and neat. She wasn't snooty and stuck up with me. She was so kind and so beautiful and I loved her.

She gave me cocoa and biscuits. I seemed to attract cups of cocoa a lot. The biscuits were real bought ones from a fancy Scottish tin and not like some home made ones that smelled stale and cockroachy. Then sadly she had to go, it was so nice there and I hated her having to go.

In the time I had left in Treforest I always meant to go back and take her the biggest and nicest bag of grapes, but I never did. I just daydreamed in bed at night of rescuing her from robbers or lions or such and being her hero and she taking care of me. Just us without all the usual house full. Nurses were always nice to me but as she was my first love, she was the nicest one.

What is it about grapes? If ever there is someone in hospital, sick or even dying down our way, it is always right to take grapes. Was it because they were expensive or just supposed to be good for you?

Grapes were the 'bestest' things I could think of to take my nurse.

Mum once took us to the infirmary, part of the workhouse, to visit someone. On the way she bought a bag of grapes and spent a whole two bob. It surprised me, as it was enough for us all to go to the Flicks. She was all done up in her coat, hat and gloves like a Toff and at the gate going in we all got our hair slicked down with that horrible 'spit on the hanky' bit to pretty us up and show us off.

While they chatted and went on, we sat quietly chewing away at the grapes till they were all gone. For me it was so strange, the time I had been in the infirmary with the old men, the Dicky bird bit and then I looked at my thumb to see it was still bigger than the other from the poisoning. It was and though it all seemed a dream, it had been very real.

While I'm on about infirmaries and hospitals there was another nurse. I was always into nurses and this one was at the Birmingham hospital, a time while we were at Middlemore homes and were waiting to be sent overseas. I had bad tonsillitis and was rushed to hospital by someone, it may have been Mrs Cadbury or it was the homes matron, and I was in a plush private car. I had to have the dreaded operation with its horrible smell of ether, which makes everyone sicker than the 'Opp' itself.

I forget what I have said at the start of all this but it was a miracle that we all got tonsil trouble because my sisters and I were, without our knowing, booked to go on the next boat to leave England. That happened to be to Canada where we would have gone without a say in the matter and all my wishes and plans for Australia would have been a lifetime disaster but good old, bad old tonsils, we missed that boat.

My operation started a trend and most of the kids in due course came in for adenoids and tonsils and a bit of the luxury at the hospital away from the boring, boring home at Selly Oak and the depressing dormitories.

For me it was special to be in the big room with clean sheets, the meals, after the first days that is, coming as fast as you could clean up the tray. The operation bit was worth it all and it was special because my nurse was from Treforest, she knew our street and everything so I got all the love and attention in those two weeks to last for many years. She was sort of my own personal Florence Nightingale.

She was my second great love.

26

* The Restless Days Before *

Doreen's memories are so different to mine, she says we never had much except love and I thought that was funny. We were too busy or too often moving around for expressions of love. Maybe old Mr Price or the Tarr family across the street or her special friend Audrey Wiltshire were sufficient for her. Being so young and just going along with things, she doesn't recall the really bad times, the home traumas, no money and so often no shoes, no Dad most times and the time I spent working.

On the boat she and I could talk. She, like myself, felt it when Dad and Mum bickered or broke up. She never really knew Dad, he wasn't a drinker but Doreen said what rotten sods some men were, coming home as drunk as a skunk after spending the money from the only job they'd had in ages. I don't recall a lot of drunks, never enough dough to get that way I suppose.

For the first time, really being away from it all, we talked of how difficult it must have been to take us into the homes. We talked over the uncles, the family and where they all fitted in. We both agreed you had to work on people like do-gooders or ulterior motivators with their bags of sweets to win you over. Christians, real or so called, were also a worry for kids in many ways.

I felt a bit guilty there and then of being a bit of a bastard to her in a superior way, only then realising how good she was and that she had a mind of her own. There were surprises in the revelations, such as the box of cigarette cards Dad gave her. I thought why her, a girl and not me a boy, his son!

She too could read and remember poetry and was worse than I in looking for something to read and she devoured all she could lay her hands on.

Doreen says she was seven when she last saw Dad but I'm not sure she has that right. She and Dad, or I felt it so, lacked a great affinity but to her, Mum was OK. Mum was hopeless, a real Ostrich and buried her head in the sand with the belief "it didn't happen" or "it will all go away." Maybe our Doreen is a bit that way too.

It's a pity the others don't know much about Tonypandy or Llwynapia, they were too young and too often on the move to London, Yorkshire, Tonteg or Church village before then settling in at Treforest. They never went back home to the real Valley. I went back by train on occasion to stay a night with Aunty Doris or one or the other and it was lovely. I wish the others could have got back to know their grand parents and the little terraced houses where it all started.

At school things were settling down, interest was on about the Huns or Germans, only the old soldiers knew who Hitler was or seemed to worry about what was going on. On morning assembly we had to stand around and listen to important things like the Melbourne Centenary Air race and we all knew the names of Scott and Campbell. There were now slide nights when parents and kids went together and some companies gave stuff away to promote things, and there was food to eat. Bushells tea was a good one and we all sang, "It always will be welcome, that cup of Bushells tea." [I think it was Bushells but it was a tea advertisement].
The best nights were the slide nights on countries like Canada or Australia, they were part of the Empire and were pushing for people to go there.
In geography class we were given a break from England, India, Hong Kong and those Empire out posts and we had to do outlines of New Zealand and Australia, learn the names of cities out there because lots were going there and sending their kids too. Maybe because of the war talk or just to be rid of them?

One night the talk was on health and we were told about T.B. Not many turned up but we always went to muck up and have free tea and cake.
T.B.! This was Wales and the coalfields were where T.B. was invented and the coal dust on the lungs with its cough, cough, cough had been going on for the 150 years of the mining in and around our valleys.
I went home and told Uncle Davy about the lecture and the funny story of the cow.
It was the same T.B. they called tuberculosis and that's what I thought the poor cow had, 'Twolicklehorses.'

You don't think of the Japanese being in Wales but there were quite a few and they played Rugby. I played soccer and never got into a Rugby team so never got to Cardiff Arms Park, never actually got to Cardiff till later on and then only twice, so it was strange to have Japanese playing our game.
Even in the schools, believe it or no, there were Jap plays and kids dressing up in funny outfits, all painted up, singing songs and going all Japanese.

We used to pinch the girls fancy paper fans and jump around copying them and singing;

> **We're gay little Japanese**
> **gay little girls from Japan**
> **we know how to dance and sing**
> **we know how to flutter our fan, etc, etc.**

All that sort of thing and the biggest sacrilege of all. They played, they played our Rugby.

Not with much hope of success, what with our referees giving orders in Welsh and our front rows as big as 'tall boys.' [That's what they called our big cupboards.]

As reported in the paper after a game at Llanelly, the Japs said;

> **Paper say we not first class**
> **we just not used to five-foot grass.**

27

* The Momentous Article *

In my initial attempt to recall and relate the facts of that time I had thought that the article was in the 'Echo' newspaper. That was until Hubert Harding told me his Dad had read it in 'The People'. The article caught my eye because it was about a migration scheme where you could go to Canada or Australia. It was for under privileged kids, orphans or those from broken homes and reading all about it I reckoned that could include me, as our home was often broken up, or at least cracking up a bit you might say.

The idea was to send the children out there and after all the slides and talk at school about the places, to me it seemed a heaven sent miracle. Canada wasn't considered, but to go and be on a farm with animals and horses, even one of your own, in Australia, in the sun, it was a dream. For girls it was to go there and be in service till they married a rich farmer or such.

Just turned thirteen, it set me off on the fantasy of a lifetime. After all that had gone on as an omen and lead up to just this, nothing was going to stop me getting out there. The article showed beaches near the big city and the country went for thousands of miles as far as the eye could see. Besides horses and cows, there were animals you'd never believe and real teddy bears that lived in trees. I thought teddy bears were only make believe.

I never told a soul, not even Doreen or any kid at school who would have laughed and blabbed it everywhere. I tore out the page before Uncle Davy had a chance to tear it out and twist it up to light his pipe with.

Filling in the form nice and grown up neat was a job but it must have been alright, though after I posted it off to the Cardiff address, the days and weeks of waiting, of the God only knew what would happen, it was the worst time in my life.

Mum thought I was sickening for something and at school I was a dead loss as if it was all now a waste of time.

Not knowing what I had started, having done it on impulse, it was a shock to Mum, to Uncle Day and Auntie Gwen, when the gentleman all dressed in a suit with his little black bag, knocked on our door one Sunday morning.

I knew somehow, swear to God I did, that he was for me. The man had really come, the letter had worked and the dream was now going to come true.

He introduced himself as Mr Llewellin from the Lady Northcote Trust Fund etc, and had come in answer to their letter. It took some explaining to both he and to Mum that it was I who had written and to prove it, I went out and got the paper from my hiding place in the pigeon coop to show them. It took a few cups of tea as they talked and Mum went over it in her mind, our Doreen and Yvonne sat as quiet as mice in what seemed the now ominous disaster of my leaving them.

Mum wasn't sure for awhile but Uncle Davy and Aunty Gwen, for whatever the reason, thought it was a great idea. They all talked it over till as the clincher to everyone, Mr Llewellin suggested that, as I was old enough to care for them, why didn't I take the two girls? Then looking at Doreen and Yvonne, said to apply as a family.

It being unofficially decided, the talk developed about how, when things got better, Mum could think of going out too, taking Bernard and Myrna.

That part was all talk at the time and as it turned out, just pie in the sky and never ever to eventuate like that at all. Much the opposite in fact.

He filled in the applications, took all our details, and as the girls realised all was well, they too were going on an adventure, they got excited. Mr Llewellin told us not to be too excited or raise false hope, as we may not be even accepted. We would be notified in due course, very soon and he then took his leave. We all sat dumbfounded.

From that moment time stood still. Waiting for an exam result or to be chosen to go to Ogmore was nothing and for me perhaps more so than for the girls as I agonised over what was holding things up. At home I was unbearable and at school a real pain in the arse, I say it because I really was and everyone gave up on me till;

"BINGO"! there was the letter.

Everyone had been waiting, half the street and even Alfie Philips who was real pooey on me for having the limelight. We had been told not to say a thing to anyone in case of disappointment but in fact we had told the world we were going to Australia.

The letter said to be ready on the day mentioned when we would be picked up and taken to the Cardiff office for a check up, both medical and a mental sort of test. We knew that part was OK, we weren't stupid, just looked that way at times. A big lesson in our education had been in 'mug cunning', a lesson we got an A pass in.

At home it was hard to be normal, school was impossible because it was weird that the news was often of Australia and that I was going there, instead of being just another back street sort of kid. I was sort of an identity as we got out our atlas and looked in vain to find where Bacchus Marsh in the State of Victoria was.

28

* Despair, Hope and Farewell *

After all that, word never came, no day or date to go to Cardiff and the glamour and glory wore off. Perhaps all just a bad dream, so it was back to the old routine and the same old King St life.

At Treforest High I got a bad fit of the hates, not only for old Evans but all the bloody awful teachers who beat the shit out of poor kids because they didn't have a cap with the school emblem on or a jacket or for stuff we couldn't do a damn thing about. If you cried from the cane or ruler across freezing knuckles, they kept you in after school and you missed out on your job such as my grocery run and you lost it.

The real hate was the disappointment of not getting away from the miserable cold and never ending wet with only soggy sand shoes to wear. It was a hate of this poor-as-piss place we had to live in and though I cried to God, he never got the message as he had his hands full looking after the rich ones who put paper money in the collection plate at Chapel. Never missed it, as they had plenty left over to have lights burning in every room of their bungalow or mansion.

I hated my Dad for always pissing off and leaving us and Mum, who was good at reading tea leaves and looking posh when she went out but never seemed to know which way was up with us, her kids. "Christ!" I hated the whole bloody lot, hated it all and in a rather beneficial way, I got it all out of my system.

I never really hated my Mum or my Dad, just the rotten system. You could blame some of it I suppose, on this depression thing that they endlessly went on about.

With all that out and said, happy, happy days, the word did come. Be ready, no need to take anything except personal things as we were to be provided with everything from the funds of the Lady Alice Northcote who owned the scheme. She was by now dead of course but had left all her money to take care of kids such as we. It couldn't be all that bad a risk to take if she had done that. It sounded better than where we had been so far and to go back to school now would be worse than dreadful.

Our farewells were terrific and we were heroes. At Chapel everyone said prayers for us and there were little gifts from people who normally didn't give us the time of day but gave out Bibles and prayer books to anyone who could be a sort of missionary. We also got all those twelve side threepenny pieces, a pocket full of them.

Leaving King St, our old No.49, for all the bad things, it had been home but with all the excitement it was in an instant all left behind, as we turned out past the Druid Stones and it was all finished and done with.

For Mum it was all a bit much now the time was here and was really happening, she looked a bit forlorn with Bernard and Myrna, one on each hand. Old Davy and Gwen, our cousins and all King St waved us goodbye. Mavis Richards was missing and I would have liked to have seen her, perhaps had a last hug for all the good, bad or naughty times. Alfie, bossy and thinking his poo didn't stink, for all I've said, he had been a good friend and he too just stood and stared as we left.

It was Mr Llewellin who picked us up, we also picked up Hubert Harding and Rex Chamberlain along the way and then the five of us were magically in Cardiff at the big railway station to catch our train. Doreen got a prayer book from Mr Llewellin which I know she still has.

Other than the small parcel we each brought with us, that was it and we were in our carriage with the leather seats and big window. The window or shutters were let down on the leather strap so we could see out as we left without much fuss and then very soon, that was that for Wales. The land of my fathers that I wished to escape from but now with dreadful premonition, I wasn't quite sure.

Hubert was my age, wild and a revolutionary, his old Merthyr Tydfil wasn't big enough for him and he was glad to be off. Leaving was no trouble for him. Rex was an age between Doreen and I, they were both good for each other while Yvonne as usual, went along with everything. The actual leaving of King St, the Rhondda Valleys and Wales, never hit us all till the first night at Middlemore.

29

* My Recriminations *

For me it was different. We went through the countryside, getting greener and cleaner as we left the pits and industry behind and before I knew it we were back in England and what I'd started began to hit me as all sorts of things went through my mind. My Mum, back there alone, none of us to look after Bernard or Myrna and God knows how they'd feel when they realised we were really missing and gone, possibly and even probably for ever.

I knew Mum would manage, she always did. God and Jesus and Dewi Sant, all of them, only knew how but what if our Dad popped in to see us and we were not there. Gone!

I thought about it for mile after mile of the clickity clack as we went along. Would he try to find us and as it has all turned out, if he really cared? He had better be quick anyway because we would soon be at the bottom of the world, for that's where it seemed we were going.

Much later, with time to think, I wondered who signed the papers, if there were any, Mum didn't and isn't it up to the father to have some say. He had to sign each time we went to the Cottage homes, I saw him do it. Maybe to be sure, to be sure! I had signed for him, anything at the time to make it all work out.

The music of the wheels with the, 'Diddley do -- diddley da,' and the 'clang, clang, clang' of the crossings as we went across made me think of Doug and I climbing on the gate and watching the people inside in comfort go by. I wished he was with us and, not having thought of him for a while, wondered if he'd ever get to know what I had done.

We went to London again and never having seen much of it in the time at Hayes when Doreen was in the pram and Doug and I the only ones to remember it as real and not a dream we had once had. This time we went to Australia House and saw much of London on the way, the enormous size of it. I'd read the book, [History books and photos] but this, the big real picture, was much better.

All the kids went to Australia House at some time for interviews or such. Our files were there and new notes added to them so that in years to come, they would be ready if needed in 'that future' to identify us or anyone involved with us as migrants of the time. The secrecy act was in place to forbid anything being divulged and lots of kids were never to know or find out who they were or really what happened to them in those early years.

It didn't matter to me all that lost or stolen children thing, it had been my choice and decision and even taking my sisters with me was left to me to decide.

As pointed out later, the advertising was certainly exciting and appealing to just such as I and in cases of not much enterprise, could have been a disaster and possibly led to a life of drudgery in some remote outpost.

The Bindoon, West Australian, shocking and shameful era of child migration was in the future to stun the world, could that have been for us? Leaving as we did and it happened so quickly, though it seemed to take ages. With the war in the offing nobody really knew where we all went this time, to those down in the valley at Tonypandy, we were all up and gone without a word. It was to be many years before the mystery was unravelled or anyone in Britain with their own problem of war, got around to thinking about us and things.

Who was to know in the years to come that such series as 'The leaving of Liverpool' or 'Lost children of the Empire' and revelations of child migration were to cause both England and Australia to seriously investigate what had gone on. Perhaps our only true and selfless champion is our Margaret Humphries O.A.

30

* Leaving Cardiff Station *

Leaving Cardiff, the busy Welsh capital, was an adventure for the five of us children off to whatever fate had in store for us. British rail in those days was superb, the leather seats with a rich smell, window seats to look out of like Lords in comfort. I've already said it but here I was as one of the rich folk Doug and I had wistfully watched go by as we swung on those crossing gates a lifetime ago. We bored or entertained anyone who would listen as we madly talked of where we were going, right up till we arrived at London's Victoria Station.

Actually starting to believe we were pioneers we received a welcome at Australia House suitable to such or the new citizens we were soon to become. We met up with kids who were in a way family for the next fifty or more years. Additions were made to our files which, happy to say, someone kept till our maturity at age 21. Every child got a file, if they didn't, there is still one in the Archives of Liverpool University where in 1993, our Bernard finally found his. I have mine to this day and it is a treasure as it includes all my letters to the Farm school while at work on the sheep station and right up to my time in New Guinea in the Airforce where it was I turned 21.

It was a quick, vague look at London sights before we were in Middlemore.

31

* Middlemore Homes and the End in Sight *

There it was! We were driven up to the building, the group of buildings that was Middlemore, the name mentioned in Cardiff and London but in the enthusiasm of it all was never thought of for what it was! Just another children's home.

Not only a let down after weeks of excitement but a bit scary in the middle of the strange city and with all the people and children talking in different lingoes, I could have died. I could have made an idiot of myself too and cried but instead just laughed till they thought I had gone potty.

All these stupid dreams and fantasies about boat trips and new countries and here I was back where I started from, in another bloody home.

As my thoughts get out of hand, I think of how fate and that fickle finger, was to see Bernard here one day, in these same homes. He, the lucky one, to follow us in due course while our poor Myrna, unable to join us, she being too young and with a war in the offing, was adopted out. Can you believe it? !! Something she and all the rest of us would have to always live with.

It wasn't really that bad, there were five of us Taffys and we had the experience of homes, we could put it up to any of those foreign speaking kids gathered by the hundreds. There were Scots, Geordies, Cockneys, Liverpuddlians and even some Irish, always some Irish.

At Middlemore time dragged on and nothing looked like happening, no word of boats to take us away so we had to go to the rotten school. Another school to add to my list of non events and here too we were picked on and never taught a thing. The war talk was getting serious and we were told we were lucky to be getting out of England.

The diversion to break the monotony as Xmas came along was the tonsil thing and most had a stay in hospital. Mrs Cadbury used to call with her basket of chocolates, she thought of the children as her little pioneers and took some of us to her home called Bourneville and not far from Selly Oak, with its gardens and home estate bigger than all Llwynapia itself.

John Middlemore was a pioneer in 1872, rescuing boys and girls to give them a new start in a new country. Mr Paul Cadbury was chairman for 25 years and Mrs Cadbury was a director of Middlemore and opened her home at Bourneville as I have mentioned. In 100 years, Middlemore cared for 8,000 children.

Convalescing or resting after coming out of hospital was supposed to be doing nothing but they had funny ideas at Middlemore. You stayed back from school alright but were given floor polishing to do which meant miles of floors and passages. The heavy block of wood as big as two shoe boxes together had a long handle that swivelled as you pushed and pulled it back and forth. You put a pad on the bottom with wax on it and worked up and down, section by section to the end. Then you changed pads to the polisher and did it again without leaving any streaks or you'd have to over do it again in the afternoon. It was OK if you took it as a muscle builder, but most kids were scrawny and hopeless and never got it done.

This was a running away place like in most others we'd seen. I think Rex might have had a go but only just for fun as he really wanted to get to Australia but Hubert wasn't going anywhere but on a boat out of there. Yet there was always a runner and they would be back in hours or at least a couple of days. The tedium of waiting was catching up on boys and girls, kids were picking on each other and fights were on all the time. Even Rex and I were jeered and teased into having a go and punched the tripe out of each other just for the hell of it. I threw a right, he ducked his head and I almost broke my hand on his hard, thick as a Welsh plank head.

The dormitory full of boys was becoming an uncontrollable riot at lights out and filthy mouthed kids from the slums of somewhere were f---ing and cursing, making big talk of girls fannies and stuff. They didn't just call them that either but to we decent kids brought up with sisters to respect, it was disgusting in front of the little ones.

Some of them were worse than others and always at themselves playing with their man sized dicks and messing up the blankets. The worst thing was that we other big boys were surreptitiously making tents of the blankets and getting bad ideas too.

It was really and truly time to get out of there.

Then it happened, so quickly as it often does, our big cases which had been ready for ages and ages, full of the new outfits to set us up in that Bacchus Marsh place in Victoria. It was, as the name on the cases said, The Lady Northcote Farm School, Glenmore, Victoria and at long last with the sigh of the 'Oh God,' unbelievability of it, we were on our way.

As I had started out with us at the Hotel in Southampton, spoken about everything including Captain Gwyllim Williams on the 'T.S.S. Largs Bay' and all of that, there is nothing more!

Except perhaps. Where was our Dad, our Mum and the others? Were they alright? As I think back I can't recall any news or hearing of them since we left King St. Is that where they still were or were they off again? Would we ever see them again?

However, nothing was going to worry us now, having got it out of our system that life here in Great Britain was almost over and done with.

Only time would tell if our family, any bits of it, would be around in any of the places we'd been or if there'd be a welcome on the hillsides or in my 'Vales' when I came back rich and important. Would there be no more need for big boys or for anyone to cry?

As 'Con the Fruiterer' was to say sometime in the future, "Gooda Luck, [Or Iechyd Da, in Welsh] to your family." Happy to say, from here on in, our family got their fair and deserved share.

2nd Party of Northcote Pioneers. Doreen and Derrick at top right.

32

* Middlemore and Beyond *

We polished and waxed floors, ate Mrs Cadbury's chocolates till, when the party was getting a bit rough, we escaped to our lovely 'Largs Bay' liner, just in time.

It would be remiss of me not to mention our brave, intrepid but very innocent escorts, Miss Marshall and Miss Merinden who became our good friends. One severe gripe I have is that one of them borrowed the diary I meticulously wrote, a foolscap sheet every day, a collector's item I humbly believe. I never saw it again. In 1993, John Stocker, the boy from our farm school who became professor of English, taught in Japan and South Korea and who was awarded the British O.B.E. for services rendered, went and found Miss Merinden. She remembers the diary but with that old timers thing, it was now a forgettery.

Mr Herrington who later became a Squadron leader in the R.A.A.F. and later still, a trustee of the Northcote scheme, was in charge. He was enthusiastic, overly so when he gave me a great kick up the backside when he caught me! We became great mates in the years to come.

The boat trip was heaven to us all. We had our own cabins. There were snacks at all times and so much food, fruit and cakes, everything. My thoughts after a few days at the shear profundity of it were, 'what do they do with the leftovers?' It would fatten and feed Alfie Philips' pigs for a whole year.

The Bay of Biscay at the start, like the Australian Bight at the finish, were days of disaster with everyone doing the big chuck up. My sadly lost diary would have told the magic of Gibraltar with Morocco off to the right. Valletta harbour was inspiring as we picked up new migrant Maltese. One lovely man, Attard and I think it was Joe, thought it funny that I called him Sir. He looked after me in a kind way and went on to Sydney where the name Attard became a token of success. I hope Joe was a part of it.

At Port Said we all went ashore to see the sights and marvel at the 'Gilly Gilly' man making his day old chickens disappear. As the Empire was still strong and an Englishman still well respected and as children of the white Sahibs, we were given the royal treatment.

Though we lost six weeks of schooling, the trip as a history and geography lesson more than compensated and for me, like the others I suppose, the whole school bit had been a non-event. Thinking about it, of our misbegotten lot, we finished up with teachers, an accountant, my mate Peter Meyrick, a few large city identities, a mayor and a Shire President. There are a couple of millionaires in there too, not bad for the 161 of us to arrive at the farm pre war.

Down through the Suez Canal to Aden was unforgettable, as was the visit to Colombo in Ceylon, which I geographically lost for awhile till the realisation it was now Sri Lanka.

What historical places we were passing, down through Egypt and what is now Saudi Arabia, Sudan, Ethiopia and Yemen, all just names meaning nothing to us as we sailed into the Gulf of Aden. What an explosive world this was to become in 1991 and continue to the new millennium.

I must mention Colombo and our tour of the city where we saw the monkeys and the snake charmers, gay looking street vendors, [This was before the 'Gay' of today when, like in the song, folk were happy and gay.] and colourful entertainers.

We saw the Zoo and the gardens where lunch was a feast of food and fruit we had never seen the like of. A fruit salad, an exquisite taste experience, so unbelievable. I spoke about it and raved to everyone for years until one day on my round Australia trip at Bowen, Queensland I had my first mango. Not in a salad but on its own. Eureka! This was the taste flavour from Colombo.

For many years, the people we had met at Groper Creek out of Home Hill, Ayr in Queensland, sent us a case of Mangoes each Xmas at a cost of $2, that was for the freight only. Happy Xmas.

Aboard ship there were fun and games. Sunday school was still a goer with a party of young missionary type do-gooders to teach us all those lovely, "I'm a H-A-P-P-Y," or "Jesus wants me for a sunbeam" songs you never forget. We were singing and it was something in Welsh we were into when we saw the portly gentleman with a big father Xmas beard, watching us. He had a uniform, gold braid all over and he looked a bit scary but impressive. In my nationalistic and poetic way I pictured him as how our Welsh hero, Owen Glyn Dwr, would have looked.

He spoke to us, just like us, but a bit more posh. He asked who we were and found out we were part of the group going to Australia. In the days to come he stopped for a chat and his interest seemed genuine as he talked of the whole fascinating idea, it and our becoming a part of it all.

We soon discovered the best part, he was the Captain of the Ship, the big Boss. Captain Gwyllim Williams was a countryman of ours, stern as hell to others, but a lovely man to us. He allocated a steward to care for us at all times, the whole voyage and see we wanted for nothing, Captain's pets so to speak.

Then it was May 17, a difficult bit of navigation through Point Nepean, all of us up and dressed in our best clobber. I've just had a look at the newspaper photo of our party on arrival, all so smart, happy and enthusiastic! On the outside that was and then, only till that night in new bunks in a strange world of new sounds, when it all hit us.

Arriving Melbourne aboard 'T.S.S. Largs Bay'. Rees' top right corner.

33

* Enter Colonel S.J. Heath *

We had our first introduction to our new principal and to we little kids he was awesome. Colonel Sydney John Heath, O.B.E., M.C., M.B.E., and M.V.C., there with his wife. Mrs Heath herself was a big, strong, dignified lady to suit the Colonel but he was even more impressive. Ex Grenadier Guards, six foot eight inches in his socks, moustache to suit and only one arm! His right, the left was missing at the elbow, a war service injury.

We were to find out soon enough that he was able to hold a naughty boy under that stump and hand out a deserved smack or wallop.

Mrs Heath, ever the true lady, could always produce her boiled lollies to quieten a crying child, a sure system that seemed to always work.

The Colonel had been principal of Fairbridge Farm School at Pinjarra, West Australia for eight years. He was back in England on leave when approached to join Northcote and was persuaded by the challenge, to come to Glenmore at Bacchus Marsh and start the Northcote Farm School scheme as its first principal. He was able to see virgin bush cleared, the first cottage built, others well on the way and all ready enough to receive the 28 boys off the 'S.S. Orford' on the 26th July, 1937.

It was the start of a village and the homes for the 161 children of the pre-war parties and those to follow post war.

There must have been a hold up for a while as we later found out and the reason we, the second party, had to cool our heels at good old Middlemore and where we Rees' almost went to Canada instead.

All the principals, besides the Colonel, to name the ones to do with me, Mr's Brown, Philips and Wignall were incredibly dedicated men who did so much for we children.

The Australian appointees to the Northcote committee were similarly sincere, including such notable and important men of influence such as;

Sir Earnest Henry Wrexford K.T.

Sir Harold Daniel Luxton K.T.

The Right Hon Lord Richard Gardner Casey C.H, D.S.O, M.C.M.

Major General Sir Brudenall White K.C.B, K.C M, K.C.U.D, D.S.O.

Sir William Angliss.

Sir Arthur Coles.

These and others too many to mention were the sort of people who had the interest of Australia's future at heart. The enthusiasm of all Northcote folk for the new arrivals was shared by all and whatever the furore and recriminations, the media and the press frenzy of the years to come, the majority of us were assured of a more successful future than ever possible back at what we, through deep rooted heritage, called home.

So, in our convoy of cars, we headed off, not through expected green and luxurious countryside but dry and dusty, strange looking landscape. We were off to the 'Marsh' as Bacchus Marsh was henceforth to be known.
At the Mechanics Hall there was a turn up of locals and officials. The Shire President, Councillor E.F. Prime, welcomed us himself and on behalf of the residents of the district. We were hopefully to be a welcome addition to the district and its numbers in the years to come. I can report, 60 years later, that some are still there having contributed to the Marsh's growth and wealth.

Sir Harold Luxton responded with a fine speech. It was like a party with sandwiches, cakes and drinks galore, all so much appreciated but we were now most anxious, having got so far, to see our new home and meet the people who would have such an important part to play in our new way of life.
With thoughts of previous homes and people therein, the last few miles had a quietening and tempering affect.
For the little ones, it was getting a little too much, the strange places, stranger people and all the excitement. All they needed by now was a home, if possible! Lots of T.L.C. and attention.

It was eleven miles to go when we left the Marsh, our first look at the Australian bush, tinder dry with a heat haze giving the countryside a look different to anything we had ever seen before. We could see rabbits and sheep huddled in the non-shade of dead looking wattle trees. The only relief being the Willows in the distance across the barren brown flats, indicating where the creek was before its last trickle of water gave up like everything else. Even in May, it was still a high temperature, with the country in a desperate drought situation, which was to be worse in 1939 with bush fires beyond belief. It would take many years to recover.

On the way and to the left was 'Greystones', Billy Angliss' place with its fine country home where many children were to visit and meet our own Sir William. This was the man who gave the almost three thousand acres of his property to enable the Northcote dream to eventuate. He loved we Pommie kids and all we stood for and meant to him. It was so fortuitous he being there with his land. Knowing something about how we felt too because at the age of nineteen with only a few shillings in his pocket, he too had arrived in Australia in 1884. He may have thought seriously about us, he himself had become the great 'Meat Baron', the success of the century, earned a Knighthood and therefore saw in us a similar success.

We passed the Victorian State School No.3688 there on the left and just a short walk before the main gate. A typical Aussie school, weatherboard, iron roof with verandahs, a bell out front and just a handful of children from scattered, horse riding distance farms. The little school was soon to erupt with the arrival of all the multi accents eager to learn and become 'Strine'.
Turning in off Glenmore Rd, we drove passed Angliss House and round to the assembly hall and dining hall.
There were twelve cottages in all around the top of the open area, not all completed at this stage if I remember.

The staff and the 28 boys of the first party were there to greet us, the boys were so happy to see new faces, faces with a word from home, but more especially to have the twelve girls who would make life different and more like real home.

We were sorted out and allocated our cottages, bungalows I suppose and not like the two story brick institutions of our past. We met and quietly had a close look at our new cottage mothers, for most of us who had been institutionalised before, it was lottery time, whether to be joy or despair? It is happy to report that those chosen in roles never undertaken before, were, with one exception, [We will mention Miss Woods later], all kind and caring people.
More photos were taken and we still have the ones taken outside our cottage, where we looked the child migrant part in our suits and ties, long socks and shiny shoes. These were soon packed away as sandals, shorts and shirts were the order of the day from now on.
That photo, the one of our party on arrival at No.6 cottage, was to become famous and used often in the, 'Lost children' sagas of the years to come.

The first morning, after the shock of the compulsory cold shower, we were allowed to wander round and settle in. Except for us, there was nothing but hills and fields forever. The tired old Eucalypts, which were Gums from now on and the strange Peppercorns, the scrubby withered Wattle, looked so very different from the trees of old England or my once Wales.

Perhaps my first unwitting thought of the country's beauty was the big peppercorn tree over the water tank on its stand alongside the brand new Tassie Oak cottage. Our home, all so new and a feeling at last that all was going to be, how did that man say it? 'Real Beaut'. It was also, a new word to me, 'Bonzer'.

Several new trees had been planted in the plan to put trees and shrubs all over. Each cottage had its own water tank but they were only a few rungs full so water for garden or trees was not available till an improved water supply was worked out. We each had our own trees and every drop of waste was religiously carted out. At the 60th Northcote reunion at the Farm, I was proudly able to show off the magnificent Gum trees, the result of our gratifying perseverance.

The cottages were brand new and built to last forever, timber framed with weatherboards outside, the floors and most timbers of Tassie Oak. They are all still there today, as good as the day they were readied for us. The cost is a laugh as each one, and they housed up to 20, was just 1,149 pounds, or $2298. The large galvanised iron rooves were hot as Hades but good catchment for the big tank we relied on for our water.

My cottage was No.6, later named Yerawia and meaning, joyful. We found our mother was to be Miss Enid Scholes, a spinster lady from Moonee Ponds and a devout believer in the Christian faith. Her teachings and principles were beyond reproach, though somewhat tested by some boys. We accepted her strict teachings, I thank her for my love of poetry and we all bless her for those early years of transition from what we were to what we became in the few short years together.

Colonel Heath settled the boys in to blend with the first party, the so-called oldies. The girls had their own cottage and all together, we were to get the other cottages and the surrounds ready for the others soon to follow us here. The staff was to be about 40 strong and with 161 of us kids, it was a tidy sized Aussie township. We were in a very short time to become amazingly almost self supportive. Not child labour, as in other schemes, but by the work the senior boys took to with new found energy and enthusiasm.

Bernard ('Bugsy') told me in later years that he and all the little kids, six years and up, used to weed the carrots, lettuce and other vegies in 100 yard rows down on the farm after school. In bare feet and no hats or modern muck smeared all over to protect from the sun. That, you could say was child labour and in retrospect if you wanted to make a fuss, was not nice. As the senior boy with them at times and supervising, they were having fun, doing a good job and as far as the bare feet bit, who amongst country kids those days bothered with shoes? That is if they had them!

There was Elsie Heath, the Colonel's daughter, almost as big and as strong as him. She was the general help, man Friday and friend of every man, women and stray dog. Elsie drove everything, especially the truck which went to the Marsh for supplies or to take kids to the doctor or dentist. Many is the trip into town we had and we had a happy association to last many years. She and Pringle had us save our penny a week to buy a fishing rod at the first Xmas, then on the holiday camp to Pt Lonsdale, they initiated me into my life's sport of fishing.

Miss Pringle, a spinster and life long friend and companion of Elsie was known to all as just 'Pringle'.

In years to come, when I was settled down and married in Sydney, The Colonel and Mrs Heath, together with Elsie and Pringle were to become almost neighbours. Colonel Heath, on retirement, bought a poultry farm at Casula, out of Sydney which they all worked on.

We visited them often and it was our pleasure and honour to have them all to our home. He expressed how good it was to see the result of what Northcote really meant. Indeed, his strict teachings and especially the military part which included the discipline of marching and drilling was to be a great help when I soon joined the armed forces, [Air Force]. Sydney John Heath, I'm happy to say, nursed my son Evan.

Glenmore school was in the hands of Henry J. Parker at the time the numbers started to increase out of all proportion. My time with him and at the school was short lived, as with three others, being the senior boys, we attended for only two weeks before we were allowed to leave for duties around the property and on the farm itself.

Most fortunately, by someone's good thinking, we were tested and found to be generally at Intermediate standard and good old Parker issued a letter to that affect and with a reference which went into our ever growing files. Both were of prime importance in time to come.

Though I always wished for a better education, which would I'm sure have fitted me for a different if not better way of life, I did at that time think it was great to be finished with all that stuff. I had never been at any place long enough to learn a lot, sufficient must have rubbed off along the way but it was now a chance to get on with life and what was ahead.

I suppose I could now add, 'By now I was Fourteen.'

My record from Northcote, the file I received when I returned from war service and having turned 21, the file with all the nitty-gritty in it, showed me to be a workaholic and always keen to please, even to a nervous breakdown from over work, happily fixed up by a couple of days rest.

At No.6, a joyful place as the aboriginal meaning states, we learned the good manners and etiquette most kids missed out on, we had to behave as gentlemen and say our prayers each night. Miss Scholes made us all read good books, Treasure Island, Robinson Crusoe and such and I was in my glory. Poetry too which was, as the name Yerowia says, a joy. Rudyard Kipling's 'If' I learnt in one night and loved, especially the last line which says, "And which is more, you'll be a man my son."

There were lots of poets to come out of our farm school, a few books and lots of interesting stories written.

Good old 'Scholesy', a strict spinster who thought little boys should be kept busy with no time to be naughty, if only she knew the past. She believed the cold shower we had to take each morning, rain, hail or even snow, were necessary to cool the blood. We would line up stark naked with only our towel and one by one go under the spray, no chance to cheat or pretend and I swore then never to have a cold shower ever again. Even in winter, the dormitory having no windows, just louvres where the wind whistled through each morning before sunrise, it was still difficult to rid oneself of that confounded erection and many a boy copped a whack with a ruler and told to get rid of that bone.

Miss Scholes, never having been with boys, only saw good in everyone and never imagined what naughty little boys reaching that age were doing as they went through the agonising time of growing up, little hormone factories in fact.

As it comes back to me, it was the time of the relieving cottage mother, a time of trial for her and us I suppose. She was not used to a mess of boys our age and I suppose we took advantage of her in a way. At the same time she was different and not being that old really, with some of the boys looking older than they were, she unknowingly or whatever seemed a bit of a tease.

It had been a time of no girls, no sexual interests whatsoever and we were easily stirred up. Fantasy had been the only relief.

There was the big dormitory, then the sick room, no one ever sick so the two senior boys, Henry Simmons and I had it as our domain, next was the bathroom belonging to the mother's private quarters.

After all were bedded down for the night, Miss X would run her bath, she would hop in but leave the door slightly ajar and it didn't take long for the first rotten inquisitive kid to sneak up for a peek.

We sorted them out and took control. Henry had a good go and I peeped in to see the bath of suds, two bare arms splashing two breasts, voluptuous, a word I never understood till then but they really were. Back in bed it was sheer hell and the hormones of over active suppressed youth took over.

We regulated the taking of a peek before it all got out of hand! Miss X, by her demeanour seemed to know what was going on. In later years, at reunions when the times, 'The good old days' were discussed, Miss X had carried on the same in other cottages, a bit of fun and games all round.

It was a difficult time and when you think that all the boys and girls were away from those who would normally give them love and attention, it was missing. Whilst the staff were most caring, it was not possible to give a child individual attention, it would not be fair and only cause jealousy and upset.

Thus it can be seen that we were more than susceptible to anyone who showed a little more than the usual interest in us, but who had ulterior motives or an intent to take advantage. My experience shows it does go on. The records show and I cannot or must not mention names, but some people did interfere most seriously with some of the girls. There was a pregnancy and a prison sentence for a person in high office. The children involved took years to get over the trauma but went on to an almost normal life.

Like before at Middlemore or any of the places of the past, there was always someone doing a bunk or running away. Some kids, boys or girls, never accepted being in a home, nothing against them but were always taking off. Even Doreen ran away for a time and Yvonne and friends went off for quite a spell. The trouble was, out there, there were few places if any to go to and the few bits of bread and dripping saved or bits of fruit soon went. Raw rabbit was there by the ton, not an apple orchard in sight so it was back to home the only option, there to face the consequences. I never ran away as I was too busy working.

As we were intended to become farmers, the actual real farm duties rather than general muck about stuff was the order of the day for senior boys like Harding from Merthyr, Wilkes, Goofy Miller and Gray. We, with other older boys were soon to move down and fill the bunkhouse. As big kids, so we were called, we were sort of the elite, the others were littlies as class distinction crept into the system.

On the farm our mentor, teacher and confident, [He talked to us man to man, as an equal], was Mr Norm Hancock. He was the perfect gentleman, one to pattern oneself on and aspire to, he was always so clean and tidy, well spoken and was able to talk and impart all his knowledge in a quiet way, so we took all he said to be true. Norm Hancock was unruffled, even the first time I helped to deliver the calf from its mother when it needed turning around inside for delivery. He was up to his armpit reaching in to the cow, a really pooey bloody mess but he still had his collar and tie on, explaining it all as he delivered the poor little Poddy calf.

Everything was going well on the farm and the intention that we should be self supporting was going better than expected under Norm's guidance. He was always Mr Hancock, a due respect we were taught for old folk, only the Colonel got the 'Sir' bit of old England. I got to call him Norm when we worked together at Colac where he was Show ringmaster for many years. I, as a reward, was taken to meet his family and be assistant to him in the show ring. Colac is the jewel in the western district of Victoria.

At just fifteen, did dreams come true, was this lad on his thoroughbred, in suit, collar and tie, jodhpurs and riding boots, the obligatory Squatters hat firm on his head as he rode round the ring with messages. If only his 'nurse of the bandaged hand' back at Treforest could see him now. How proud she would be of him.

We took to milking without a thought, by hand at first and only five cows in those days and the tumble down milking shed with its ever mucky, yucky, post and railed yard. It was falling down and too close to the big house where the Heath family lived for a start and where the farm manager took over later. It would have to go from there.

The herd rapidly increased through necessity and a dairy manager was employed. Someone to improve the herd and really teach us all about farming. Enter, Mr Les Graham.

Mr and Mrs Graham arrived with their brood of kids and life was never the same again for us. The old cottage across the road from the dairy had been dollied up, a few additions, a bit of paint, [It had never seen a brushful of paint before], and it was ready for them. Baby Ken arrived and in respect I called my pet Magpie after him. Les ran the show but we boys did all the work, we were keen, it worked and we got on well together.

Though boys by age, we were men now and doing more than a man's work. The Graham's house was always open to we farm boys, cups of tea and Anzac biscuits or even a breakfast. Mrs Graham, of the many talents, made scones endlessly, home made jam, the thick cream from the separator bowl, biscuits and fruitcake. Home made bread, the smell even wafting across the road above the warm cow shit aroma.

The parties of children from overseas were arriving regularly now, we were growing up and just as well as the work was now full time. We started at about four when the first of the herd with full udders calmly chewed their cud as we relieved them by the big stainless steel bucket full. From then it was all go till nearly dark time and bath time before dinner. Our herd grew from five to eventually become ninety odd, this included a herd of about thirty pure bred Jerseys. These put our milk production into the top class with its high butter fat content.

Until we got the milking machines, it was twice a day by hand and took some effort. We developed strong hands and could fill a bucket in record time, competing to squirt the milk to foam in the bucket between our knees sitting on a three-cornered stool and finish stripping our cow first.

We by now had plenty of chickens for eggs and cooked poultry, chooks as they now were to us. Our sheep and lambs were up to about 3000 and we had fixed the shearing sheds and mustering yards to handle them. I liked this part of farming and it helped me get the good position later on as I picked up the shed work, piece picking and crutching. It was there I had my first initiation into shearers, their colour-bloody-ful swearing and joke telling.

For Hubert and I, who on the train from Cardiff and while at Middlemore had planned our horse ranch, here with the riding of horses, a necessity and priority, it was just heaven. They were good horses, not just nags and we rode them more often bare back than with a saddle. We had 'Fidgety' the retired racehorse, seventeen hands of irrepressible bone and muscle. We were told and it was confirmed that he ran third in the Melbourne cup before he was retired and sent to us to have a good home. His mouth was as hard as hell, he was great to ride out of the yard but when you turned for home after a muster he took off and it was hang on hands and heels for grim life. No bare back with him. He only threw me once, right at the gate and almost home and the crook knee is still with me to this day. Old Bill Gilson was shocked at my burst of shearer type swearing.

Harvesting was great, the first crop of wheat and oats was a time for all hands and the cook to turn to, a time we built up muscles as we stooked and stacked finding out the real meaning of Chapel harvest festival and the song, 'Bringing in the sheaves'. This is what it's all about. Our river flats produced about three crops a year of lucerne and rye grass. These were cut and baled for winter feed. We still used the draught horse and it's sad to see that the only ones around now are those at the Easter Show pulling fancy brewery carts. We built stacks of bales and artfully created hay stacks, homes for mice and monster brown or yellow bellied black snakes. Though hard work we were artisans of the pitchfork, the good companionship and smokos made it worth while.

There were men employees of course, they did the jobs we were not allowed to handle, driving etc though tractors were not classed as driving. About four men and they had the spirit of the place to heart, told or made up fantastic stories of their working days all around Australia. Old Bill Gilson was my friend, a veteran of the first war with injuries that kept him awake all night, he always brought enough cakes and biscuits back from visiting his family in Melbourne to share over a cuppa.

Enthusiasm is great stuff and you can see we had become proud of the farm and our personal achievements and I haven't mentioned the pigs yet. Pigs! Heaps of them and more coming or evolving each week. The Boar was a massive great frightening beast, the biggest you've ever seen and we all loved him and his prowess. He was given to the farm by a kind supporter who believed in the work being done at the farm and he was no ordinary pig, but third prize at the Royal Easter Show. By the progeny he produced, he really was a champion.

The pig sties extended down the back paddock forever with the constant noise and rich pongy smell. It all continued after I left to go to work and even increased as the war escalated and the large U.S. staging camp at Darley Bacchus Marsh came into being.

The farm had a contract for the swill from the camp, this was brought in trucks loaded with 44-gallon drums of the stuff, truckload after load. There was a ginormous steel boiler, an oil burning heater I think it was, and the swill was tipped in and cooked up, [The smell!!! Not to mention the flies]. It was later mixed up with crushed wheat to make a lovely feed and the pigs really thrived on it.

Every so often a truck would return to the camp with a load of dishes and pans, crockery and cutlery, anything the extravagant Yanks dumped in the swill. Doreen's note says that the kids came down with a fever from eating apples and God knows what out of the Darley swill. She was working in the hospital at the time, Michael O Halloran was one of the boys. "I fell in love with him," she said. "He brought me a box of chocolates, God knows where he got the money from." But they had come out of the swill too!

It was very bad, very sad news too, to hear later that a fever had gone through the camp, all our pigs were destroyed and the whole area strictly quarantined. While away on overseas service I actually studied Pig farming on a correspondence course which was a dumb idea, as lessons never reached me in the New Guinea jungle, so the idea fell flat. I also studied from the Australian Sheep and Wool, [The book], but never became a grazier.

The self-supporting bit meant fruit and vegies too. We were lucky to have stone fruit trees in the old orchard and we planted more. Apples and pears, of course, I was into them from past Tonteg and Hayes, Middlesex times, and the bonus of Bacchus Marsh was the biggest Mulberry tree you ever saw.
Being on the river flats we were able to grow vegetables, it was vegies by the 100-yard row, every kind you wish, all neat and tidy. The work of weeding and thinning out is where the kids we mentioned were put to that slave labour thing after school or on Saturday mornings. It was fun and saved our knees. Doreen recalls collecting and sending frogs to the Zoo from somewhere there and baby carrots were chewed by the kids as they thinned them out, Tonteg like turnips were my first choice.
When the old dairy fell apart and couldn't cope, someone, a good Samaritan or ones the Melbourne Trustees had convinced it was a priority charity, came to our aid. The end result was we had a new, modern dairy, clean concrete yards everywhere with solid posts and fences, a water supply and hoses to wash down after each milking or have fun in the scorching, ever constant heat. There was a shiny bright stainless steel separator and milking machines to slap on the cows udders. Everything so modern and simple to clean, no more milking by hand, a miracle for we boys to celebrate. The celebrate bit was a big

opening with officials and dignitaries making the usual speeches, lots of patting each other on the back and a day out for us all. Bigger than opening the Opera House or as they were to say, 'Quo Vadis.'

We gave each cow a name, each boy choosing the nicest looking cow for his favourite girls name. Yvonne got a creamy Jersey cow with big eyes and the Friesian I thought was the best in the herd got called Doreen. Sadly when she saw it she said, "It's ugly," not knowing the compliment and that my idea of beauty at the time was in big udders.

More boys were at work and it was a hassle getting down from the village to the farm so when the Bunkhouse was suggested the plan was put into action and before long the twenty or so boys moved in. It was built just across from the farm itself with the big dam at the back door almost and where frogs by the thousand were to keep us awake on hot nights as they croaked for a mate to fornicate with. Like the Cicadas of the bush, the noise was deafening but nostalgically memorable. We could wade through the reeds and red-hot pokers for our swim. With the level being low, we usually had a pale shade of mud to hose off. As boys, we needed a raft and with 44-gallon drums, scrounged timber and number eight fencing wire, we built a beauty.

At the bunkhouse we were put in the charge of a married couple who were to be a cottage mother and father. They had their own living quarters at one end. They were a brave couple, happily oblivious of the trial of taking on so many boys in their teens because at that stage we were a lot of two legged walking hormones ready to go berserk. When later asked, why he took the job, Mr ---- simply said, "How was I to know? We had needed a job."

And rabbits!!! A plague of rabbits, the biggest plague since that one in the Bible. The pair or so brought from England had multiplied to squillions, spreading across the whole continent. Foxes too were in super abundance, sadly for them at this time we were in the middle of one of the worst droughts of all time, there was nothing to eat, not dry grass, thistle stalks or scrubby growth. The rabbits were mangy and skinny poor as were the foxes that ate them.

The White Elephant, our local mountain had become one massive rabbit warren. A rabbit could go in there and come out miles away, so many skins, but mostly mangy and not worth a cracker. Though it was futile, we did employ our own rabbiter who did his best with traps and ferrets. The boys took turns to go out with him to learn to set traps and skin the bunnies and foxes. It took but four seconds to skin a rabbit and any trap set by Gerry O'Keefe was certain of a catch. Gerry had his own hut beneath the rocky outcrop of the mountain. After a busy day out we would go back there and put the billy on to drink the black concoction out of his chipped enamel pannikins. We would eat all his biscuits, stale fruit cake from his sisters, who worried about him, and we would listen to his stories of the bush and wondrous places he had been. He loved us as an audience and relief from an otherwise lonely life.

All the children have great memories of walks over the Brisbane Ranges or down to the creek, practically anywhere we liked as there was no restriction, bush kids already, not even snakes in abundance worried us. The old gold mine was a favourite spot, lots of gold won there in the early days and ever the dreamer, fantasies were in order. It must have made an impression on me because I was to do a lot of fossicking and gold panning at Pyramul and Hill End in the years to come.

Letters from Britain were important though few and far between. We wrote, telling about the new life and how great it was at the farm school. At first it was sufficient to have Bernard arrive aged six just twelve months later. With so much to think of, we didn't know what was going on, just wished Mum and Myrna would join us as arranged but times became so confused we never knew what was going on back over there.

With a family already here, it seems Bernard was processed with priority and on the 13th of April 1939, after his six weeks cruise on the 'S.S. Esperance Bay', the happy little kid arrived to join his brother and two sisters. The fifth party of 17 had arrived.
Bernard, with his cottage mates Richie, Sivier and Blackwell were the babies of the farm, little Coleshill had already been here a year. I never got anything out of Bernard, leaving Wales, where was Myrna, where had they gone? There may have been a mention of Middlemore before the docks, the boat and the trip but for him at that time, it was all an experience more to befuddle than be able to relate.

As you now know, the back to Goole, the Middlemore, the adoption business, everything about the time was yet to come out. The war escalation and no further kids were to come out here, it was all a shambles that thank God we were able to resolve.

My Dog, 'Roscoe'

My Horse, 'Cedace'

Station Hand, 'Mooleric'

34

* Back at the Farm *

Back at the farm, a time to remember in 1940, where we find the whole Northcote School getting ready for the brilliantly suggested idea of a Xmas vacation by the sea at Ocean Grove and Point Lonsdale. It must have seemed an impossible task to move all the children and adults en-masse, or to find a place big enough to accommodate us all for two full, hectic weeks. Where there is a shopping complex and park now, we made camp under canvas, a huge dining room and kitchen, tents every which way. Heavens knows where we all washed and pooped etc as it was all a heavenly bedlam at the seaside. My memories of old Ogmore by the sea back home paled into insignificance and besides, here it was warm.

This was our very first Australian beach type holiday with untold miles of sandy beaches, the water in the ocean surf so warm you felt you could swim any hour of the day. Basking or sun bathing, freezing Barry or Porthcawl came to mind, as did the icy water in the tank at the railway yards at Treforest.

I've mentioned saving our pocket money and buying the fishing rods, the first of many for me, forever hooked on the sport. Pringle and Miss Heath took us out to fish under the bridge or down at the beach where in those days before pollution and over population, whopper whiting and bream were in super abundance. It was the start for me of a hobby that would take me round the whole coast of this massive continent on two occasions, even to the catching of barramundi at the Oenpeli crossing on the East Alligator river up Kakadu way.

The whole camp was fabulous, not only for our first taste of life in the sun I had only dreamed of, but for girls.

While at Ocean Grove, we older boys had our first chance to look for girls. Not since we left the Old Dart had they been a real thought with so much work to do on the farm. We found the girls camp close by, what a joy and each of us met the girl of our dreams. I met and fell in love with Valma Smith from Geelong, we evaded the chaperones for our exciting liaisons of kissing and attempted touching, and then when, on the last day I went to say goodbye, she was gone. It's stupid I know but on the drive back to Glenmore I searched every corner of every street of Geelong in the hope of a glimpse of my lost love.

That, the one great holiday, was that. Back at the Bunkhouse it all went on. Porky Harding and I won the competition for the best garden, the only silver cup I ever won for anything. It was really a very neat and tidy garden but the plants were miniature, miserable and small with no water and no rain in the whole season of the competition.

It led to something else when Mr Hancock announced that the boy with the best work report would accompany him to the upcoming Colac Show. He, having been the ringmaster for many years, would require an assistant. My work experience and guile then and from the past was my forte and I worked hard at it for that job.

I went or was taken, with "Yahoo's" and "Teacher's pet" etc from the others, by Miss Heath to buy and put on the Northcote account, jodhpurs and jacket, shirt, tie and boots, such beautiful boots, for me with my boot and shoe complex, it was Heaven's reward. Mustn't forget the new Cockey type hat I soon bashed into shape to make it look old and experienced.

We looked the part as we loaded into Norm's Ford with the dicky seat at the back and took off for the Western district and Colac for my best time ever.

With my borrowed pony, I rode around the ring area with messages, trying to be useful as general dog's body. My self esteem, confidence and most of all, ambition to be someone took a distinct leap from there.

Many kids never changed from what they had been, Miss Scholes must take credit for the good manners and demeanour she insisted on and which gave us a head start on the others.

There was another trip I was fortunate to get, it was with the Colonel and Mrs Heath on a visit to their sons farm at Trafalga in Gippsland. The farm needed an extra bit of help, I being now capable of managing a dairy, among other things, needing a change they said, and would be handy for two weeks and for me it was a holiday.

It was 1939 and the time of devastating bush fires as I recall, probably the worst in a history of bush fires. Everything was tinder dry and we saw the flames roaring through the tops of the tallest gum trees, hundreds of yards ahead of the oncoming onslaught of fire below. Just an incredible sight with palls of smoke reaching into the heavens. It was taken by the winds and as reported, deposited as ash as far away as New Zealand.

We were all growing up, men before our time and in the bunkhouse, it was inevitable that one of the boys was caught masturbating. We had poked fun at poor old Tosser Evans at Treforest and now a fear it was happening here. A terrible time for over active boys at our stage and each of us suffered with the problem of an erection at the worst times. In a semi religious and strict control situation, we still feared the, 'Hell and damnation' teachings and suffered the nightly emissions we called 'wet dreams', in uncontrollable agony.

The outcome of it all, with our cottage parents, good Christian folk but ignorant of boys behaviour, sent a report to Colonel Heath. We would really cop it now!

Gathered together in the big dining hall, it was asked that those who practised this nasty habit, step forward. Unwittingly but in the strength of numbers, we all stepped out.

Good old Colonel Heath knew what boys were about, frowned ferociously with a stern lecture on the dangers of over indulgence or giving in to sinful thoughts. It was all a relief as we had expected six of the best from the strap and being out in the open, the worst was over and under control.

Except for depression time experience back there at home, we never had lectures on the birds and bees or advice on any taboo sexual matters. Maybe not thought necessary, as we were farm boys with animal goings on all around. But something was missing in our lives and it was girls, female company. At the farm, we seldom saw the girls of the village and they were like sisters anyway.

Sadly for many, we were not prepared for mixed company or taught how to behave in just the ordinary every day life of suburbia. Those who went to work on lonely farms, or outback stations, were quite old before we got into meeting and handling girls. I don't mean going the uncontrolled grope, but just how to behave and compete with other city kids.

We did meet the ladies of the Bacchus players who at any age looked gorgeous and somehow along the line we were taught to dance, an advantage for life, even dances like the Valletta and Quadrilles etc, etc.

Who can forget 'Crack Hardy', spruiker and comedian, he like most of the group, worked at the now sadly defunct Lifeguard Milk Factory in at the Marsh. He would bring the concert party to sing and dance for our entertainment. Always a treat and the first time, Mr Hardy told us without thinking, "When you're in town, come and see me and I'll give you a can of sweetened condensed milk to suck on."

Little knowing the result because on a holiday about thirty of us were allowed to walk into town. "Stay together and keep out of mischief."

It was a trial of our trust so with eleven miles there and eleven back, off we went with one intent, to present ourselves at Crack Hardy's factory.

The management came out to see what was going on and laughed when they heard why we were there. "Go ahead and give them their tin of milk," they said. With a big thank you, we put two holes in our tins and happily sucked our way home. 22 miles, but fair enough for a treat and a day out.

As once Pommie kids, we had to be good at soccer, the Welsh better still at Rugby, the real footy game. So when the Victorian School Boys Association found the team to play them in the preliminary lead up game to the International match, was not available, someone said, "What about those children at that Northcote farm place?" There was just one week to practice together as a team and the result, I'm pleased to report was a 2-1 win for us in a game said to be better than the big one. It was my only moment of glory as right half on what I tell everyone was the M.C.G., which I think it really was.

It's hard to believe so much was packed into such a short time, I wondered what I'd be doing if back in the Rhondda Valley, Harvest Festival came to mind as a highlight time for us all, the Royal Melbourne Show. We never dreamt such a world existed. Aussie kids were brought up on Easter shows but imagine us on the first, gob-stopping visit. The animals, side shows, sample bags and grand parade all in one day was too much to absorb. You may not know or realise, but sample bags were mostly free in those days and filled with goodies we most appreciated, what with ice creams, fairy floss and all the food, we were fully satisfied. I did wish our Chapel in Queen St. could see the district exhibits, which I had to be dragged away from in awe of the abundance. So many pram loads to cart away.

At the farm school, as in all such places, religion was maintained as of great importance, each to their Old World denomination. All of we 'C of E' mob regularly attended church and when old enough were given our training for confirmation. For me it meant a trip to Melbourne to St Paul's in Swanson St just across from Flinders St station and Princes Bridge. There we were confirmed by Archbishop Head, funny name but he was the Boss cocky at the time. The singing by the choir brought back thoughts of home and the men from the mine in their deep harmony.

Hubert Harding and I are still good mates sixty years on and have been since we met at Cardiff. Our dream horse stud or ranch is still to be started but we did win that silver gardening cup. I'll mention the 1979 reunion and some of the success stories of the kids. Hubert was there with Phyllis, the lovely wife he went back to Merthyr Tydvil to marry and bring back. We asked him about Rex Chamberlain, the other Cardiff kid and were told he was at Wodonga. "Call and see him," Hubert suggested.

On our return journey to Sydney we intended to stay the night so Wodonga was as good a place as any. Doreen, Bernard, Patsy, Heather and I booked into a motel and I asked the receptionist if she had a directory. She asked who I wished to find and I said, "Mr Rex Chamberlain," With no further hesitation she rang a number, spoke a while and asked me, "Who shall I say is calling?" I replied, " just say the Rees family". Putting down the receiver she told us Rex was in his gardening clothes but would be around in a moment. She then said, "Rex is the Mayor of Wodonga you know!"

Isn't that just beautiful, the little kid from Wales, not a relative in sight, all on his own and here is the big business man and Mayor to boot. It gave us and the weekend a feeling of satisfaction. There are many Northcote families, many success stories. Don Coleshill, five and a half years old in the first party, became President of Philip Island Shire but maybe more of his fabulous saga later.

Derrick and Bill Wilkes, " At Work on the Farm."

Derrick and Hubert Harding (2nd and 3rd from the right)

35

* Time to Leave *

There came the day that Doreen Tuck, a mature girl, was leaving to go into service. It was not long after that the first three boys were considered ready to go out to work in the big world. Suddenly, the days of hard work and fun together as a large family were to be over. The security of numbers would be gone and each of us would be rather frighteningly, on their own.

Three were chosen, Bill Wilkes and Eric Miller, we called him 'Goofy', good fun, good for a laugh and myself. The three of us crammed into Mr Hancock's car with our luggage, all we possessed in those big brown suitcases brought out for this, the next foray or whatever in our ever changing lives.

It was just a blank, leaving the farm I mean, in fact as I edit this, it was actually Hubert on that trip and if he reads this he will excuse me. I can't recall saying goodbye to a single soul, not even my sisters and brother. Being such a momentous moment I suppose, it was nevertheless a blank and we had suddenly left the security of it all.

I claim to be the first boy to leave to go out to work because I was actually the first delivered to his job. Hubert Harding was next. For me it was the sheep station, 'Mooleric' out of Birregurra in the western district and owned by Major Bob Ramsay, a gentleman of Scottish heritage. He was a grazier and the owner of what was really one of the finest stud properties in the district.

The homestead was built at the foot of Mount Gelibrand in 1871. Mooleric's 4 acres of historic gardens were designed by William Guilfoyle, who also designed the Royal Melbourne Botanical Gardens. Mr Hancock and he were friends through show and sheep associations and from my visit to Colac, I was chosen for the position of general hand and rouseabout. I called myself a Jackeroo, it sounded better though the name was usually reserved for sons of wealthy families. More than likely I was just a 'Saddle frigger' to quote a crude expression.

We said goodbye, as they left for jobs at dairy farms the other side of Colac. God knows if we would meet again. They would have preferred something other than the dairy work for a change but at least they were out at work and it could lead to better things.

How strange it was being cut off from all the people I knew, the blanket of security, to be out in such a quiet and strange environment. In my little room that night, the only noise, the rattle of a dog chain, little sleep as I wondered how it would all work out.

Major Ramsay was really a gentleman, a canny Scot who wanted his pound of flesh for the ten bob a week and keep that I was to receive. Both he and Mrs Ramsay made me welcome to their way of life, he the master and I the servant but that was OK by me, just give me time! They showed me great kindness and in return I gave them good service and with youthful exuberance carried out my duties better than ever expected. It may sound egotistical but they never had a better worker or one to carry out any and every task, especially lamb marking.

Mrs Ramsay, at first, looked the stern and haughty Mistress of the mansion, I'd never met the like but she was a lady. She had a quid or two of her own from wealthy New Zealand parents who I believe owned that most famous racehorse Gloaming.

We had the best horses to ride, strong and healthy, of the Tamashanta breed, famous for riding over the rough and rocky terrain of Major's Scotland. They were well suited for the stony rises of paddocks such as Bleak House here at the Mooleric station.

So here I was at last, a sort of a dream come true, a Dinky-Di Aussie worker out in the sun, earning my way and self-supporting. It was not a fortune at ten shillings a week and my keep. The keep part, meant a hut to live in and all meals supplied. Five bob was taken out and sent back to Northcote for my savings account, This was done for every child till they reached 21. The other five bob was mine to do with as I wished.

At first, my quarters were in a room in the married couple's cottage. He was the 'milk-kill' and she did the cooking for all the men who had their meals there. 'Milk' means he looked after the dairy and 'Kill' means the slaughtering and dressing of the animals for the station's use. It became part of my job to take over these tasks when Mac was away or ill.

At the farm we had learnt it all, butchering and cutting up. We used to do 3 sheep on Monday, 2 on Wednesday and 3 on Friday just to feed the hordes. Nothing deterred us and I soon showed my prowess, per Hancock's teaching, at delivering a breached calf. With my small hand, up to the armpit, standing on a milking stool, I saved my first Poddy calf to later watch it grow up.

Having small wrists and a musicians or conductors hands, or so I thought, on the way out on the boat, the pompous Doctor had said to me,

"You'll never do hard work with those hands boy." What a dumb thing to say to a kid and to be so wrong too. There at Ramsay's or as the plumber and builder of the years ahead, no one did more hard Yakka than I and the thin wrists.

Soon settling in, I got used to the routine of a sheep station and was accepted by the workers as just another Pommie kid, one of them and not a ten pound a year remittance man as used to be the case. Restless and restricted, it wasn't long before I was allowed to move into the men's quarters. This was an old cottage with the fireplace in the lounge where we would sit and read, listen to the wireless or they would tell exaggerated tales of the bush.
My room was on the left-hand side facing the dog lines across the horse paddock. I could open the window and shout 'Lie down' when the twelve of them howled at the moon or a stray bunny smell. They woke the Ramsay's and the Major would wrap on my window, "Shut them up, or I'll shoot the damn lot." They by now only shut up for me.

Some of the workers were quite old and most station hands were itinerant so there was often a new face to relate new tales at night. They had been all over the vast continent, to Tasmania and New Zealand, they had shorn sheep, cut timber or sleepers, fossicked for gold and every job imaginable. All the fascinating stories and name places put in place an urge to go and see for myself and as it transpired much later, I did see it all. There was a song to come out, "I've been everywhere Man" and in sixty years of moving around, it could certainly apply to me.

One can dream of the times that were special, one is 'Barramundi' time.
Some of the men raved about the top end and the fish there, it stuck in my mind and in 1974 I was there to see it all come true. We went out to Jim Jim, stopped at the yellow hole and then out to Owenpelli crossing on the East Alligator River at Kakadu. It was there I caught my first barramundi, as did Kurt and Judith the Swiss couple we met down the track back at Port Hedland and Broome. Marge and Rex were there too to share the most magic world in the pre-pollution and the 'Click, click' camera crazy days of the tourist. We were on dirt tracks in four wheel drives before the time of bitumen and big buses on four lane highways. The tourists were not to see the wonder of it all or to cast out a line with the certainty of a catch.

I wrote a little poem which I feel tells the magic the men described;

'Barramundi'

East Alligator
River of the stone aged man
At dawn its silent flow shows spreading swirls
the promise of the magic moment when
The cast is made,
a slow retrieve
all hell breaks loose
with action as the water boils.
A pounding heart
while taking in the strain
the cry of joy which wakes the peaceful calm
tells all!
It's 'BARRAMUNDI'.

The property, Mooleric Station, is one of the wealthy ones, with planted blue rye grass, excellent feed for baling as winter fodder. We cropped and harvested and on a wet day outside, cut chaff sufficient for the station's needs. There were only two native or natural trees on the whole property but lots of plantations of sugar gums along fence lines for wind breaks and shelter. It was an annual event to choose a section to be chopped down to a few feet height off the ground to allow for regrowth. It was a time for all hands and the cook to take two weeks to fell and cut up a wood supply sufficient for the whole year. Having read about the sleeper and shingle cutters of the old days, I fancied myself as an axeman with eyes on the Royal Easter show as a competitor. Seeing all the rows and stacks of cut up wood, all the left over sticks and branches, the thought of my wood run came back from the past that seemed not to belong to me. What would Uncle Joe think of such a bonanza of sticks for his depression days business.

Chopping wood was fun but the other chopping was the job we all hated, it was the dreaded saffron thistle. In quiet times we roamed the property for an offending patch and had to get rid of it, bag and burn it as it was an agony to the shearers when it got into the wool.

The dogs and I clicked and got on well together, it was just as well as I inherited the job or duties as rabbiter and it took a lot of my time. The pack consisted of about a dozen dogs of the Heinz variety, every sort. There was a greyhound, a whippet, a blue-heeler cattle dog and for a while, a useless golden pointer. The rest were mongrels of all sizes, making a most excellent rabbit pack.

It was dreams come true and we had fun together, on my horse with lunch and accoutrements, a miners pick for digging out burrows tied to the pommel and a 4ft length of No.8 fencing wire for pulling bunnies from under rocks or burrows. With the pack at heel we would set off at daybreak for a days hunting.

There were hares by the thousand. I caught them in snares set at holes or runs along the fence-line, they were too fast to chase, just one early morning run and the pack was done in for hours. At first it was hard to stop them taking off but a loud, "Come in behind", a crack of the stock whip and a bit of a tickle up soon taught them it was not on.

The Major had a bug about bunnies and kept the only, almost rabbit free property in the Western District. If he saw just one on his rounds, it was, "Derrick, take those dogs and clear the area."

It suited me as skins were my bonus and the sale of all skins my private, undisclosed to Northcote, income. I never missed any pest that moved be it rabbit, hare, fox or the huge feral cats that took birds and day old lambs. I even skinned snakes there in their thousands but it was too tedious and I couldn't find a market. The property was rabbit proofed with wire all round so there was never enough skins for me but, over every fence were bunnies in super abundance, so in my lunch break I would hop over with the dogs to get an extra dozen or so.

To make money and I had got the urge back in the Treforest days, I even collected the bones from years of dog feeding and sold two truck loads to the bone merchants, forget it! Too much work for no return but all this helped pass the time, a post office savings account was started and by the time I was 18 and enlisted in the Air Force I had 250 pounds in the account, a fortune in those days. My wage, under a threat of leaving, was increased to a pound, [Two dollars] a week.

The only time I got to town was with Mac in the Vauxhall utility truck to pick up supplies at Birregurra, or the once a month visit to Colac, about 16 miles. I made the visit there to get to the skin merchants before he closed so I could get rid of my skins.

As can be seen, transport became a problem if I was to get out to meet people, go to the pictures or eventually try to visit the boys way out the other side of Colac. One evening, having got rid of my bundle, I passed the bicycle shop down on the right hand side as I went to meet Mac.

It was Doakes' Bicycle shop, I went in and after a long chat about the weather, work at the station and skins in general, I was the owner of a beaut Malvern Star Roadster. My first real proud possession.

The deal was simply, ten bob down and ten bob, 'whenever you're in town' till it was paid off. There was no signed agreement just a shake of the hand, a great way to do business. I think working for the Ramsay's might have helped and I actually paid the bike off in a couple of payments.

Biragurra was our railhead, next to Winchelsea. We were always there picking up parcels or equipment. In town itself there were just a few shops set in among the peppercorn trees and the general store took pride of place. Such a place was new to me, they sold everything imaginable and waiting for our order to be ready, I examined the tools and wonders of modern farm machinery. Going to town was a treat but cost me a fortune on lollies, not sweets as back over there, magazines too or anything to read.

The blacksmith shop was just like the real thing you only see in the movies today. It was under the shade of a semi green dusty tree, a sadly sagging post and rail fence allowing rusty machinery shapes to encroach and clutter all around. Such a picture as the Smithy pumped his bellows, a sweat patch on his holey blue singlet but with time to chat and it was a great place to wait for a lift back to the station.

Like back in the Valley, everyone went to church and it was part of the arrangement by Northcote that the Major saw that I attended each Sunday. I would sit quietly in my 'go to meeting' best clothes in the back seat of the imported eight seater Vauxhall, [Biggest car I'd ever seen]. The Ramsay clan went to their Presbyterian and I would go to my Church of England. As we had learned in the early days, to get on you had to go along with it all and believing or not the advantage was evident. On the way back we would stop at the store for the papers and I would stock up on a week's supply of lollies. It will be seen that all we kids, all our lives, were hooked on sweets, even pastries such as chocolate eclairs or those puff pastry matches full of jam and cream.

With a bike I could now go to town at weekends, never staying the night, always riding back. Sixteen miles each way to Colac, just a few miles of bitumen to the first gate, then miles of dirt road across tracks and trails with endless opening and shutting of gates. Often it was pitch black and with only my faithful carbide lamp to try and avoid cow pats or even the cows themselves. The modern invention of the dynamo fitted to the front wheel was great if you got up speed but through the pooey black of night that was not always possible.

There were by now quite a few boys from the farm in the district. It was great to meet in Colac, talk over exploits and have a night out, usually it was pictures and a big aluminium container milkshake afterwards. It was a great time of growing up, having someone, sort of family to share thoughts and make plans. Also, and so importantly, someone to talk to about women and sex, the sex we were so starved for.

After the flicks, some nights we would go to the dance, dancing was one thing we knew about from Crack Hardy's teachings. After 10 p.m. it was only two bob and the first night, I will never forget. They were playing 'Margie', a song I'll always love as a favourite. The band was really belting it out, we country bumpkins sitting round the edge when this gorgeous buxom girl, more beautiful I thought than the magazines under my bed, asked if I would like to dance. "Yes please". It was so nice, first time since forever to have a woman in my arms, one to hold close and take in the woman smell rather overpowered by the powder and perfume as we did our quick-step. It was love at first glance until she asked me rather forcefully to go outside with her. Too shy and stupid, I declined and she gave up on me. The bubble burst when I got back to the giggling mob of mates. I couldn't believe it when they said she was the local bike. That's the common name they gave the local prostitute.

Country girls, it seemed, were more with it and quite unabashedly forward, and in my ignorance I wasn't quite up with it. Riding home one night a utility stopped and the driver said, "Like a lift mate?" He said he would drop me at the main gate, "Stick the bike in the back and hop in." It was a pleasant surprise to find the girl of about sixteen in the back under the blankets. A shy introduction and with no time to waste she gave me a lesson in intimate touching and fondling so that by the time I got to my stop I was a real mess of embarrassment. I could hardly say thanks, but thank God for the dark as I took my bike to ride the rest of the 'cooling down run', back to my bunk to mull it over in my mind.

While at Mooleric, Major Ramsay took time to teach me the basics of sheep and wool, I had a genuine interest so he explained everything. He was in his 40th year of breeding a pure Polwarth and never imported inferior stock but culled heavily. Even his reject rams, when available, were in great demand. There were about 200 of the ones he kept and somehow I got to know them individually, not easy with sheep. He liked to show this off to visitors or buyers and for example would ask to see B.C.2, 150. I would go into the mob and bring out that sheep as indicated by the individual ear tag they all wore.

They say sheep breed like rabbits, it was an experience to see rams carrying out their duties. A ram was selected to suit a number of ewes, usually about 50 and they were penned up for the night. Raddle, a sort of greasy chalk, was spread on the rams belly so that in the morning it could be clearly seen how many he had serviced and with seldom a miss.

Shearing was a time of hectic rush and bustle, every boy should spend a season in a shearing shed in full swing. It's the hardest game there is and that includes the wool pressing old style and all the rouseabouting. I loved every bit of it and copped heaps. Still youthful and green, with a Welsh accent, I came in for lots of friendly abuse.

It was initiation time and on the occasion of being slow to clear the board of the fleece, the N.Z'er [A Kiwi.] who had cut his old ewe on the long blow, looked me over and barked out, "Tar here and piss off quick, I hate the smell of a bloody Pom." I treasure the opportunity to have worked there. He had been the gun shearer round the track for years and was knocking out his two hundred, only a little piss fart of a bloke but made of steel.

The day the machine broke down, they all conned him to give a demo of blade shearing. Hand shears were the only way before an Aussie invented the hand piece to revolutionise it all. He said, "OK" and we all watched in a silence of appreciation as he shore with his flashing blades and never a nick or sight of blood. Or the embarrassment of my need to apply the Stockholm tar with the accompanying, 'P.O.Q. Pommie B.'

Besides mustering in, penning up, piece picking and wool pressing, I had to carry over the kerosene tins of tea, the blocks of pretty rough cake and heaps of scones. Smoko was just a great time with pannikins of tea and much acting the nanny, they were always having a go and giving me heaps.

There came a time for me to have a go at shearing, blade only, not the machine. It was when the mob had all gone and it was time to do the stud rams. The regular staff did this by hand, no one else was trusted. It was fun till the first night of sore wrists, hands full of blisters and an aching back to prove how big and strong the beggars were, for this little Pom anyway.

And then there was the lamb marking time when the ewes had dropped their lambs and they were running around with their long little tails having a ball. Having a ball, not for long if I had anything to do with it. They were ready to be mustered, penned up and marked. It was always a big day getting the mob, ewes and lambs penned by smoko if possible. Every available hand and his dog would be out cursing the stupid bloody things as they were, trying to make a break and taking half the mob each time till we eventually won and the gate squeezed closed.

They seemed to know something awful was awry, it was the castration of their lambs, the lopping off of tails and wrecking of ears with identification numbers or tags. Before that, it was time for smoko, the fire had been going long enough for the kero tins to boil ready for the tea, and hot red ashes for making thick slices of toast. No mucking about, you just helped yourself to thick slices of cold mutton, poured on lots of tomato sauce and got into it. Such a joy, all washed down with strong black tea, heaps of sugar for energy. The dogs, in their well deserved rest would be too tired to move, just lay panting in the shade and only finding enough energy to snap up the scraps lobbed at jaws reach.

Then we got into it with a long day ahead. I put on the old raincoat, back to front, a sou'wester on my head, the Joseph Roger's knife ready and keen with a spare in the hip pocket. There were two or three men to keep routine going. They picked out a lamb, holding its front and back legs in each hand and offered it up to me breast high on the rail with it's bottom facing me. It was my job to slit the little purse, take the two tiny balls, [testicles] in my front teeth, bite and spit them out in one motion and then in one continuous move, cut off the tail. It took but about three seconds, after which someone else marked the ears, left or right before the bewildered little things were sent back to the panicking mother.

This method of castration, if there was someone able to perform it, was much preferable to others, as the lamb recovery rate was better. Those cruel emasculator pliers were used and elastic bands also for awhile. These methods saved mad operators such as I from being covered by the end of the day in blood and mess, but soon there were no more mad kids to tackle the job.

In passing, I should mention the snakes. Snakes everywhere, all of a deadly stamp. On the first muster I saw a ten foot King brown, fat in the middle with two tails. At the end of the day heading home passed where it was, there was a seven foot snake, fat for three feet with the other snake it had swallowed and the rest of its tail slowly going in. Gyp, the blue healer dog, was the only one allowed to tackle snakes. All others soon carked it from snakebite but Gyp would dive in, grab and shake, drop it and grab and shake. I'm sure as she stood back, she smiled as if to say, "How's that."

My dog was Roscoe and almost human. With him doing all the work we could muster a paddock faster than three men and their dogs. He was given to Major Ramsay, as were many other unwanteds, to try out in the rabbit pack. He was part Alsatian and part Heinz 57 varieties and we were warned he was a lamb killer if not watched. We took to each other, each of us loners from the start but he was a dead loss in the pack. Sure enough, at the sight of a lamb, he took off after it and I after him on horseback giving him hell with the stock whip till he stopped, bemused. Growling at him and threatening with the whip he got the message and learned to, 'Come behind' like any dog should to the whistle or call.

The Major gave him to me as my own sheep dog and he never harmed another animal till the day I left. His photo is still sitting on my bookcase and it was the worst day of my life, worse even than leaving Treforest or England, when having joined the Air Force and being called up, it was time to leave. I told him to go sit on his box, [The big kennel I had made], as I did most days and to stay. He stayed there as I was driven out in the station ute, I couldn't look but he knew it and the fun days were over between us.

As no one could handle him, nothing else to do and as I found out years later, he got the lead aspro [a 22 bullet] and was put down.

Having graduated from general hand to boundary rider or saddle frigger, as we were commonly referred to, I had my own horses and carried the requisite first-aid kit to be used on sheep and lambs caught in fences or such. As a bush doctor I felt I 'done good' when a lamb got caught and tore a three cornered section out of its stomach. Seeing it happen I was able to catch it and the intestines and stuff the lot back in. With horse hair and a bag needle I sewed it up so Miss Scholes would be proud and carrying it gently back on the pommel, got it back to the station where it was cared for. It recovered to become a pet, thinking it was a dog it soon followed everyone around.

Doreen, at fifteen, with me there being now responsible, was sent out as house maid and general dog's body. Mooleric never had one better. We had our first visitor, never had such a thing as a visitor since the Uncle from Rhydfelin. I say we, but it was for Doreen, the word had got around she was here. He was one of our boys from Colac way and the start of a bit more getting together as we grew up.

Having Doreen there was just great, we needed each others company and the security of a confidant. I'm sure we would have gone bananas without someone of the same age to talk to, in the evenings I'd be allowed in her room in the big house to listen to the radio. Our favourites were the 'Comedy hour' and the 'Hillbilly hour', where we learned every monologue and cowboy song by heart. We out sang and yodelled Tex

Morton and Buddy Williams, even Harry Tarrani as we had grown up to yodel in Tonteg.

Between us we read every book in the huge Ramsay library. In my time there I even read the Bible front to back plus Tolstoy's, 'War and Peace'. That's besides the western 'shoot em ups' and thrillers by the dray load. It was by hurricane lantern through half the night and it was murder on the eyes.

Doreen is the one in the middle of the family, not old enough to be bossy or young enough to get attention, just the one to be there and help everyone. Never nasty or picky but often in her life, taken advantage of. At Treforest or Tonteg, I was not always nice to her and didn't let her read my comics and books but I did love her. She was always around, Doug and I both, as boys, thought she was a menace to look after all the time but when they met again in 1979 it was different story.
Doreen and Yvonne looked after each other in all the 'Homes' and both had cared for Bernard and Myrna so it was a follow on that Yvonne also came to Mooleric to work, after I had gone though.
Doreen kept in touch with the Tarr's in King St. and with Audrey Wiltshire in Pontypridd. I thought how proud old Pricy in King Street would be of his friends the Rees girls if he could see them now.

36

* The Man *

Life on the sheep station was daylight to dark hard, great, but a routine of repetition and one needed a break. On the bike, the heavy roadster, not the lightweight speedster of today, I would make the trip to Glenmore and the farm. Sixty miles, there on Friday afternoon and back on Sunday, it was never easy. Sometimes I would take toys I had salvaged, repaired and painted to give to the little kids. Something inherited from the cricket bat Xmas time in Tonypandy I suppose.

1942 and all the conversation had turned to the war and its rapid escalation. So many workers had enlisted or were joining up, labour was becoming a problem. With this in mind I'm sure and with my 18th birthday coming up, the sly old Major Ramsay took me into the Army recruiting depot in Colac. There he spoke to some old cronies and I was given a medical check, asked a few questions and that was that, but on the way back I gave it all great thought.
To most, I was a country bumpkin but my early training gave me lots of mug cunning. By this time I was an experienced station hand capable of carrying out any task they threw at me with a Taffy youthful exuberance. I was now a top station hand. Major Ramsay, under pressure I might add, had recently given me a ten bob rise, ever the canny if miserable Scot.

So, having decided the score and what it was all about, never having taken days off, I asked for time to go to Melbourne for shopping or such. It was all strange to me but OK and I found my way to the R.A.A.F. recruiting office. Amazed in fact at all the others with the same thing in mind as we found the officer in charge. We filled in the papers and went through the whole procedure. Physically fit as the mallee bull they always quoted, mentally I thought I could cope, though the non-event schooling in those early days was a worry.
They told me to go home and I would soon be notified of the result.

It was coincidental not to be out riding or rabbiting as we had been kept back to clean out the chaff cutting shed, so coming out for a breather, I was there when the mail arrived. There was an official letter for me, which I opened and read immediately. I sat on the horse trough to think about it. It took a moment to sink in that my life was about to change because this was my call up and acceptance into Air Force service life. In retrospect, it was the second most important letter in my life, the first being from Mr Llewellyn in South Wales, which enabled me to get to New South Wales.

Just then, the good Major came up to inform me I would not have to go into the army [Sneaky old bugger]. I was exempt because of my priority job. When I showed him my letter, he just smiled and said, "Good luck boy, I understand." He also then told me that when I returned from duty, there would be a position as station manager for me. "Keep in touch Derrick, write occasionally."

Perhaps my experience of rural life was to come to a close because of the Japs, perhaps the best days of my life, every boy should have such a time. It is so character forming and with a little time in defence service, gives one a practical approach to life somehow sadly missing today.

Jimmy and Cedace, my two lovely horses were given a last feed, a pat and a nuzzle. They with Roscoe, my very best mates. Major and Mrs Ramsay said farewell and we parted the best of friends. Doreen was sad to see me leave, it was for the better and she, perhaps with thoughts already of moving on didn't feel so bad.

It seems I'm so wrong there as Heather reminds me of Doreen telling her how she missed me, having never been away from me. She had hugged the clothes I had left to breathe the smell of me. Whenever the Bing Crosby song, 'San Antone,' came on she had cried at the 'Deep within my heart' bit.

Mary, my good pal, said little, just stood back, eye to eye for a moment. Worst of all as I've mentioned, my dog Roscoe was left behind.

The first thing was to get back to Northcote farm to leave that big brown suitcase of personal belongings. Not much to show for my 18 years, one suitcase. Being one of the first to enlist, I was a minor celebrity for a moment as I said goodbye to them all. Yvonne and Bernard were not too sure what was going on but change was ever a part of their scene. Many of the kids joined the forces and proud to become Aussie diggers in true tradition.

In Melbourne, the big smoke at last, it was all adventure. A country bumpkin? I must have looked it too, staring at all the sights, the best being girls, so stunning and confidently capable. Dining on my own and not knowing how to behave or looking like a hick was an experience as I took it all in and thought of what was to come.

Having spent time reading the posters, I passed the Tivoli in my lost wandering of the city, my mind was made up to see the show the first night. So fantastic then and now in retrospect still is. The Tivoli girls were just gorgeous and knocked my love-starved eyes right out, the comics were hilarious and all the acts for me, were just superb.

Being a hillbilly or country and western fan, as they now call it, the Tennessee Hillbilly was terrific playing his banjo and singing 'The Death of Willy.' His wife was a yummy chorus girl and as Dolly, was to become Bob Dyer's partner in the 'Pick-a-box' show to follow later.

Bed that first night was in the Y.M.C.A., a place we were to stay while on leave, there or the 'Toc H'. A stinking hot night, sleeping in the raw, my money belt was stolen right off my waist. It was a rotten restless night and I was glad to see the sunrise so I could get to breakfast before presenting myself for the induction into the Royal Australian Air Force.

No further worries, we were in their hands, all green rookies together for the first time in great trepidation, kids again wondering what service life had in store for us. The medical didn't worry me as it did some because I was used to being starkers in a group from Miss Scholes' into the shower trick. The embarrassing time came when we all had to line up before the doctor. A lady doctor for God's sake! As we inched forward to face her we were told to hold up our shrivelled manhood and "Milk it forward", perhaps necessary in future times to look for a discharge. She then, can you believe it, lifted it up on a H.B. pencil and stared at it. At innocent 18 it was a bit of a shock but as it happened at each change of station unit, it was par for the course, commonly referred to as the 'short arm parade'.

Once we were sworn in and taken the oath, we were off, still in our mixed civvies, on our first march through the streets of Melbourne to the cries of, "You'll be sorry." Colonel Heath, ever the soldier, had taught us boys the basics of marching and drill so it was all a snack for me, not like some of the chaps with two left feet. I soon learned it was easier to become marker on route marches so as to set the pace instead of struggling along in the rear.

We were soon fitted out in full issue, boots and all. After being bussed for miles, we found ourselves in a rough camp in the bush, back of the beyond it seemed, but it was only Rocklands Dam near Hamilton where we were to spend three weeks of 'Initial training'. A toughening up time of drilling and route marches, rifle and arms training, hour after boring hour of it till we were all, perhaps only nearly all, fitter than that Mallee

Bull we've already mentioned. The tucker, a la mechanic turned cook was basic but plenty of it. The tuck-shop sold only lolly water, all grog a strict no-no.

After stand down each day, a communal shower and dinner, we sat around and talked till one evening bored with the inactivity I suggested we go and chase rabbits. Mostly city bred they said, "What do you mean chase rabbits?" So we went out and I ran and caught a rabbit. When I brought it back it was to a chorus of, "Bloody Mad Pommie bastard."

It's funny that on the first day I was called a Pom, I didn't like it at all and the fact my name was Derrick made me introduce myself as Taffy. I was to be known as Taffy from then on. The only ones to call me Derrick are Heather, Mum, Doreen and later some family. Even my grandchildren call me Taff. When Sebastian, Evan's son was asked, "Is that your grandfather?" He replied firmly, "No, that's just Taff."

All the boys, skinny and just out of school, were now men and had to prove it by their drinking and they certainly got into it wherever the chance. They, and by they, I mean all the mates in my years of service, thought I was queer because as you know, at Treforest in the Rechabites, I promised to not touch the demon drink till I was 21 years old. For what it's worth I didn't drink till after I came back from Borneo with the war over, my 21st was forgettable up in the jungle but over the years I've tried to catch up, with a special preference for a good red.

Being fit and ready, rearing to go, the next move was to the old Exhibition Building in Melbourne. What memories of that place. The grand old lady had been completely fitted out beyond all recognition with floors and decks in every inch of space. The kitchen and all amenities and recreation rooms fitting in where possible. There were rows after rows of iron beds, straw palliasses and every item to Air Force regulations or no leave pass. Air Force bods everywhere, just a human beehive of personnel with a serious intent to finish this training rubbish and get into the real war.

The smell! or odour of cooking from the kitchen below made one chuck rather than eat. The food was rubbery scrambled eggs, tinned dog [Bully beef] and endless baked beans on soggy toast. The evening meal always had watery mashed spuds and soggy greens, prunes and rice became standard issue. Luckily I loved them to survive almost four years of them.

There was an instantly erected 3-ply timber wall canteen where we could gather and talk over the day's events and girls. Nothing alcoholic, just lolly water by the truckload and a penny back on the bottle. There were so very many empties lying around that, restless as always, I couldn't resist collecting them and stashing the stack of money into my savings account. It became considerably more than the six shillings and sixpence [65 cents] that we received as pay.

In the evenings, the busiest place was the row of telephones instantly installed. Queues of blokes ringing mothers and girlfriends, wives and lovers. Some, first time away from home, missed their loved ones but I never rang. Actually, I had never spoken on the phone and didn't till a later time at Mt Druitt's new camp just out of Sydney.
Study was priority and leave was restricted to Saturday nights and a rostered Sunday so we had little time to get it on with the W.A.A.F.'s in the camp nearby. But once started, I lost no time trying to catch up with what my Mavis Richards of the 'up in the ferns' times had taught me. City leave in the months ahead crammed years of experiences into a brief but exciting time. The patriotic ladies put on house parties at their homes to entertain the brave heroes to be, girls willing and able were there to make a fuss over us. After years of milking cows, sheep and cattle or all that stuff, this was the life for me.

I had my first look at 'Chloe' in Young and Jackson's, the watering hole opposite Flinders St station. With a million others we danced to the continuous loud bands and music. We jitterbugged up a storm to Benny Featherstone's band and you never heard 'In the Mood' like it as the perspiring conglomeration of uniforms clapped and cried out for more.
The trouble with the Americans [Yanks] was just starting and they were everywhere in a massive troop build up. With their starched and pressed uniforms and big pay packets, they were winning the best looking girls and rivalry was quite a problem. It was once, an Army versus Navy or Air Force thing but now was becoming US versus THEM. It was really all good fun, a few busted heads and a trying time for all service police.

Our six weeks preliminary training started at daybreak with us all shaved, dressed and fed. It was 'On Parade' to form ranks to the W.O.D.'s satisfaction, he then stood us 'At ease', while the 'Adje' took over to have the 'daily routine orders' read out. The Adjutant usually became the 'Silly old bugger', they were often first war veterans having put their age down to have another go, great blokes.
It was hard keeping awake in the monotony of it and the bright morning sun after busy days and nights. In the gardens round the Exhibition Buildings, the doves and pigeons billed and cooed, picking industriously

at whatever they picked. This was their terrain and they took little notice of the upheaval we caused, even of the drunk covered in 'Sun' newspapers, asleep on the park seat oblivious to this, our war. He looked a Digger himself by the R.S.L. badge on the hat, near the brown paper wrapped bottle dropped from the dangling hand. Had it been full of metho and boot polish or cheap red, 'Fourpenny dark'? His last, as it turned out. He had curled up for the big sleep and when we came back from Tech, he was still there, him and the doves. He! Dead as a Dodo.

We drove to Brunswick Technical College in double-decker buses, not yet petrol heads but urging our drivers to race each other down busy streets. At the Tech, in new overalls and boots, we were shown the tools for scraping, gauging, filing and rasping. We used the micrometer and gauges for accuracy till ready for exams and an assessment of our prowess to allocate a trade accordingly. The future was to be decided for us, be it mechanic, electrician, fitter or armourer. In the forces, any civilian qualification excluded you from that in the service. The idea was to teach you only their way of doing things, a system that was hard to follow, but with the pressure of an on going war and the desperate shortage of tradesmen, there was no time for old ways and bad habits.

It was a no time to waste, pressure time. The average course of six months turned out qualified personnel ready for immediate active duty. It was revolutionary and something of a miracle that the five year course of civilian days, could be satisfactorily completed in that time.

A miracle of war time organisation perhaps but also a shambles of endless bull shit.

I chose to be an Armourer so they gave me a mechanics course and it wasn't going to be easy. Unlike city kids, I didn't know a piston from a carburettor and had never driven a car. Never the less, on completion of the time, I received my certificate saying I was a fitter, an aircraft fitter no less and with just a little practical tuition was soon able to pair up with another fitter and carry out the ultimate job of a 240 hour inspection. It didn't take us that long to learn. The engine had done 240 hours and needed stripping right down, testing and then re-assembling.

When we worked on Kittyhawks for example and the job was complete, the test pilot would collect the plane from the dispersal area and with one of us sitting on each wingtip, he would taxi to the airstrip where he would rev it up a bit before take off with us listening intently to the tune of the motor. After throwing it around the sky in test manoeuvres, it was a thrill to see him taxi back and give the thumbs up sign. He signed the 'A.OK slip' and we felt just great as if we had put another nail in the Japs coffin. It's funny or perhaps a bit strange, but after the war when we all had cars, I never even changed a spark plug and my mate Warren, a mechanical nut, said I kept the worst looking motor he had ever known. Though by then a most practical and thorough tradesman, grubby things mechanical were not my scene.

Going back to the classroom was for me, the hardest part of all, my time spent there in the past was minimal and never a great help. Only my reading and practical application saved me but just the same it took all I had to get through. With two others I missed out on Component parts and Airscrews, one of the last exams and we had to join another group and repeat. This was another stroke of good fortune, history repeating itself, because the others went to Canada for their overseas duty. Like the leaving of Middlemore, the next half of this story would be so different.
So with the course completed, a short leave to say goodbye to 'All the girls I've loved before'. Billy, Dick and Eric Coombes [The Mallee kid] and I, instead of the ice and snow, were to eventually be together in the warm tropics of New Guinea and Borneo.

The tropics already and I haven't even started to tell of the six months in the show ground at Ascot Vale next to the Flemington racecourse. For the many thousands who passed through there, it is impossible to explain what the weirdest way of life was like but so unforgettable.
We were in No.2 cattle pavilion, roughly and hastily fitted out to house troops. It was draughty and cold, the straw palliasses were lumpy and hard and only 'He' knows how we kept warm enough to sleep. We wore overalls, socks and overcoats and being young, mad and commando fit, we managed to survive.
The food was mostly so so, yucky and monotonous but as they told us, war was hell! There was a canteen where as insatiable hormones on two legs, we could fill up on junk food and drinks. There were food stalls outside the main gate for pies and peas, chips or such.
On weekend leave or nights of A.W.L. over the fence, we lived and loved as though there was no tomorrow, house parties and girls, dances and girls. I took girls home to suburbs I'd never heard of and spent all night finding my way back to camp, often only just in time to don overalls for parade. Staying awake in class was murder.
The transition from farm hand to man about town took so little time, all those early years stood me in good stead.
Then it was all over, only the passing out parade, a pat on the head for being good boys and a short well earned leave.

I won't forget it, it was Melbourne Cup day and we figured it out we would be dismissed from parade in time to cut out the back way, across the camp and into the racecourse through our hole in the fence, in time to see the cup run.

A first for most of us on a steamy hot day as we stood in line in full uniform, impatiently waiting for them to do whatever they were going to do. The drill sergeant, a sadist who seemed to hate all airmen and enjoyed our total discomfort, kept us standing there till we reckoned we would miss the race.

His "Squad... Dismiss" was the last order at Ascot Vale, hard to believe the horror six months was over and we were now A.C.1's [Airmen first class] on ten and six a day. Kit bags had been ready for ages so we grabbed them to race away as the crowd could be heard over the fence and horses coming onto the track.

We were sweat balls but the Gods were kind, there was just time to place a bet, a real roughie but a nice name for me in my betting ignorance. It was not only my first race but the race of the century. 'Old Rowley', ridden by A. Knox came in at 100 to 1, an introduction into racing that was to lead to a part-time career later on. Even though I was to see our famous Billy Cook ride Rainbird and J. Letts a bit later on Belldale Ball, it was the thrill of Old Rowley coming down that Flemington straight that gave me the greatest thrill.

We thought we were now ready to go to war but after sitting on our backsides so long it was a fitness camp for us before the Pacific zone. Three weeks intensive commando stuff, armed combat, rifles and grenades, bush and jungle survival and night manoeuvres. We received our own heavy old 303 rifle to cart round for the next couple of years.

Billy, Dick, Eric and I received the first posting together, to strange country for the city type Dick and the Mooleric me but not for the Malley kid with his home just up the road so to speak. It was the Catalina flying base at Lake Boga out of Swan Hill and we were to work on the famous Catalinas plus one three-engined Dutch Dornier. The Cats were fabulous, flying at sea level they were hard to shoot down, their surveillance and coastal operations part of the history that helped win the war.

Combs and I were to become a concert act in our years together, he with his banjo and I singing with my comb and paper, Jews harp and mouth organ. I'm told not to mention playing the spoons which I did, so I won't. There were fun concerts between here and Tarakan, Borneo. The only paid engagement was two pounds from Rex Taylor, our C.O., who asked us to fill in at Noemfoor Is. when the big act was booed off stage as hopeless.

On the long bus trip to Swan Hill we met some local girls, we were new blood in town so we had a head start at the dances and shindigs at weekends. Everyone, everywhere was friendly to all in uniform, a bit of patriotism with the hope of a bit of fun and games thrown in, in the case of the lovely ladies.

At the camp just out of town, our dispersal area and workshops were on the foreshores of Lake Boga, a fantastic place to work. The actual campsite was a bit of a hike away, set amongst vineyards and stone fruit trees, I'm really into fruit trees as you know. The fruit and grapes were in full season so we made pigs of ourselves. There were two lakes, one full of tortoises and in the migrating season which was right then, they tediously toddled to Lake Boga in their millions, many thousands at least. They would queue up to get through the few openings under the railway lines or scramble over one into the miles of twin steel extending forever. Those that got through then had to cross the busy road which became utter mayhem. The hundred yards of road became a bloody mess and total hazard.

The short time we spent as fledgling mechanics was hectic but exciting as, with the escalating war, we wondered where our overseas service might take us. Cats [Catalina Flying Boats] were big bulky beasts and when they had to come out of the water for service, in summer it was OK but in winter volunteers were called to swim out and fit the undercarriage. The incentive was a tot of rum before and after so the real booze artists were first in line even though, as they said, it would 'Freeze the balls off a billiard table'.

It seemed an age but it was only six weeks for us in this great spot and super Swan Hill before the exciting posting came through. The three of us were to report, post haste [Right away], to an as yet unheard of unit, No.11 R.S.U. at a lesser known, Mt Druitt, somewhere west of Sydney town. Not a soul knew where it was, not even Air Board itself.

In what was a needless urgency, we were processed in record time, handed in the issue gear and extra blankets. Passes and movement orders were issued and transport laid on for bus to Melbourne and train to Sydney.

It was a shock when I went to say goodbye to the W.A.A.F. in stores section, we were just casually dating as I thought but I found her in tears and distressed. "What had I done?" The W.A.A.F. Sergeant told me to just leave, get going and be on my way. Was this my first broken heart? I don't even remember the girl's name.

It's a bore now to relate tales of wartime travel, suffice to say we did lots of it. We arrived at Central station in sardine like packed dog boxes, we were all crushed and sooty from the flying ashes. The lucky ones found a luggage rack to try to sleep in. We had the keys made at the Brunswick Tech so that we could go from carriage to carriage to check out the girls, share a blanket and a bit of 'Hows your uncle' if you know what I mean.

Arriving in Sydney late on a Sunday afternoon, we cleaned up and used our travel chit voucher to get a meal in the railway refreshment rooms, the first of many ordinary meals at stations round the country. Then with all our gear, we looked through the departure boards for our Mt Druitt. Not a mention, the guards didn't know of it and it was stalemate till a traveller from Katoomba told us it was on the western line. We found the train, a cattle truck edition and were told, hopefully, it stopped at Mt Druitt.

This whistle stop, soon to be a hive of activity was just a wooden platform out there in the sticks. In the dark we could see what was a general store, cum newsagent and you name it. There was a Church across the way and way down on the right in a paddock all alone, the ever present in lonely places, the 'School of Arts'.

This was Mt Druitt, Vintage '43, the Mount itself was just a rise in the distance and the airstrip over the back was just a stretch of dirt and gravel undulations.

Two Dad and Dave characters were attending the railway crossing gates, for a moment the nostalgia of Doug and I watching the Flying Scotsman roar by on that first night out of London, hit me. Where on earth was he now?

The two blokes looked us up and down as we asked where the Air Force camp was. We got a 'Buggered if I know' from one and a casual 'Some codgers in uniform went that way', pointing up the road.

Lumping the kit bags and gear on our shoulder we tramped the dirt track to get to some old cyclone wire gates on the left, no guards on duty, just a few lights but it looked like this was it!

The temporary C.O. was Sergeant Reg Johns who was in control of about thirty service type personnel. He, for a moment was Boss and this was the nucleus of what was to be the 11 R.S.Unit, 'Taylors Tigers' and the pride of all Air Force non-flying units. There was an old, run down mansion-type house on the rise, it was known as headquarters or Bull Shit Castle.

We had another C.O. arrive who, never having had a unit before, stuffed everything up and wasn't with us long before Squadron Leader C.R. [Rex] Taylor arrived. He and we had a few hiccups at first, till a compromise was arrived at and a relationship between officers and men started as an example to all units.

Rex took us through the war, became an Air Commodore with distinction and an O.B.E. and just recently had the honour to lead the Anzac Day march in Melbourne with a contingent of us, his men and mates, to take the salute at the Cenotaph. Rex died a happy man just two weeks later.

Briefly so as not to dwell on it, Rex started in the ranks, went from L.A. C. right through the ranks to Air Commodore in a career of distinction as C.R. Taylor O.B.E, C.Eng, F.R.A.E.S. and father of the 11 R.S.U. family.

Just recently Blacktown Council, at our 11 R.S.U. committee instigation, carried out a lot of work and with a lot of personal effort, cleaned up our then derelict garbage dump old campsite. It is now a picnic place with trees and gardens and as an Air Force memorial it has a brass plaque with our story on it. What I'm getting to is that at the dedication and flag raising and as we took the salute I was smiling and Bert asked, "What's up?" and I mentioned the mottos.

The Air force motto is, 'Per adua ad Astra'. 'Through adversity to the stars'. That soon became, 'Per Torres Excreta ad Astra'. 'Through Bull Shit to the stars', as the services were full of it.

There was also, 'Per adua ad Asbestos', which loosely and crudely translated is, 'Stuff you Jack, I'm fireproof' and I might as well finish it off with the classic, 'Nil Bastardi Carborundum' or 'Don't let the bastards wear you down'. Sorry about all that.

In the months ahead we would reach our full compliment of over 400 officers and men. It was a hectic build up to be fully equipped and ready for our salvage and service duties. Bearing in mind no such unit had been before, there was no precedent and we were all on a learning curve.

In crews of about 14 we travelled the state recovering crashed aircraft, bringing them back for service and repair. To be in a crash crew was a bonus, fun and adventure, but rough.

My best trips were to Bulli, to Tuncurry across in the punt from Forster, where there is now that beaut bridge and the one to Coffs Harbour which was to become known as 'The Banana republic', with its 3 dollar bills and El Presidente.

While at Coffs we knew the war was getting closer than folk were told, or that Australia was aware of, by the Jap submarine activity along the coast. We spent many a long night in the silent dark, moving stores and supplies including endless rows of back breaking 44-gallon drums of fuel. I won't mention here about the occasional drum we loaned to the banana farmers for 10 pound a drum to buy beer and stuff for a dance at Woolgoolga, the entire town invited, about 50 in total at that time. I gave our unit the name 'Taylor's Tigers' at that time, but I will surely mention that often enough.

Heather and I built a house up there at Emerald Beach in 1980 in the 'Famous' Pete and Jill Doig country, they had the famous caravan park. [Everything they did was prefixed 'Famous'] They entertained us while staying there and building our shack, we played Canasta and drank any and everything. That Rechabites thing had long gone by the board. We did the twelve months round Australia trip with the Doigs. It was fun and games and a laugh a mile.

At Druitt, we were there longer than expected so we received leave every night except Monday which was closed camp to all. There was a dance every night and one at the Blind Institute on Sunday afternoon. On Monday night, while most others were in closed camp, Alan Jones and I snuck out to a fabulous dance at the lower Town hall where the Lebanese ladies held their dance. The girls there were so beautiful, it was dance, beaut supper, but strictly don't touch.

At Air Force House there were hundreds of quickly created rooms or boxes for the troops to stay. The A.D.C. [Allied Defence Canteen] was great if you could get in early enough, because you could get the Yank type apple pie and ice cream with lots of real coffee available till all hours. Four or five hours sleep was standard and we were up about five to catch the train to be back to Mt Druitt and be on morning parade at 7-30 a.m. If late, it was closed camp for a week so we never were.

The train we caught was the munitions factory train the girls caught to St Mary's. It was an education, really something. Those women, some girls, mothers and the other type, were rough but honest, they gave us kids hurry up with their pranks and teasing. St Mary's, with its munition works, was the next station to ours and lots of time was spent there in liaisons with the girls, there or the pub. My mate, Sergeant Barford of 'Barford's Bastards,' met and later married his wife, Benny, there.

Being on the western line and Katoomba being further out and up the mountains, it was the in place, a must for tourists and where everyone spent their honeymoon. Up to this Blue Mountain town and resort, where the dances were great and airmen were received as heroes, we often gave Sydney the miss. Out by train through the then vacant west to Penrith, to the Three Sisters town soon to be famous worldwide.

It was in this holiday setting I met the shy little girl who in time was to become my beautiful wife. She was then only fifteen, still a school girl, young and innocent but old enough even then to captivate me, to change my life and so many of my family henceforth, Amen.

Russ French and I had joined the weekend crowd heading up the mountain this fine day, [A bit of fog and mist but that's Katoomba]. We walked down the hill past the Carrington and the Paragon, just a coffee and chocolate cafe but as nostalgic times slipped by, it was to go on the heritage listing. We found our way to the Villers Brett guesthouse where the landlady always made a fuss of us. She said how handsome we were in our uniforms, which was good for our girl chasing morale. Having lost her husband in that Villers Brett Flanders campaign, she had a special feeling for servicemen.

Russ didn't dance much, he was Tasmanian and more than a bit shy while I was now a dancing nut, so we headed for the dance nearby. She looked very nice, shy and petite but just about my size. She was a bit bemused as I said, in my apparently still strong Welsh accent, "My name is Derrick but they call me Taffy, may I have this jazz waltz?" Heather Jean told me later, "What a funny name, 'Toffee' " but we danced every dance together and the whole time was just terrific. It was my intro to the Gwynne family, to the roast lamb dinners, apple pies and passion fruit meringue pies, to a style of living so new to me, but that comes later.

Going back on the train, not having given much thought to it before, I thought of my Dad. He was Air Force too, he was young and enthusiastic, he was called Taffy too. Under different circumstances, his World War 1 and mine World War 2, what really was in store for me?

37

* Katoomba…. Heather *

Back at Katoomba where Heather and I had been dancing the night away, we met Hazel Lynch who was having a night out too. Heather was being kept an eye on by Hazel who was being chaperoned by Heather's mother, Mrs Gwynne [Aunty Jean to one and all]. Hazel's husband Gerald was a sergeant cook at 113 R.G.H. Concord and on duty, little knowing I might add, that his lovely wife was out gallivanting about.

With Miss Scholes' teachings I must have made that good first impression, though they all thought I spoke funny and me thinking I had got rid of my accent. Mrs Gwynne took me for a gentleman, I was a bit of a mystery to everyone and being from Melbourne, not having anyone in Sydney, she asked where I was staying. With the result that the next day after the dance, there was a note at Villers Brett guesthouse asking me to contact them when back at camp and if I wished, arrange to come to Rhodes for a nice home cooked meal. It was the magic words, 'Home cooked meal' that did it but to see Heather Jean again was a nice thought too.

Managing to get the right connection at busy Strathfield, I got off at little Rhodes station and asked at McIlwain's shop for directions. Mrs Gwynne met me and introduced me to Mr Gwynne. George, of Welsh derivation and I were to become the best of mates, right up to the night he died in my arms, much too young and only in his early sixties and just enjoying life.

Both Heather and I were so very shy at the time though everyone says I was never ever shy, but I was. Only fifteen at the time, it was hard to know what her thoughts were of unusual me as she showed me around what I thought was a very expensive solid brick house with it's lovely garden and shrubs. An impressive vegie garden too and even a chook shed up the back where big black Orpingtons laid big brown eggs.

All of this made a lasting impression on me so new to suburbia. This was it, the sort of lifestyle worth working for and I never realised ordinary folk lived so well.

Having met Hazel up the mountains, I now met Gerry, newly married with baby Robyn. They were renting a room while Gerald was stationed at R.G.H. It was Hazel's influence saying I was a nice boy that convinced the Gwynnes to allow me to take Heather to the pictures at

Concord West, a first for her, to be allowed out alone, with a boy I mean. The first too, of our suppressed passion as we kissed and cuddled in the back stalls. Though possibly just a passing phase, my 'passio magneto' told me in a way of a future development.

Rhodes was unique, rather undiscovered and to me at that time, a fabulous place. Thomas Walker, about 1791 built his home at Uhres Point, he named it Rhodes after his family home at Rhodes Hall in Leeds, England. At that time Rhodes was a most beautiful sweeping tree covered section of land on the banks of the Parramatta river which was full of fish and prawns there for the taking. By the time I arrived it was becoming an industrial area, a new bridge across to Ryde where the punt had patiently putted across. The acrid smell of Timbrol's Chemical Factory was even then driving folk away and the prawns and fish were almost gone.

We did our courting in the little park on the left over the bridge, it's now gone too but the swings we'd sat on together in 'early romance and getting to know times' are a pleasant memory. Rhodes was my first real home in Australia, it was there I took part and became someone in a real live community.

Heather, being an only child, born as something of a shock to a mother of 42, was thankfully not a spoiled child, perhaps more of an over protected little girl and her own natural character was subdued and not allowed to surface for some years. Her good upbringing and kind nature was an influence on me.

We were to see quite a bit of each other in those few months while at Mt Druitt. Good friends, nothing more at this stage with me living the life of Riley in Sydney town and leaving shortly for overseas.

While I was away we wrote reasonably often to keep in touch, I later found out I was only one of dozens she wrote to. Other servicemen back there had a better run, the locals and of more importance at the time, half the British Navy. In fact Mrs Gwynne, in her patriotic vein, entertained so many of them. Much to Heather's approval I think, with the greater freedom it brought.

In retrospect, no longer a boy but still full of youthful exuberance, I turned 19, life was a ball and I was coping with whatever came along, though a rather late starter. We forget nowadays how everything was moving at top speed in those wartime years and no time for indecision or to dilly-dally.

Having no one to answer to, no parent or guardian and after the years of confinement of the farm or sitting on a saddle day dreaming, I must have gone berserk. Uniforms had an attraction, an air of mystery and my apparently still pleasant Welsh accent, all put together had a seemingly magic attraction for girls.

For the short time before Air Board choofed us all off, we laughed about going on leave and said, "This war is hell." The good times we had were to keep us going in the extended time we were away. White women would be a memory and in two years time the dark native female was to be looking almost white!

It was a funny time, funny peculiar perhaps as events moved apace. There was a girl in Melbourne I fell madly in love with and though there were others to confuse the issue, it was the real thing. When away in N.G. we wrote regularly at first. I didn't notice the dropping off of her letters till one awful day at mail call, I got my 'Dear John' letter. I had heard of them, it was the easy way for them of breaking off a relationship, a couple of our boys had them and my mate, the best man at my wedding after the war, Johnno, lost his wife to a Yank that way.

I was prompted to write a poem because of all this, it may give us a break from the monotony of my ramblings.

The Dear John letter.

> **At Nadzab camp**
> **I wrote, dear heart**
> **At Noemfoor**
> **Dearest mine.**
> **At Moratai, 'twas sweetheart**
> **as time passed slowly by.**
> **In Borneo at Tarakan**
> **with two years nearly gone**
> **My heart stood still**
> **the letter starts**
> **those dreaded words**
> **"Dear John"**------------.

38

* Mt Druitt to War in New Guinea *

Finally at Druitt, everything was fitting into place, from utter chaos we were now a complete unit. Ready or not we had to move out of the great camp we had created, to make ready for the next R.S.U. to follow, No. 22. We were to leap frog them through the islands campaigns and even meet up again at Noemfoor Is.

The war was however not ready for us and as a complete unit we were sent to cool our heels at Bradfield Park to await our orders. What a disaster that was! We were in full tropical gear, all ready and rearing to go, discipline and uncalled for bull shit not our strong point and here we were amongst green rookies and new officer types who thought their poo didn't stink. All of them in neat, well pressed uniforms and hats at regulation angle as per Air Board orders.

That was the elite Bradfield Park base and they won't forget us in a hurry. We were still waiting, ruining the discipline of the whole camp till Air Board in all its great wisdom said, "Send them away, anywhere, but a long way away."

So it was pack up again, most of our gear was stored but ready and waiting. God knows if we would see it again as we boarded one of those mile long, infamous, ash and cinder spewing troop trains. Destination Queensland, supposedly a secret.

To praise it up, it was a rotten trip and took forever, food in transit is always lousy and there is a lack of it. Very few stops to get anything extra, no grog or even lolly water, just evil tasting warm water. If your carriage pulled up near an R.R.R. [Railway Refreshment Room] you got killed in a rush for a pie or piece of that stale fruit cake. A chat to the girls too was a relief over free, warm cups of their tea.

Nearly everyone smoked, endlessly, with nothing else to do and the whole train became a moving smoke cloud on two steel tracks.

It was boring, boring, boring but somehow, quite forgettably, we arrived at the end of the world by the name of Coominya. It was out from Ipswich on a branch line and the two towns we would get to know were Esk and Toogoolawah, but then only by truck when leave was granted and we all went to town, and how! The locals up here were fabulous and friendly.

The women, young or old, single, double or married, were all friendly and patriotic to us with half the male population gone off to the war.

Coominya had an airstrip, just a satellite, a cow paddock of gravel or a one-time melon patch. It was seldom used except for an ancient Avro Anson, so we used it for endless hours of left-right, left-right marching in full combat kit, like mad Englishmen out in the midday sun.

We built our canvas township, mess halls, ablution blocks and everything and we waited. As time eased by we gave up, drill sessions became half-hearted strolls, playing Pontoon or Five-hundred was a bore and the whole camp had severe fits of the lethargies.

Christmas was coming up, it was hot and dry, the flies were taking over, millions of the little black b------s, so for something to do two of us snuck off. Who really cared anyway as we went off to case the area? It was bonanza time when we found miles of ripe watermelons, we ate as many as we could and carted a shirt full each back to camp and then next day went back for more.

He was waiting for us, the farmer that is and we were in real strife. It was "G'day" all round, we introduced ourselves and had a good chat over who we were and what we were doing.

"Take the bloody lot," he said about the melons in despair. The rail strike was still on and he had no way to get them to the market now. The grapes were almost ready too and they also would go to waste.

What clever little buggers we were, we suggested he bring a cartload to the camp and flog them, we'd give the word and he could get rid of a few. It's a nice story and true too, that he did just that and over the next few weeks he got rid of the whole lot and as he said, shaking our hands in his big grateful paw, "It's the best year I've ever had."

The local people were really great and before we left Coominya and that camp, it was suggested we have a barbecue, a real, fair dinkum Aussie barbie. We emphasised they bring all wives and daughters along. One of the locals supplied the bullock and we gave him better than top price. It was put across the enormous pit we had dug in which the roaring fire had settled to red-hot ash. The beer, usually rationed and unavailable, was laid on by our mate the publican who incidentally must have made an instant fortune in our short time there. Local wines came from all sides and all in all, it was the mother of all barbies, the likes of which that neck of the woods would never see again.

Thank heavens it was summer in a way, because one night the end of a cyclone hit our comfy canvas camp with four and a half inch diameter hail stones causing absolute devastation. Everything washed down the now river like airstrip but it all gave us something to do to fill in time as we rang out our things and started again.

By now Xmas was almost on us, if we didn't receive our overseas posting soon, in the day by day expectancy, the problem of leave would become a major issue. Air Board said no one was to leave the area, we were on hourly call.

Our unit, No.11 R.S.U. made 'unofficial' Air Force history that Xmas when the whole unit went A.W.L. [Absent without leave]. There was a skeleton staff who had no one to go to, they could cope and plead innocence of where everyone was. Before we took off, we set a day and a time to be back in camp without fail as we then spread out across the country. Some husbands went interstate to be with families, all of us without passes or travel permits. Bert Marshall, our transport officer made it to Kalgoorlie in West Australia to see his lovely wife Dell. We met years later and she told me what a wonderful surprise it was. Jack Hamilton, or Bones as we called him, [Like in ham bones, get it?] travelled miles on every transport imaginable to be home for Xmas with Thelma.

True to our word, we arrived back in Brisbane en masse, I mean by the hundreds, the railway station full of us, each one liable to be up on a serious charge with a barrage of service cops in every direction. Wally Potts came along, Flying officer Potts, Engineer officer and a quick thinker. He lined us all up and took charge because like us, he had no pass but he marched us up to the gate, told the guard we were on secret pre-embarkation orders and filling the little Queensland train, we were home free.

The parade next morning was a farce, no one to chastise the other. Our W.O.D. [Warrant officer Disciplinary] 'Wally the Wod' put himself on extra duties with all of us to help. Our C.O. Rex Taylor, who had been off somewhere too, covered for us in the few reports that came in and it turned out a very merry Xmas for us all and no damage done.

Silently and without any fuss, the advance party slipped away to prepare our first camp in New Guinea, supposedly a secret destination, but we all knew it was Nadzab out of Lae. The packing was for real this time and a hell of a job getting it all aboard the Liberty Ship, 'Edward D. Baker'. These Liberty Ships were made by the thousand just for this purpose, moving troops en masse around the globe. They were pure economy and made of steel, in the waters of the tropics they became sweatboxes, the steel decks as hot as an oven in the day, never to cool down. My only knowledge of ocean travel was on the good old 'Largs Bay' and how very sad it was to hear of her being sunk so ignominiously in the rotten war.

Jack Burgeson, a wireless nut, set up his primitive P.A. system which he had begged, borrowed or stolen while at Druitt. He had only about a dozen records, all antiques which he played endlessly. There was a Mo McCackey [Roy Rene] comedy, a Conrad Veight classic and a sad old western, 'Little Joe the Wrangler' which drove the C.O. mad. We had a good laugh when he grabbed it off the turn table one monotonous morning and cast it way out into the blue Pacific. I searched for years for a copy to play at our reunions, in vain but I could still sing the stupid thing word for word.

Monotony was the order of the day and except for the D.I.'s dumb exercises on the deck, we played cards, bet on crown and anchor or unders and overs and wrote letters. It was too hot to sleep and those who could squeeze a space, slept on the deck hoping for a breeze. The food was crook as usual, worse even and washing was in saltwater with a special saltwater soap. It took the skin off leaving one all sore and itchy. When it did rain, praise the Lord, it was a sight to see with hundreds of bodies hastily soaping up all over and rinsing off before the cloud passed.

Shaving daily was murder, beards were a no no and moustaches only the prerogative of the baby faced pilots trying to look like a suave Errol Flynn.

Milne Bay appeared on the horizon, our first sight of the tropics and the evidence of bombings and war damage. We were allowed to have a swim, diving from the decks and having fun till some smarty noted the place was chocka block full of sharks. Not wanting to be the first casualty, end of swim!

Arriving at Lae, with its huge ship wreck half out of the water, there was a scene of feverish activity. Troops and equipment being unloaded and dispatched in great haste in convoys of camouflage to camps and depots in cleared jungle space.

We were disembarked into troop carriers for our trip through dense jungle and giant high Kunie grass. How could any one fight in this was just one thought as we arrived at the partly prepared camp at Nadzab, our home for the unforgettable months to come.

Almost instantly the track from Lae to Nadzab became a super highway, built in days it seems by the amazing Yanks and their endless equipment. It was soon to become as busy as Parramatta Rd, with heavy trucks and a jostle of Jeeps driven by smiling, gum chewing or cigar smoking black Yanks. They were always happy to give us a lift, they liked our Aussie, free and easy way of life and our acceptance of them. That was something mostly new to them.

On one occasion we were invited to a Chapel meeting to hear the quartet sing, Bible songs amongst others. Ray Addlington and I went and it was the most magic night of music and rhythm that I ever had, spine-tingling stuff.

Nadzab! How could you describe it at that time in history? It was set in what had been endless, impenetrable jungle. A plague of bulldozers had cleared miles of it for camps and airstrips to spring up everywhere in preparation for the big push north, hopefully to Tokyo now that the tide of battle had turned. This is the home of sparrow sized mosquitoes in their millions. There was scrub typhus and dysentery which, combined with ptomaine poisoning from punctured bully beef and herrings in tomato sauce tins, it was at times a little tedious! The mossie repellent on issue was deadly, not to the mossies, they lapped it up, but to us. It stung the eyes to blind you and if it got in your hair it took the teeth out of the comb.

The one thing we did religiously was take our Attebrin tablets against malaria. They tasted like hell if stuck in a dry throat and not swallowed right down, we all soon turned into a sickly yellow, hard to distinguish from the enemy themselves. Salt tablets and I think of all the 'Hoo-Ha' today of the 'no salt diets'. These were as big as marbles, impossible to swallow but without them and with all the sweating we did, we'd all be dead.

This was once again a canvas camp, a bit like Coominya, but that was bone dry while this one was damp humidity, with a tropical downpour at four o'clock every day, then the heat. It rotted and made everything mouldy right before your eyes. We were used to sleeping on straw stuffed palliasses but here we found it imperative to scrounge packing cases to build bunks to get off the terrain of scorpions and centipedes as big as zip fasteners. In due course we made tables and chairs for a little comfort in the rotten and rotting conditions.

Until we became attached to the American Fifth Air Force, our tucker was just bully beef and dog biscuits, tinned gold fish, [Herrings in tomato sauce,] rubbery scrambled and watery eggs. Prunes and rice of course.

Then came the change and we could not believe how well they fed and stuffed themselves. There was grapefruit, cereals, real meat and vegies, chocolates and dried fruit. I could go on and it was nice knowing them for a short time just to share their rations.

The reason for our being there, after seeming to be stuffed around for so long, was to service the aircraft in urgent need and to prepare the number of planes ready for the big push north. We worked in shifts day and night in primitive conditions, the early discipline and training we had thought was garbage was now proving its worth. There were now aircraft of every description from Moths and Kittyhawks to Liberators, filling every inch of dispersal space. The sky, with now only a lone, lost Jap reconnaissance plane in sight, was a bedlam of take offs and landings.
The logistics, if one thinks of it, of supplies for this mass of men and machinery is just mind-boggling. We criticise bureaucratic bungling but it is amazing how they come through in times of dire need.

As real as it all was, one part seemed a dream. It was a time when we were losing Liberators, the enormous four engined monsters. All Nadzab waited for the next one as we watched them crash to the ground. There were eleven by our count, though records may show otherwise. Each one could be seen to take off to gain altitude, then as they climbed the motors would start to splutter and cough, next moment down they would come, resulting in the death of the full crew. One crashed near our dispersal area with wreckage strewn for miles around. We were among the first on the scene to find charred wreckage and the stench of burnt flesh.
The story that came out of all this is that two German saboteurs were found putting cotton wool in the fuel tanks. As the planes started to climb, the jets became blocked, the engines failed and down they came.
The two were tried and sentenced to a public hanging there and then. It is all a little vague now but some of the boys went with a thousand others but it was not my idea of entertainment.

While talking of entertainment, ours was mainly open-air pictures where, courtesy of Uncle Sam. We saw new releases before the common public. There was a large screen set in the middle of a cleared area where servicemen of every variety flocked with home made, fold up stools. They sat on them where they wished and if it rained, just sat with their ground sheets around them and hats, fur felt, airmen for the use of, pulled down around the ears.
Even if it rained and the picture got blurred and drippy, it was quite comfortable. It was only crook when the siren went for an air raid, we waited patiently saying, "Go home you bastards," till the all clear went or we dribbled back to our lumpy bed in disgust.

On our tour, as the Japs moved back, we saw most of the fabulous U.S. shows with Bob Hope and his gang. We had famous stars such as Gracie Fields and John Wayne plus a multitude of gorgeous girls to send us all blind! Just doing their patriotic bit gyrating and looking lovely had men going bonkers at the sight of a scantily clad girl.

I know I go on but, of all the hundreds of units massed there, our 11 R.S.U. was the most innovative and we built, [With official or unofficial? sanction], a boxing ring, full sized with all facilities, all in our leisure time of course. It was there we held boxing competitions between Army, Navy and Air Force. The Septic Tanks [Yanks] brought all their best boys to have a go. It was before its time but we had a totalisator for betting, all in the name of necessary recreation. With Syd Hardy as trainer we put on the best nights of fights seen in N.G. Many Golden glove boys of the good old U.S. of A came but found it hard going against Archie Kemp, our light weight champ or the tough timber cutters from up Dorrigo way.

I never did beat Rex Chamberlain at Middlemore or the farm, so I only made it as a second to towel down the boys, but with the inside information I filled my money belt with pounds, dollars and Dutch guilders and never a bloody nose.

We would have gone troppo without some time off, evenings and some Sundays. In that time some of us made souvenirs to sell, mostly to the Yanks who had money to burn. Russ French, my mate who was with me when I met Heather at the dance at Katoomba, had a brother Earl in a construction unit and he had shown Russ how to engrave. With some coaxing Russ helped me make a set of tools from pieces of tool steel, shaped and tempered. With these, we engraved any and every article they could produce, rings made from two bob pieces, bent and shaped, a heart or shield piece was silver soldered on. The favourite was a silver, shaped, single or double heart, heat pressed into perspex. The usual inscription was, "To Mum" N.G. 1943-4 or, "To my Darling" etc. It later became S.W.P.A. [South West Pacific Area]. The charge or cost was six bob, sixty cents or two guilders in Dutch currency. My piece de resistance and no one else did it, was the Lord's prayer on a filed down and polished two shilling piece. For these I got five pounds or ten dollars as it is today. I also did it on a shilling but it was too demanding in a home made hand vice and with just a bit of steel and no eyeglass.

All the extra effort enabled some of us to take home a nice bank roll, mine alone was about 2,000 pounds, on top of all this and with money to burn, I had no need to draw on my service pay which accumulated over the two years. Being on active service it was now 12/6 per day or $1.25 in today's money.

A few of us in the know put together a few figures and our little unit of enterprise with its foreign orders and souvenirs made 100,000 pounds, a little of it playing two up with our affluent buddies. We were the only ones to do this in such style.

The war was moving on and we had moved back a bit by now, supplies were getting through and most importantly there was now a beer ration, two bottles per man when the boat came in. It was a morale booster for those who had missed their drink and a chance for a bit of a grog on. Those, like my Rechabite self, who didn't imbibe, sold the ration to a rush of buyers for ten bob a bottle. Talking of grog, being only a service unit, we had no heroes or awards, the only casualty and a bit of a laugh, was while we were in the beer ration queue. Mick behind me, went 'Ugh', flinched a bit and staggered. On investigation, it was found he had been hit in the back, in the beer queue no less, by an almost spent sniper's bullet. Mick was awarded a Purple Heart by the U.S. authorities but the Air Board wouldn't let him keep it. At a reunion in 1998, he inferred he did finally get it.

The task was almost over at Nadzab, we had done the job and supplied the aircraft as requested and the war had moved on. Time again to join our advance party and prepare for the next push. While the unit cleared and packed, a party of about eighty now fully competent tradesmen were chosen to move up to assist No.22 R.S.U. to settle in at Noemfoor Is and take up duties.

It's a small world as they say, my neighbour Cyril Roberts of Copacabana, having read some of my material came up with the revelation that we had been mates under C.O. Del a Rue at that very time.

We were ready and quite happy to get out of Nadzab, we had done well in our foreign order making without affecting our war effort. Rex Taylor told us that the task of preparing the aircraft was thought to be impossible with engines and spare parts so unavailable. Rex, his officers and men, Island hopped round the clock scavenging parts from the Yanks or any crashed plane. In later years, we found that that part of his career and our combined effort helped him in promotion from Squadron Leader to Air Commodore and not wanting to brag, I believe we are the only non flying unit to be mentioned in official history. We have seen wall sized pictures of our campaigns at the Canberra War Museum, but not the records.

Noemfoor, unheard of by one and all, was once another pleasant tropical island, but not for us. The pressure was back on and 22's dispersal area near the shore was a feverish hive of activity. Our little mob were in temporary tents longer than expected, waiting for our big mob to arrive so we could set up camp with the mates we missed. Ours was a tight little group, in our tent I mean. Ross Smith an old man of about thirty, Russ and I the big wheel money earners, shy little corporal Ernie Lord in control and good old 'Diddlington', Ray Addlington, who looked after us like a drunken father in every way possible. His 'Battered Bully beef' was the specialty of the tent.

We were now looking like natives and some of us spoke quite a good 'pidgin' English. On a Sunday off, [No R&R those days], we would follow a jungle track to the native camp and soon were made very welcome. There was always paw paws, coconuts and bananas for us. It was an education just to sit with the chief and watch real New Guinea native life, a relaxing world away from reality too.

The chief or boss boy was a former N.G. police boy and one of the famous 'Fuzzy Wuzzies' of that epic Kokoda trail. He still had his 45 automatic and a letter he showed us to be able to retain it. We had brought him a carton of bullets, which he found difficult to obtain, it was a Godsend for pig hunting to feed his mob. I think he wanted to give us a woman in return but, with due respect, we were put off from watching the woman feeding from the pendulous hanging breasts, a baby on one and a piglet on the other.

When the rest of our unit arrived, we made our camp and got on with war demands of fixing planes. 'Eureka!' The Comfort Funds parcels started to arrive with the little things we sadly missed. The Red Cross was also there with some goodies but best of all the 'Sallies', Addlington's mob, the Salvation Army, who were always there with that cup of tea and a biscuit, the only fair dinkum, true believers in charity and the love of God. Dig deep for them whenever you can.

In most parcels we received there were letters or notes from women, ladies or girls, it was your guess, but they wished us to write. Many a romance came from them and thousands of letters were written in answer, filling in many a long 'Dreaming of my love of thee' night.

It may have been about now that my mate Val, later best man at my wedding, received his Dear John letter. He lost his wife, the beautiful Tivoli girl who I had met back stage at the Tivoli, to a visiting Yank and not till many years after he got back did he get over it.

After our wedding Val lost touch, disappeared completely but a bit more about that later.

Something a bit different, painful for me, but a funny anecdote for others. All these simple stories are fact and if I don't tell them, who will? They will be lost forever.

I knew about the shape of things from the homes days and times together in the raw were not a bit embarrassing. Being in the tropics, in the humid heat and with infections so easily contracted, it was only now, showering with the mob in the open air that I realised how different we all were. Most still had foreskins, mine was different! I couldn't get it back and technically it was called a 'Pin hole'. At times irritable and leading to other things but most unhealthy. Doc Stephenson agreed and I was booked into the rough and ready hospital, 'Rooma Sakit'[Sick or hospital], for the little operation.

Coming out of the anaesthetic I was sore but that was to be expected and it would soon be OK. Or so I thought because as soon as I dozed off there would start an erection and my cry of pain brought the Sister with relief in the form of a spray of Ethyl chloride and it was magic. Every time the beast raised its head, 'Squirt, squirt' and down it would go.

Now this was the hot tropics and I was a hot blooded frustrated youth. The Ethyl chloride ran out and in the rest of the two weeks I had to use a flannel like my Mam Rees once used. This one was in iced water to cool the blood.

'It' was still sore when they let me out and 'It' was bandaged up, sticking erect out of my open fly and supported in that re-dick-erless position with a tie around my waist.

The reception back at camp was hilarious with remarks unprintable, all the mob of native workers fell about in the Kunai grass in total hysteria, pointing out and calling, "Pooky Sakit, Pooky Sakit," which in native talk meant 'Sick Cock'. To them I was 'Pooky Sakit' for the rest of my time on Noemfoor.

Doc Stevo did a couple of encores for practice, he even did Salty Reastons when he was only in for his tonsils and the shit hit the fan over that lot when Salty woke to a pain down there and not up here.

Bill, Doctor Stephenson, had occasion to visit and stay with me years later, he is a very good friend and a brilliant medical man. He met my son, smiled and said, "It worked" and only then confessed that I was his very first operation of circumcision, or as the boys crudely called it 'Ring Barking'.

It was at Noemfoor that the surprising letter arrived out of the blue and found me. The one from Douglas, my elder brother, who had lost touch so many years ago. I got a photo of him in his Canadian Army uniform with his wife Doris and her little girl. I never really knew if it was his real wife or if it was his daughter. He looked so handsome, so good looking and very happy too.

Further than that, we wrote of current events, unconsciously putting off about the times and events since we last saw each other, he at the end of the railway platform in Yorkshire and I off to Wales. We planned to take up things later when this stupid war was over and we had settled down wherever. As the story tells, it would be years hence with so much water under the bridge.

It was a good time in some ways, Doris wrote me lovely letters and we looked forward to becoming brother and sister in law when this was over. The parcels she sent me were just incredible, full of Canadian food, chocolates and candy bars, the cigarettes were appreciated by the mob. I think 98 % were smokers during the war.

The letters somehow, somewhere in the next month's confusion, stopped and we lost touch. It's all part of the story, Doug and I too, involved in our own war efforts at the time, we were to make a new start in life at ages 22 and 24 respectively, it was getting later than we thought.

My Captured 'Lakatoi'

New Guinea, 1943/4

Tent life, Nadzab, N.G.

39

* Still at Noemfoor and Then? *

Our tour of duty went on and once again we were behind the line of battle, the war front being many Islands ahead. We had to catch up with a move to Moretai in the Halmaheras group of Islands, Dutch N.G. It could once have been a paradise! A good camp, experts by now and the dispersal area where we did our aircraft servicing was near the ocean, though the water here was always warm and not really refreshing, we could sneak down for a relaxing dip.

By now the war in Europe was reaching its closing stages and at last Churchill and his cronies admitted there was a war on out here in the Pacific and we got our first Spitfires, one of the planes that won the battle of Britain. It was great to see it do its stuff, looking skywards we had the first hope of an end in sight. The Yanks had their Lightening P.38 twin fuselage fighter plane. The two superb flying machines put on a dog fight for all to see and though biased, the 'Spitty' had the best of it and it was now Tokyo or bust, that was becoming the daily wish.

Though I refer to them as Yanks or 'Septic Tanks' in these pages, we held them in the highest regard and black, white or brindle, they were our best buddies.

The war was ongoing, we carried out our duties while the rest of the world was another time, another place away. Each unit had a case of "Going Troppo", tropical fatigue. When it really got to them they were sent home for honourable but embarrassing discharge. The once mighty Japanese fighting machine was feeling the pinch as the power of the allies was taking affect and signs of panic and the Hari-Kari of failure was in the air.

Our main source of news was latrine rumour and humour too! Such as, "What has 10 seats and flies?" Answer; Sitting on a ten seater 'Thunder box'! We heard it all, what was to happen and this time it was what we were waiting for. It was to be the big one and once more the advance party was chosen, oddly enough, again 80 men and officers. I really wanted this one and luck or sucking up to Wally Potts had me included. If this one came off, we could be on our way home at last.

We knew it all except the destination, Tarakan, an Island off the coast of Borneo. It looked like the real thing as we had to prepare a full kit, rifles and all this time.

The beaut camp at Moratai would, I presume, go back to the jungle and all the amenities we had built would soon disappear. In the back of the camp the sly grog manufacturing machines would lie idle. These were copper coils over borrowed containers and little bits and pieces with a fire underneath, heated by methods we called 'Choofers'.

These ingenious gadgets were 'Stills' for making grog, something like the men of the Ozarks in the U.S of A used. What we produced was almost pure alcohol, clear, taken neat or mixed with anything you could find. It sold for 10 pound a bottle and the buyers were lined up for it hot off the pipes. You must give our mob credit for ingenuity, they used Mercuracrome, a red chemical from Doc's supply used for cuts and sores. It made a very nice, potent red drink. With Mycasol, the green stuff for tinea or such, the grog was passed off as Creme de Menthe. The stills may have been flogged to another unit who would have got little use of them because in a flash, everyone was gone. Our customers had moved on with us.

When we boarded our ship, it was with trepidation and a 'What the hell were we doing here?' Were we to see one of the last major beach landings of any size? The convoy was a shore to horizon fleet of every craft available and as birds do on instinct, we steamed off as one, row after row and the excitement became intense.

Arriving in the dead of night we were just offshore, few slept but all awake to see the wave after wave of the bombers in aerial bombardment at dawn. It was awesome to watch the systematic destruction of the oil tanks and shore installations. The big guns of the destroyers and naval craft then took over to pick out what was left. Watching in the ponderous silence of a moment's lull, the buildings and palm trees had disappeared as if by magic.

There was a moment of calm, of prayer too I'm sure and then rows and rows of L.S.T.'s [Landing Ships Troops] set off like a million mothers and ducklings. After the devastation of bombardment they quickly made a beachhead as the enemy moved back. The main worry was the snipers in a Kamikaze situation, tied up in the palm trees taking pot shots till located and blasted into eternity.

Our little detachment was set ashore just to the left of an old jetty where the mangroves started and where I captured my native Lackatoi, luckily with the out-rigger intact. The mangroves were good cover for we, non front-line troops, safe but in a mess of black mire and mud. Tarakan was by now a 'Dantes' inferno of fire, smoke and flame because it had been a major oil base. The loss was a major blow to the Jap war machine and the crack Japanese marines stationed here who fought a no mercy, desperate last stand battle.

Being the only R.A.A.F. group in the invasion, we did as we were told and that was, "Keep out of the bloody way." Happy to do just that too.
Our landing orders were 'Zero plus four'. I really believe this story to be true though in all the years it was never admitted to. We obeyed the command. Dumped and standing around like headless chooks, wondering what next but ducking for cover from whistling sniper fire.
Then this very senior, big brass army person came charging down, screaming along the jetty side, "What the bloody hell are you doing here, you stupid bastards, there is a war on." This was 11 R.S.U. and we had been sworn at by better men than he ever was. It was explained about our orders being 'zero plus four', as the penny dropped and it dawned on them it was zero 'days', not hours. We should have been snug on the ship for a while. Apologies and a giggle all round.

The foreshore, the shops and most buildings were soon cleared as the soldiers moved out, our No.1 was told to find temporary quarters and being the only ones interested in real estate at this time, we had first choice. The building chosen was brick and though battered, still substantial. It seemed a bit unusual and had that strange smell about it, even the furnishings were unusual and unfamiliarly odd. [To me anyhow.]
It was odd all right, a Major rushed in, in a panic it was too and told us to find something else. "This is the Japanese brothel and probably booby trapped." My mate Bones Hamilton, on his 50th wedding anniversary I think it was, said to me, "Do you remember the heaps of French letters outside the window that day at Tarakan?"

On the serious side, our task on Tarakan was to secure the airstrip as soon as it was safe and then prepare it to receive aircraft A.S.A.P. The strip was an absolute shambles, potholes and bomb craters, some still ticking away and we didn't know if it was mined. Worst of all, on Tarakan, being a low lying island, the whole airstrip rose and fell with the tide.
Just the same, our group working with every able bodied man, levelled and then laid a complete new strip of steel mesh. Of urgent necessity, it

was back breaking and if I did nothing else in the war, that was sufficient.

We had planes, not too big yet, arriving with supplies and re-enforcements and none too soon. We had time to build workshops and to strike a camp, to quickly make quarters for the unit soon to arrive.

Tarakan had a small, civilised township, a few scattered houses with some amenities plus a little hospital but eerily in a way, all the natives and town's folk were missing. We scroungers were able to collect lounge chairs, fancy glass and marble card tables and all different bits and pieces to make this camp the best ever, very comfortable as we wondered, how long?

This one was a bitter campaign, some said nearly as bad in a way as El Alamein, considered to be one of the worst. It was here that Tom Derrick V.C. lost his life leading his squad and could easily have got his second V.C. These men of the 2/23, 24th and 48th Battalion of the 9th division were long overdue for a well deserved trip home, six years at war is too long for anyone.

As we settled in, some folk returned. The Indonesian women began to reappear, so small and petite, they looked so beautiful in their bright sarongs as they walked past our camp each day. They looked so tempting and except for nurses and sisters, excluding the native ladies, they were the first women we had seen in almost two years.

Everyone looked almost white by now and a group of us decided to take the plunge and visit the ladies running a 'You know what' business. Strictly off limits and a dishonourable discharge if you got a dose but five of us showered and shaved and set off down the road. Two turned back almost straight away. Snowy and I decided it was not on and the other instigator soon followed us back to camp.

I can remember well, the last enemy bomber to come over, it must have been a very desperate Jap pilot that dropped his last stick of bombs, causing no damage what so ever, just a harmless jungle eruption as he flew off into the futility of it all. Our side lost people in those last days as desperate infiltrators sneaked into tents at night but it was almost over and the casualties ceased.

In crash crew, free of other duties, we did little, our service tents on the side of the strip, the rescue tender ready and waiting, as we watched each take off and landing. Experts now, well trained and ready for any eventuality, we could be at a crash in seconds to turn off the fuel and electronics and get the pilot out in a hurry. Our main customer was the, 'arrived too late for the war Cowboy', coming in too fast on the short strip, only to finish up in the creek at the end. To fill in time we played endless five hundred with Red Cross cards, now paper thin from over use. It was a long and tedious day from first light to dark, thank God for the lousy strip being unfit for night flying.

It seemed by now we had been in these Islands forever. Houses in streets, footy games, cafes or drinks at the local, all that civilian lifestyle forgotten. SO!, we stood around the 'on duty tent' that morning, looking like stunned mullets, to hear the news that it was all over. Victory in the Pacific was finally achieved.

It all came and went without any fuss at all and those remnants of us scattered throughout N.G. and Borneo, as in all the islands, just waited.

The excitement and celebrations back home in cities and towns, never touched us, as rather dejected in anti-climax, we were forgotten men. When we did finally manage to get home, no one seemed to give a damn for the stragglers, the would-be heroes who missed the moment of glory.

It was now time to use all that street cunning and early enterprise to get in line, wait for the travel orders and find transport home. It was sad in a way to see the rookies, newly arrived and a little lost, to find they had missed the bus.

With a bit of luck, or from favours owed, my name came out of the hat and I was one of those chosen to board the old Avro Anson and take the first stage back to Moratai. To pack more men in, the kit allowed was absolute minimum and we had to leave all the goodies we had collected in two years. It was basically shirt and shorts, boots and gaiters and hat. All the hardware and rifles are probably still dumped up there, bloody good riddance to bad rubbish.

On the '72 trip overseas, we took off and landed over thirty times, none of them to compare to the feelings as we eased, heavily over loaded, off the metal mesh, squishy runway, we had miraculously made. Our camp, the devastated jungle and even the big brick brothel building in the landing bay up from the jetty where my forty foot Lackatoi still lay in the slime, were only too soon, just memories.

Back at Moratai, the scene was unbelievable, men from every unit in the South Pacific or any zone were there, all dying to get back and despairing of ever making it. There was just not the transport, nothing flying or sailing available.

To maintain a little discipline, keep the mass of troops out of mischief and give them something to do, the N.C.O.'s had everyone on 'Emu

Parade', that is picking up rubbish round the area, even to the last match or fag butt.

Some of our mob had arrived and handed in their movement orders, they quickly gave us the drum, don't register and it was a blessing that we didn't. Everyone slept where they could and there were canteens catering for the mass of humanity. By this time the powers that be had lost track of where half the bods were. We were strictly on our own.

The procedure, we soon found out was to be at the Airstrip early to check out everything that could fly and see if they could squeeze you in. We were in luck and found a Yank Liberator, refuelled and bound for Singapore. The obliging officer told us there was lots of planes flying from there to Australia. "Be here early in the morning 'Ossie' and take a ride. Go home from there."

We were in time alright, first 'Dags' off the rank so to speak but, it was disappointment, they were over-loaded and a "Sorry Buddy."

It will seem I'm making this up but it's true, as we headed off for something to eat, she took off and was certainly over loaded to our realistic eyes because it only went a little distance, gained hardly any altitude when it crashed a few miles passed our old camp. The story came out, there were broken bottles everywhere, the over-load was bottled beer for Singapore. 'That' was the Lib we were not meant to catch a ride on.

There were three of us and we never gave up, we just stuck together and persisted till we found the D.C.3 which they said was heading for Darwin. Hallelujah, the jackpot. The fitter was doing his inspection and said they would be off shortly, "Why was everyone calling me, Shortly?" We guarded our positions from the thousands who would have taken our place till we were allowed to clamber aboard.

We took off from another strip of memories, circled and said bye-bye to good old Moratai.

Now Hollandia is just a short hop across and we had to call in to collect mail. This had been a big base such a short while ago but was now almost deserted with only lots of surplus and lonely equipment on an empty tarmac. Except for one lone plane in the dispersal area.

When we landed, we got out to stretch the legs and sticky beak around, we were met by a skeleton staff, a disgruntled pilot and navigator too. Hearing the orders for our plane to go elsewhere but Darwin, we were getting really pissed off, left posted and absolutely nowhere to go, worse in a way than back at Moratai.

That plane on the strip looked OK from here, "What's up with that?" we asked and the two officers told us it had a broken under carriage. They were waiting for fitters to arrive and fix it.

Thinking, thinking, the parts were there and waiting. So we came up with, "We are all fitters, we fix it, we get a lift out of here, OK?"

"Bloody oath." Picking up the necessary tools and gear we got stuck into it and by the coming up of dusk it was done, the last task of service for us in these Pacific Islands.

It was a quick snack in the depleted mess hut and we were away, a 'Thank God' once more. We left in the extreme heat of the tropics, in just our summer gear, worn thin shirt and shorts, then night fell and a severe tropical storm hit us and we had to climb to the maximum altitude the tired old bus could handle. In that unlined body of the plane, it was an icebox where we almost shivered ourselves warm till we reached 'Milne Bay', where we swam on the way up, a lifetime ago. Ice blocks, but so happy to be this close to home. There had been little time to think about that and where in the name of heaven was my home anyhow?

It was almost midnight when we landed and couldn't wait to get to the canteen, which was now open all the time to cope with the busy flow of traffic.

The hot meal and cups of tea soon put us right. When we got back to the plane they were loading it with stacks of canvas mailbags among other things ready for an early morning take off. "Sorry mate, we're full, can't take you any further, report in at the movement office."

Our immediate and outraged thought was, "Like bloody hell," after us being the ones to do the repairs to get them here, "No way."

We just waited and when their backs were turned, we crawled aboard and pulled the canvas bags up around us to spend a lousy but secure night.

At take off that morning we breathed a sigh of relief when airborne and too far to turn back. Patting each other on the back with joy, it was finally next stop Australia.

It was and we flew over the coast and landed in Townsville, Queensland, it was all down hill from there, that's the way I thought looking at the map of Australia. I was to get a much better look at the place in '74 and then '84 on the round Australia trips that we did.

You should have seen the look on the faces of the crew as we climbed out of the aircraft door. They just laughed, felt a bit guilty I reckon of trying to put us off last night. "Just hang around a bit chaps, we'll have you in Brisbane before you can say Jack Robinson." [I never ever found out who this Jack was]

As they walked off, a funny old bloke strolled up and had a chat, "Going home?" he asked and we said, "Yes." "You wouldn't have a bit of tobacco on you mate?" he asked. We told him no, "Sorry mate, we don't smoke," so off he went. When the crew came back, they asked, "How'd you get on with old Cooper the customs man?"

"The sly old bugger," Snowy said, "I've got a kit bag full of cigarettes and tins of tobacco I've been saving for months." He could have claimed the lot.

So we took off for Brisbane, got a lift to the railway station F.O. Potts had marched us through in that other life and we caught a train to Sydney. Once again it was without passes or tickets and this time we wouldn't take no for an answer.

It was quite anti-climactic really, our being back, everything so strange and changed. By our figuring, we were at least six weeks ahead of the rest of the mob. They could take ages to get here so why not use the time to catch up. We could be anywhere and no one would know. Money was not a problem, we had money belts full and no need to use the pay book and give the plot away prematurely that we were back in town.

A much different man from the boy that went away, different in outlook from that Valley kid and the farm or sheep station green hand that was. Money was no object, no roots or parents to burden me or answer to, it was time to meet old acquaintances and have fun. I suddenly felt I had to find Doreen and Bernard to make sure they were OK. Yvonne was an unknown quantity and heavens knew if and when we'd next get together. The first visit to Rhodes was like taking the first step again and I wondered how I would be received! I hadn't written as often as I now realised I should have. Heather was grown up and quite lovely. The two years had made a difference, we were both quite shy with each other and now I realise how I was a bit too pushy on my first visit and then shouldn't have asked her out so often but Mr and Mrs Gwynne thought it was alright. At that stage it was house parties, pictures and a dance or two. We were still just good friends and with plenty of opposition for me.

I flew to Melbourne and saw Doreen. I visited our Northcote Farm, so quiet and empty now. I chased up some of the farm kids and generally caught up with things.

Major Ramsay had told me to come back and work at Mooleric and to that end I had studied sheep and wool as well as the pig farming thing in my spare time, and that's a laugh. 'Some time', very soon now, I would have to start thinking seriously about these things, come down to earth and get serious.

But really, how could I go back to being a farm hand, a station manager even? I loved the land but my future was elsewhere.

I flew back to Sydney, back and forth a few times in fact because if you had that magic movement order and looked Atabrin yellow from overseas, it was easy to cadge a lift.

Six weeks unofficial R & R before we three met up again to get our story straight before reporting in, which we did. We were issued new equipment, a full outfit and looked like rookies except for our weird colour. Someone in an official capacity gave us a pat on the head for a job well done and our pay books were brought up to date. So much back pay it seemed a fortune and then we were told we were granted a months long service leave plus? It was to be another month or more of visiting and travelling until it felt good to report back.

My posting was there and waiting, it was to the R.A.A.F. station at Parkes out in the west and not far from Fairbridge at Molong.

Parkes was full of rookies, green and raw youths all fretting to do something or go somewhere but with the war over, it was too late. We met up with quite a few of our unit and we were sort of veterans and treated very well, did almost as we liked in fact as in the days of mass demobilisation there was little to do.

Lorna, the W.A.A.F. girl friend who took me in hand, knew everyone, the hotel proprietor, the sergeant of police and anyone of importance. We all met each day for drinks on the house at the pub. Lorna and I spent lots of time sleeping it off at the council swimming pool and only reported back to camp if really necessary. I've told about the bike for Bernard and riding it in the stinking heat.

It was ongoing, the station at Parkes was given leave for good service and special war effort. Leave was something I didn't need so I volunteered to do guard duty. For this we received double leave and it was slowly getting to me and reaching the time to get out, back to the real world in fact.

While on guard duty, Mick, another boy from our unit with connections in Sydney, a bit Mafia sort of thing I suppose, suggested he get a truck up one night from Sydney. We would take the sixteen tyres and wheels off the semi-trailer sitting doing nothing, they would flog them and we'd cop our fair share. I can honestly say it was not for me and backed off but he saw nothing wrong in it at all, it was something that went on.

Getting a discharge was a slow process but I couldn't take much more of this stuffing around as in farm talk, I chaffed at the bit. My urgent request for discharge was a tear jerker, a sad family sob story and it must have worked because shortly after, I packed once more and this was to be the last as I took myself off to the Victoria Barracks in the big smoke. There I handed in my gear, keeping little but my overcoat and some shoes. I'm stuck with that having shoes complex. We had a medical, this time no lady doctor with a pencil doing her 'Short Arm Inspection'. My pay book was stamped and handed back as the souvenir I still have today and there was a nice severance pay.

The Officer in charge, on behalf of Air Board or whoever, shook my hand and I left. Four years of service, all my mates and perhaps my best youthful years.

As I walked out the gates my thought was, "That's the end of that." It had been a somewhat fantastic time in many ways but it was done. I had made hundreds of mates and like at the farm school had been secure in the numbers but, suddenly, perhaps for the first real time, I was alone.

They say when you die, the past passes before your eyes, just then, for a moment, Llwynapia, Mam Rees and our Valley, the walk back to Goole and Aunt Mathews, the homes and the rest of it, was there and then gone.

40

* Discharge and Home at Rhodes *

When this was written I can't recall, I found it again later in amongst my private papers.

No title, just;

He stood alone in Martin Place
lost soul in civvy gear
from four long years in uniform
"Where do I go from here?"

From Tarakan, the last all clear
sent weary warriors home,
heroes dime a dozen
mates gone, just him alone.

His several calls to girls he'd met
had left him in a daze
with lovers, husbands, boyfriends home
War just a passing phase.

He picked his worn out kit bag up
and caught the Hornsby train
got off at Rhodes and shoulders hunched
he walked in dismal rain.

To come alive as Heather's Mum
with welcome so sincere
said,"Come in son and rest awhile,"
you're always welcome here.

He found a home, he found a wife
a fruitful life began
alone no more for war matured
a youth to thinking man.

A bit sloppy I know but it said it all, for as I stood on the footpath the shit hit the fan, where do I go from here? I was just one of the thousands in this situation, most of us had lost four, five and six years of the time we should be establishing ourselves in a trade or profession.

Thinking of the getting out of London, the workhouse and the homes at Church village, things had been crook in the past so I picked up my bag and headed for Central station. They had told me there was always a spare bed at 16 Cavell Ave. and the bed on the back verandah for servicemen staying the night sounded pretty good to me right then, so I caught that train.

From and for that particular time, I thank Mrs Gwynne. In her early days she had run boarding houses with her mother so she was used to having boarders, only men and especially World War I Diggers and now our lot came along.

Being there was nice and convenient, it also helped eliminate the opposition, some boyfriends still calling. It was rather off putting to them when they brought Heather home to find little old me in bed on the back verandah. The locals soon gave up and the last of the English sailors went back to Blighty leaving me a free reign. In an unknown way, I was home free both metaphorically and practically speaking.

C.R.T.S., 'The Commonwealth Reconstructional Training Scheme'. It sounds impressive and talking to local returned men I found it was available for advice and assistance in choosing positions or selecting a vocation.

At my interview we chatted and I was told there were courses in everything available, the nice man said, "You can do or be anything you wish," so I said, "I would like to conduct a Philharmonic Orchestra." I was dead serious too, but the interviewer was a bit taken back before saying, "Sorry old chap, that's not on the list," and handed me the list.

I asked him which ones were suitable to becoming self-employed and one's own boss. He pointed them out, I ran my finger down to stop at plumber, not having a clue what a plumber really did but with my Mum's psychic thing, it sounded lucrative. So that was that, I was to be a plumber.

It was a good trade and gave me a good living. Music or the stage could have been my forte with satisfaction and success but as the song says, 'Que se ra', I think that's how it goes and 'Whatever will be, will be,' seemed OK then.

With thousands like me waiting, it was to be twelve months till my course came through and so it was necessary to find a job, the first frightening time it had happened to me. A phone call told me of a job at Richard Hughes' canister factory at a place called Fivedock. Somehow getting to Homebush OK, I asked where Fivedock was. You guessed it, "Just down the road," that famous Aussie reply.

Now buses were a mystery to me, a taxi ride out of the question, so I walked and walked for all those miles in a suit, collar and tie till the sweat poured out of me. The employment officer at the factory took pity on me, fascinated at my story and that this was my first job in the city, so he gave me a start.

I did lots of menial stuff but, for most of the twelve months I stood at that whirly gig testing machine and helped make 1lb Horlicks cans, twenty thousand per day. It was a nothing job but an education in life and how factory workers existed. We played cards in the break, soccer at lunchtime and I learnt about S.P. betting and dog cards. It was there I had my first introduction to footy, as N.S.W. knows it.

I went by bus, the 459 from Rhodes station and it was sheer hell some days. Sitting in the warm sun, on the jiggling bus, hormones going crazy in enforced pre-marriage celibacy, I would arrive nearing my stop thinking pure thoughts and of ethyl chloride spray or ice blocks to get 'It' down before I could get off and race back to bundy on late again.

At home, as I was calling Rhodes now, all was going well. Heather and I were going steady or 'Tracking Square' as they say in the bush. Mr Gwynne, George, had me sharing a few bob each way in S.P. bets on a Saturday, which Mrs G frowned on, as she did the few beers we shared now that my Rechabite restriction was over. I was a welcome male support in a woman dominated house as it allowed us to go to the long since banned Hare coursing at Rooty Hill, next to our old camp at Druitt.

Then millions of cans later, I was released from the boredom of inside factory walls when the starting date for my plumbing course arrived. It was to be at the famous old jail at Darlinghurst which was now the East Sydney Technical College. Except for some on site training at Pagewood, it was to be our classroom for the next six months, so many thousand ex servicemen were to pass through there doing every training possible.

The great wage during the course was to be three pounds, ten shillings, [7 Dollars,], on completion it was to be six pounds five. An employer was chosen to take each of us as apprentices, there would be three monthly checks for the next three years when we would be assessed as fit to receive a license. Many dropped out of the Tech. College part to become just unlicensed journeymen.

Money at that time was not a problem. I had savings and the other seemed enough to live on so Heather and I became secretly engaged. We were keeping the announcement to make it official at Heather's up coming debut. What a great engagement party it was at the once notorious 'Roosevelt' nightclub, the 'In' place of the time.

The practical work at Tech was a snack, easy for me but I found the theory and tech drawing most demanding and hated the three years of night classes. Old Craddock Evans at Treforest copped some of the blame for not doing more with and for me.

On the way home, late at night it was off to sleep hoping not to hear the train rattling over the Ryde Bridge and missing my Rhodes stop. Getting out at Meadowbank, it was often a long walk back over the road bridge.

Mrs Gwynne, Aunty Jean, was boss at Rhodes and necessary matriarch of the Howie family. Of Scottish descent, she was a strong but clever woman, stubborn as a mule and bigoted as all hell.

We got on so well, at first. I have so much to thank her for but that's only till I took her only child in marriage. George, who I loved, died in my arms before we were married, so sadly, it was my 22nd birthday after my missed out 21st away up north.

I logically assumed the position of man of the house and her and my relations slowly deteriorated. I was paying my way by now, all expenses for here and the holiday house at Ettalong. Over a period till the break up, I used all the savings and Heather and I came out second best and with almost nothing.

In the happy meantime, we had great times. Heather was the only one allowed to drive the big, black enamel Chevy tourer to Carss Park and Cronulla for picnics and to Mona Vale for the days I'd dreamed of at the beach. She was the only one with a license and a car, so it was with a car full of hangers on, she with the lovely hair I used to brush, in pigtails, sitting on two cushions so she could see over the wheel and out the windscreen. The police often pulled us over to check the license of this little girl and for what it's worth, at this time in 1999, after fifty five years of continuous driving, there has never been the slightest accident, fine or being picked up by the Fuzz.

By then, my last opposition and very dear friend Ken King, ex Royal Navy and discharged here, had taken off for Melbourne where he met and married Gwen. We all, our and their kids and grandkids, are still the best of friends.

Mr Gwynne had recently joined the Masonic lodge and it was at Concord West in the Masonic Hall that Heather made her debut with me as her partner. It was a rather saddened occasion, as George had died a week before and never saw her looking so beautiful in her debut gown her mother made. It was his wish the debut should go on.

George was one of a large family of Gwynnes who settled in Gawler, South Australia. It's strange that Robert Gwynne had migrated from Pontypridd in Wales so many years ago. Was it possible that her and my grandfathers could have known each other? George, being a veteran of World War 1, had served in the hellish trenches of Flanders field, the affects of the gas poisoning and endless diet of dog biscuits and tins of sweetened condensed milk, brought about his early demise. Dying in my arms as he did, he missed the grandchildren he would have adored.

As partner to Heather, I was introduced to all the local folk. It seems we made an impression when we danced the coming out waltz, the manners and decorum from those at the farm with foresight was coming out and I received an invitation to join Lodge Nth Strathfield in Blue Masonry. In due course I was to join a Scottish Royal Arch chapter in Red Masonry at Drummoyne and in fact I became first Principal or Master, the youngest to be so at the time.

All that was most important in my life, not only for its teachings but for the friends I made. Heather, half Scotch I suppose, with Patty Wardrop, catered for our Robbie Burns night. We had not one but two Haggis'.

It was a fun time with a Welshman running a Scottish night but I knew the words of their songs better than they.

I can't help wondering here at the end of the century, what has happened in the changing times, to religious orders, churches and lodges. Have we irrevocably lost the plot? Am I getting old and cynical?

Our wedding was quite a social event. I was moving up and as Dad or the Tonypandy mob would say, "Very Posh." Amory at Ashfield was the very fashionable reception venue and a great success.

Whilst the honeymoon first night at Potts Point was also a success!!! or so Colin Rankin, Doreen and the mob thought. They had sown wild oats, [those ones that squirm in to never come out,] into our night attire and it took all night to clean them out. When we opened the cases those damned grass seeds flew every which way, wasting valuable hours.

All the next day, two bleary eyed lovers, from want of sleep only, in their going away clothes. Heather in hat, high heels and gloves and I in a suit and tie, walked around Sydney all day trying to fill in the day till the train left from Central at eight.

Most couples still went by train, the only difference was, we were not going to Katoomba but to what had become the honeymoon hotel of the north, the Ritz Private Hotel at Yamba.

After an uncomfortable long night sitting up we arrived at Grafton to board our coach [Just a bus actually] to Yamba. For me especially, the run along the river Clarence, the cultivation and cane as tall as N.G. Kunie grass in blue sky sunshine, was magic. The whole two weeks was more than magic, a slight hiccup was that Heather sprained her ankle and was confined to her room for a few days, it made things hard but we got through somehow.

We had actually booked in to stay there again the next year and it was sad to have our deposit returned with the news it had burned down with a honeymoon couple lost in the fire.

With that fixed up, Tech now only a night time thing, I could settle down and get to work. After so much travelling and changes I could catch that 459 bus from Rhodes to get off at Bland St, Ashfield. The bus, rattling along in the sun was no longer a problem for an old married man. My first employer was Horrie Hatton of Haberfield, a master plumber of the old school. He had an old Hupmobile car, the back seats were missing and the kapok stuffing escaping out of the seats. In that enormous space at the back was a mass and a mess of mysterious plumbing and draining gear, the old dog slept there at night and it all smelt to high heaven.

That was a fantastic time training in service and maintenance, the basis of my future capability but, when Ken Willard and Fred Boone, my mates on the Tech course, told me of the job at Works and Housing, [Education Dept] at Chippendale where they did school repair work, it sounded pretty good and a change, so I left 'orrie 'atton of 'aberfield and worked there awhile. That became boring too and just a big bludge, we would be given a job chit and our bus or train fare and sent to a school or Dept place. The job may only take minutes or a few hours and you just hung around till 3 p.m. when you could knock off and go home. If it rained you often did nothing but play cards if enough of you were on the job.

It was not surprising to sneak off to the pictures in the city and find a couple of mates sitting there in the dark. The money was to union 'regs' and I looked for the little extras and scrap metal was it. Lots of discarded scrap brass and lead and I made a point of having some in my Gladstone bag each day for the extra pocket money, that was my way of life.

Very soon, that was enough of that, bludging and goofing off all day and learning nothing but roof work at which we were soon experts.

It was old Bert Sims, who I worked with for a while there before he left, who told me about the position as Maintenance plumber at the Repatriation General Hospital, [R.G.H], it was only a few minute from home so I jumped in and got a start there. It was as big as a large sized country town and the biggest hospital in the Southern Hemisphere. There were ten of us in our workshop and we were kept busy at the most interesting challenge of hospital maintenance.

I walked to work at first, then it was a no brakes, no mudguards push bike and with increased affluence it became an Austin A40 and before I left there it was my first of many Holdens. Living most handy to the place, I was happily on call in emergencies and for lots of beaut over time. Even one Xmas day when I was called out just an hour before the ham, pork and turkey were ready to be carved for the Rhodes special Xmas spread. It was a blockage in No.2 sisters quarters. I knew where the trouble was and had it fixed to be back home in the hour. Mac, the foreman filled in the worksheet and I received the union rates for the day, eight hours triple time for my little effort.

My knowledge of racing was limited to seeing a Melbourne Cup and the hare coursing at Rooty Hill so, to become heavily involved in the racing game came out of the blue. Stan Wellings was a bookmaker, a licensed bookie with the A.J.C. and S.T.C. and he operated at all Sydney races, even Moorefield and Roseberry, which is probably before your time. His regular clerk left and the position was open. Stan was married to Dot, a cousin of Heathers, they had no children and considered Heather as their nearest kin. So Stan said to me, come and learn the business and when I'm ready to get out, you can have the stand.

That was a terrific time and I enjoyed every minute of the excitement and glamour, though damned hard demanding work, big fields and long shot winners. With good early info from owners and trainers I took small, four bob doubles at cricket score odds to pick up better than wages money.

Dress was terrific, spivvy suit, collar and tie and a snappy small-brimmed felt hat. In the days before betting boards, I felt pretty smart standing up there calling the odds, swinging the bag and taking in the dough. After a meeting the thing was to wet the whistle at a favourite pub and there I learnt to quaff schooners of beer. I saw many of the greats but Bernborough ridden by Athol George Mulley was my favourite and he drew in the crowds.

It was sad in a way, like my wish to lead an orchestra, bookmaking was not meant to be my vocation because Stan, only just 42, hurt his instep on a ladder while painting. It was cancer and he lost his foot, then his leg and in six months he was lost to us. Stan had been my proposer into

Masonry, Carl Berg next door in Cavell Ave was my seconder, they both died the same day, a sad double funeral. As young people then and as they still do now I suppose, we talked about it and thought, "Oh well, at 42, they have had a good run." What, in 1999, do the kids think of us oldies or wrinklies now?

My regular plumbing always went on even though one way or another I never missed a city race meeting in four years and the extra was very welcome. There were many private little plumbing jobs of my own at evenings or Sunday morning and it seemed I was never at home. Evan Douglas and Rhondda Lynne appeared on the scene and I realise now that Heather did most of the rearing of them on her own. It's a wonder they knew me, only joking about that bit because not like my Dad, who choofed off for ages, I was always popping in to eat and sleep.

Not yet really settled, room for change, so while working at the Repat, I met Bill Lloyd and Alec Beeman, both returned men who did a painting course in C.R.T.S. As painters, they were doing a bit of painting and paper hanging for Mrs G. Over a cup of 'knock off time' tea, they spoke of getting out of the messy paint business and into something different. Their bright idea was to buy a milk run between them, keep their jobs but run the business in the early mornings till they paid for it and it became full time.

Money was the problem for a deposit and before they left I was to join in, become a third partner for a few months till they got ahead. The idea was that we all keep our jobs, work four mornings on and two mornings off. A great idea and I was very enthusiastic. As a result, we bought a milk run at Leichardt where we started at 1-30 a.m. so as to be finished in time to get home and to our work on time. The run included a horse and cart, which didn't deter an old farmer like me, but scared the hell out of Bill and Alec the city slickers. It, the horse and cart bit, lasted two mornings when we had to find extra money to buy the old bomb Ford truck.

On top of all this, the milk was all in bulk, involving cans, ladles and measures. It was a messy, slow process and we didn't have the time to spare.

So we changed to bottled milk, one of the first to do so and the customers all threatened to leave us till they realised that at last they had real milk as Pat, the previous Milko, used lots of water to make his lot go further.

A lot of you will know the run area, it took in Palace St just up from the depot, it crossed Parramatta Rd. at Taverners Hill where we served Briton's Brewery [Free beer on tap for the staff and us] then across into Rofe St. and Jarret St. area. Ces Smitzer had the little grocer's shop on the corner that the mob put in for and bought him when he got crook. He and I became good mates and in the wee hours of the morning I'd get roped in to have a drink with Ces who could not sleep. With coffee, we used to knock off a bottle of Van der Hum and many a morning I delivered milk by vague memory. Often Val, his patient and lovely wife, cooked us a bacon and egg breakfast.

Ces was the up and coming boxing champ till he was struck by that rotten Polio, lost the use of both legs but remained a stoic man and friend to one and all.

The partnership lasted nine months, damned hard demanding months before Bill an Alec had had enough, it was not their scene. I liked it, it was a great outdoor job and all going quite well so, after much discussion with Heather, we approached the bank [The 'Which bank?'] and easily got our first loan in the partnership of D.R. and H.J. Rees. A partnership some said wouldn't last but one which is still going strong in it's 50+ year with evident success.

It was revolutionary and I was about the first to use a Holden utility instead the horse and cart or big cumbersome vans for delivery. I did the run in two quick loads and soon took two hours off the delivery time.

In a time of change, folk in the inner suburbs were by now moving further out west, leaving only old folk who needed or could only afford half a pint per day. The run and milk demand was dropping off and we were lucky to sell it at a profit, besides which, the distance and traffic to Rhodes was a bit much and in a later change to Beecroft it became worse. We little knew that we would see the day when thousands moved back to those inner suburbs and paid a fortune for once 'give away' dumps.

Nothing in this world is more sure than change and when Rhodes became unliveable with Timbrols, C.S.R. and all the other industries around, it was time to move and we found a new, brick two-storey house almost completed on Beecroft Rd, Beecroft. This was then, and still is, the nicest suburb in the greater Sydney, the most desirable place to live and raise a family.

Strange that my first visit there was during the war when Heather brought me to meet her friends, the Watsons. The station, prettier even than my Tonteg or Taff Vale, the Australian, English combination countryside made an impression but at that precarious time, I never dreamt that I, my family and my families family, would become such a part of it in the near future.

About 1800, the first grants were made at Beecroft and in 1886 the railway station was declared open. When Sir Henry Copeland declared it open, it must have been a sight to see in its Australian setting.

Judge Fitzharding built 'Red Hill' on his five acres in about 1890. It had magnificent views extending to where the bridge would be but also to Botany and the ocean, many miles away. We were to live in 'Red Hill' for a time when Harry and Eden Lenehan owned it and we were building our 36 square three-storey shack next door but one.

As I contemplate Beecroft and its short history with the streets named after the early settlers, what a difference to where I grew up. My kids will remember clean fresh space, such things as old Bob Dunn and his horse 'Peggy' in the dray, with a Cheltenham Girls High School hat over her ears keeping the streets clean. A friend to kids on the way to school just as my friend the marble collector along from Tonteg had been.

It's ridiculous but we moved from Rhodes into 75 Beecroft Rd. on Xmas eve. By lunchtime we were almost unpacked. The garden with its gardenias and roses was a perfumed picture, the Australian Christmas bush all down one side was in full red bloom. The garden had been a nursery for a cut flower supplier. The red bush and my first real look at something so Sydney, Australian, reminded me of my holly collecting business back at that other home. Like that holly, this was in demand too and I couldn't resist it. I quickly cut and bundled up my utility full, took it down to busy Burwood where I parked on the footpath and flogged it for five bob a bunch.

I got eight pounds ten shillings for it and that was the amount of the council rates that year.

My new milk run at Hornsby was such an improvement, less distance to travel and much bigger in gallons with families taking up to a dozen bottles instead of that poor pensioner half pint at Leichardt. Except for the time of the twisted ankle, I never lost a day in my four year stint as milko, even then I drove the truck while Heather, under shouted instructions, did the delivering. I did have Xmas day off.

Many a time Heather was with me voluptuously boobed in shorts and halter top. Some of my clients had folk sleeping in wired-in verandahs out the front and she told me of the young fellow waking to see her putting down the bottles, "Jesus Christ, is that the bloody milkman!" was his waking thought.

Our early Beecroft days were fine, Evan and Rhondda went to the little school right through to 6th class. Mrs Rush taught Evan and in later years, seemingly ageless, she was to teach Adam, Sebastian and

Benjamin. Heather and Patty Wordrop, with so many others of course, ran the P&C. Between us all we ran balls and stalls, dances and even a Harvest festival like vegetable stall one year which wore me and my ute out delivering orders round the district, but we made heaps of money. At one ball, I engaged the young Frank Ifield, then only fifteen, and as M.C., gave him his five pound. Doreen said he also played for them at Ashfield, he was so keen and wouldn't stop till someone told him to P--s off.

Both of us locals, I was one day 'back in plumbing' and able to fix Mrs Ifield's broken sewer. We all knew everyone, young Trevor Williams as P&C President, Jack as patron of the tennis club and Joan running her charity do's to eventually earn her an Order of Australia. Only oldies like us will remember Les Black and his band at the bowling club in Hannah St or when the Stuuts took over the Hairdressing shop where they sold everything, fishing tackle, rifles and ammo and all, that's how long ago it was.

Still busy making money at the business and my own affairs, I failed to see what was happening at home. Mrs Gwynne was demanding all Heather's attention and not accepting that she was my wife as well. The conflicting loyalties, the demands of the children, it was all driving Heather crazy. It was apparent the intent was to drive us apart. To make it worse I had, through necessity and being my own man, taken over all responsibilities and costs but Mrs G, thinking I was taking over everything, couldn't from her matriarchal lifestyle, accept a mere youth doing so.

If I had been more mature, of a less individualised background or something, it may have been different. To make it all so much more difficult, Heather had to go away for a while, to hospital with a worrysome appendix.

The clash of strong personalties came to a head.

The end result without going into all the tears and trauma was that we had to move out. I, for one, couldn't take any more or I'd do a Dad. The only way we could do that was to sell the milk run and that morning of the final blow up, I put it on the market and it sold in a fortnight. We were reconciled it was the right thing to do. Still with the obligation to care for the old biddy, we bought a block of land just up the road at 48 Beecroft Rd, opposite Dr Cook's white house, for seventeen hundred pounds. A fortune for land in those days and everyone said we were mad. We quickly arranged a builder to draw up Heather's plans [The first of many in the future] and as a returned service man I was eligible for the war service loan which we applied for and received the three thousand, five hundred pound loan at a rate of 3-1/2% interest, sufficient to build the house.

With the sale of the milk run, we were just able to manage, not a bean to spare, but it was our own home and the first of many to come. All my hard put together savings and labour, put into Rhodes and No.125, was now down the gurgler and lost forever. There was little left for furnishing or floor coverings and furniture as we had walked out and left everything, the lot not even a tea towel taken. Heather had to work at Reid's grocery shop in Hannah St cutting sandwiches to pay, week by week for urgent things in our start from scratch.

Once we were settled in and calmed down, as far as we were concerned it was forgive and forget but Mrs Gwynne said she would never set foot in my house, ever. As will be seen, we had many houses in our time and she never weakened in her pig-headedness. The only time she did was for Rhondda and Alan's wedding at Coronet Court, North Rocks when Rhon said, in no uncertain manner, "Grandma, if you don't come, I'll never speak to you again." We learnt a lot of Grandma's funny ways in later times, such as the habit of secretly giving them a dose of castor oil or such every Friday night. Shades of cottage mothers in homes. Heather and I were shocked and knew nothing about all that going on.

That's just the domestic side, for me it was difficult and more traumatic. The milk business had been excellent and profitable and I had got away from plumbing, which I never really cared for. The milk run was almost paid for and I was about to get my second one, but the only thing to do was go back to the tools. Without Ken and Fred, my Tech mates now in a thriving cottage plumbing business, it could have been a disaster. It took only a phone call to explain my situation and they gave me a start and I was a plumber again.

The first day, Fred Juleg took me out to a new cottage at Merrylands and dropped me off with my tools and sufficient material to, as we call it, rough in the hot and cold and gas lines. He then went on to Blacktown to his job. When he arrived back about three in the afternoon, there was nothing done. I'd only done maintenance, rooves and repairs, never worked on a new cottage as such and knew nothing of measurements, the heights of basins, baths or W.C.'s etc and I'd not made a start.

I felt like a complete idiot and he was as embarrassed as I, but we got stuck into it. He showed me what to do and we finished it to get back to the yard in the dark and everyone long gone, all locked up.

Next morning they all had a good laugh over it and I was sent out with Fred to learn the ropes, which I very quickly did. Fred was, in all honesty, the best cottage plumber in all N.S.W. Modestly, I claim to be second best. It was my pleasure to later stand up for Fred as Groomsman at his wedding.

What a boom period it was developing into with the population explosion of all time, caused by mass migration, with hordes of people of every nationality flocking in. Homes were needed to house them all and we were to share in the biggest building boom of Sydney's relative short history.

After some time with Boone and Willard, as a dedicated mate, I was soon foreman of a large team. My mate from the hospital came to work there too and in time I suggested he, Alan and I should get a piece of the action and go it alone. We formed the partnership and it was an instant success so, to cope with the pressure of the drainage and sewer work, we brought in Laurie as a fourth partner, becoming one of the major plumbing firms of the time. The staff was over the forty mark.

L.A.C.Rees
No.118687 R.A.A.F.

Derrick with Doreen and Heather
" Back in civvies, 1945."

41

* Business Days *

During my business days we had the big recession, the one that hit the building trade and sent so many companies into bankruptcy. Our trouble was caused by the full time accountant we employed not sending out invoices in time, so when our biggest builder went bust he almost took us with him. That was Rothman Homes and from thousands of dollars debt, we finally received $400 which we blew one night on a party in a 'Devil may care, what the hell style.'

Up to this time all was going well but losing so much didn't help and on top of that Laurie and Alan, [Rotten Sods] two of the partners, were setting up a business of their own while still drawing wages, using our material and taking our best men and contracts.

What a rotten time, Alan was one of my best mates and I could never understand the underhanded way of it all. Kevin McGregor, our solicitor, advised Eric and I to sue for thousands but we just called it quits and with difficulty went back to a seven day week on the tools again till we were back on our feet. As time will tell, all that or whatever it was, affected Eric disastrously.

With Rothmans down the drain so to speak, one of the supervisors and builder by trade, suggested we pick up the threads and start a building company of our own. Eric, Bobby Burns and I started Florida Homes and built some of the nicest homes round Sydney. Things were at last coming together and at this rate even a mention of early retirement.

To help finance the building company, Eric and my firm of TEACO P/L, held back on Florida's invoices for all the plumbing and draining, septic tanks etc we did. If anything happened we would be the biggest creditors, curse the thought.

It was therefore another disaster to find our partner and so-called mate was spending not only most of his time but all of our money at the Epping R.S.L. drinking and playing the poker machines. Kev O'Rourke, our bank manager had noticed what was going on and suggested we check things out. It was too late, the damage was done.

Through his underpricing and mismanagement, our Florida company was out of business and Teaco P/L, as I feared, was the main creditor. It took considerable time and effort to get Teaco back on its feet but we dug in with good contracts, to soon have it going again but it was becoming hard work. Too much beaurocratic overhead and we cut back to two principals and five men. Eric, for whatever reason, always left control and decision making to me. I wish he didn't.

As can be imagined, plumbing was losing its appeal, the building trade slowing down and on a tight rope, the last to be paid on most projects was the plumber.

Perhaps with this, or something yet unknown in mind, I did a two weeks course with Toast Masters and my 20 minute speech earned me the Champion spark plug for best presentation. It was just coincidental that my favourite Sergeant from 11 R.S.U., Bert Pendergast, had reached the position of Australian manager of an insurance company and he asked if I would like to join a trial course.

It was a way out, to be done with plumbing. Doug in Los Angeles had won a monster trophy for best salesman in all California so why not me? Salesman could be my thing and a chance to join Bert's company.

At my stage of life it was the strangest feeling to be dressed in a suit all pukka, a brief case in hand and the obligatory Herald tucked under the arm, to catch a train to the office. God! I didn't know how to behave, it was so different from the plumber in shorts and shirt or, as I thought of it, the lad on the station in a back to front raincoat biting out balls at lambing time.

After a slow start, two weeks learning about this other world, I was making headway in my drastic change of vocation when early one morning before leaving for the office, I received the ominous phone call. "Eric hasn't been home all night and I'm very worried." It was my partner's wife and I had the strangest feeling come over me, a terrible premonition.

Our arrangement had been that he carry on the business and as the outstanding monies came in, we split them between us. He would then have a business with plenty of prospects. There were no financial worries, no debts and Eric's home was paid for. He had a lovely wife and three fine boys. Never a single sign of anything wrong or untoward.

I dressed and drove to the workshop. It looked instantly ominous, the desk was clear of outstanding paper work, all accounts and bank deposits were made. Eric was alway the tidiest man I ever worked with but this looked really bad.

When the men arrived I sent them out to check every job we had going and then rang every connection to check his movements, all without a clue. There was nothing of his whereabouts all that weekend.

Ringing Bert at the office, I told him of my fears to be reassured, not to worry about the job, just stay and do whatever was necessary. Little did we know at that time, my future career in insurance was already over before it had really begun.

The police found the utility at Wiseman's Ferry on Monday morning, the hosepipe was connected into the cabin and I can't express in words how I felt or how it affected me.

The next week was awful and worse than difficult picking up the threads after the funeral. Eric was my best mate, our families had grown up together, we were both ex R.A.A.F. and fellow Masons but there was no answer to the big question, "Why?" Even to this day.

It was necessary to pack up the workshop at his home and move it to a temporary place at my home. There was too much money outstanding and work half completed to just leave and walk out.

Whether I liked it or not, it was time to pick up the tools once more and get on with it.

Sadly and never to this day do I know why, the wife never spoke to me again. I never received a thank you when we handed over the cheque from the insurance company. Bert had suggested some time ago that we put in a Super scheme. Two of the partners took the two hundred dollars a year in cash. I had insisted that Eric join with me and, against his will, I put him in and this was the cheque that was received. Without it to carry on at the time I don't know how she would have managed.

That being as it was, in modern suburbia, Heather and I made so many lasting friends. The children were doing well at High school and there was sufficient money coming in for the good life. I must have mentioned that we had eight houses in all, most of which we built ourselves. The big one on Observatory Hill was Heathers design and we won the Herald homes award for it. Bugsy and his motley crew laid the 36,000 clinker bricks and cursed every one. The whole team was scared of the foreman, Heather, but loved her morning teas or play lunch as we called them like the kids did. That house was 36 squares and big enough for Evan to fix up the downstairs flat for when he and Robyn were married. In appreciation, they gave us our first grandson and Adam came home to a very happy household.

The cost may be of interest, the land was $7,000 on a good deal Geoff Cassidy got for us. The house cost $14,000 to build and we thought we did well to sell it at $46,000 just a few years later. Now it's worth up to perhaps $700,000.

When we sold it, there was sufficient to have funds to make that all important 1972 trip to see Doug in America and Dad and others in England and Wales.

Before going we purchased a choice block of land in Coronet Court, North Rocks, where we intended to build another house on our return.

While we were away our friends were looking after Heather's Mum who was getting on in age, difficult and demanding by now. Her brother George, or Foss as we knew him, had come to live with her as company. For so many years they took up so much of Heather's time in caring for both of them and it was a big task for a little girl looking after two big homes.

Arriving back from overseas we had to rent a house while we built the beautiful Spanish house. Heather had rung Evan from Torramalinos in Spain to say there were so many Spanish houses everywhere. "Mum", he said, "You're in Spain" and so she built one. Values escalated and in a few months it was worth more than the one we sold to go overseas, it was a nice place for Alan and Rhondda to get married from.

Everything was now moving apace and it was really a fairy tale wedding, the bride and groom looked fabulous while Robyn, the maid of honour looked radiant as expectant mothers do because Benjamin Luke was on the way by now.

Instead of all that fancy car stuff, we had a purple and gold coach pulled by two magnificent white horses and driven by two liveried coachmen. The drive was hilarious to watch, it was out our street, down the big dip and then up the hill to Pennant Hills Rd. With a full load the horses hooves slipped on the bitumen and it was all out onto the wheels to get us moving to the blast of car horns and much shyacking.

At The Kings School Chapel [Alan's old school] there was over a hundred guests and they all came back to the house for the reception where a big marquee was required for the wedding breakfast and the overflow of guests.

Rhondda and Robyn had swapped sisterly duties because at Robyn and Evan's wedding at the historic St Anne's at Ryde, Rhon had been bridesmaid. That was a wedding, followed by a big do at Chatswood afterwards, a spectacular merger of the Grundy-Rees families.

The newlyweds were soon settled in, at our Coronet Court of course, need you have asked. It was with us and it proved so convenient. Marge and Rex had been thinking of doing a round Australia trip so when, in a weak moment, we said we would go with them, it was soon arranged and we were off in six months time. We had to buy a caravan and a brand new, short wheelbase 4/wheel drive Toyota, oh what fun. Rex insisted on taking Laddie the spaniel for protection, the dog that would lick you to death as he played. It was a six month, right round Australia trip in a time before terrorist tourists, when it was mostly dirt and petrol at only 25 cents a gallon. There were few caravan parks and we slept out in virgin, almost untouched wonderland. That was some trip, you can have a read of the diary if you wish. Both of them in fact.

In her 90th year Heather's Mum passed away, sad I suppose but a relief for all of us. Unfortunately she was not done with me or Heather either, because when the Will was read, it stated clearly that everything, including the proceeds from the house, was to go into a trust fund. The interest was to go to the grandchildren while they lived and then the residue to go to the Blind society. It was unbelievable that Heather was to receive nothing, even though her Dad had left his half interest in Rhodes to her and that all my savings and work over the years was in there too.

We engaged a solicitor to overturn the will and that was easy with the unfairness of it all and the Blind society had no objection. It did however cost us thousands of pounds. The house was put up for sale immediately and we accepted the first reasonable offer wanting to be over and done with the whole miserable affair. Taking out expenses, we gave the two children a considerable amount for their houses and the small balance was used to resolve our situation and that finally was that part of our life's story.

On a lighter note, I should mention the brother, Uncle George or 'Foss', as he was so well known from his gold fossicking days. He was the original Aussie character and worked for the Pymble council for a brief time. He had an accident, took a small pension and left. It was just 3 pence a week. Can you imagine 3 cents every week but, what is more, he drew it almost till he died at the age of 91. It made insurance history and at the end a rep came to see us to ask us, please, can they call it quits as it was costing them a fortune in paper work.

He went gold mining at the age of nineteen and like so many others found himself in West Australia. At Kalgoorlie he knew every claim and every gold strike made there, his wealth of stories from the era would fill a library. In later years he still got around in his old-fashioned suit and celluloid collars, waistcoat with the watch and chain across the front and always looked immaculate. He was in great demand as an expert on gold and minerals and went religiously every day to Tattersalls Club in Pitt St. to talk mining and racing, but not to bet.

I still have rolls of maps of remote places over the continent, one he had casually mentioned was the mine at Orange in which he and two others had an interest. The others over the years, past caring, had left their share to him but he too did little about it.

Now this should finish this saga off with us coming into a fortune, fixing the whole family up and living like lords forever after 'BUT'!

Just before he died he talked more about the Cadia mine, quite interesting but awfully vague and then one day a letter arrived from Pacific Copper saying they were going to exercise the option on his interest in Cadia for the agreed sum of $2,000. We managed to get the story from him and shock doesn't describe our feelings. Our solicitor appealed but it was too late, the time of the option was up. Heather and I even met the Managing Director of Pacific Copper who took us through the complex at Orange where we saw the huge potential. There were eleven minerals and the gold content was sufficient to pay for the whole operation, the estimated value at that time, 1969, was eleven million dollars and when Uncle Foss died, Heather was the sole heir. The $2000 helped pay for the funeral and out of pocket expenses to wind up the old fellows affairs.

That was OK, he was a fountain of knowledge, a fabulous man and a good friend to me, it was a joy to have known him.

42

* 1989 Heathrow *

We arrived at Heathrow at the start of January after a month of Swiss Xmas festivities. We stayed with our Swiss friends Kurt and Judith at their lovely unit in Thyngen, near Shaffhause on the German border. Their hospitality in the snow and incredibly beautiful countryside was a dream come true for Heather who always wished for a real white Xmas. There was a need to wear woolly lined boots, thermal underwear and our kangaroo skin coats, causing me to compare this to the Xmas back home at Copacabana in 30(C) degree heat on the beach. It certainly was a change, nice! Just this once, as I had moved to get away from this.

As we collected our little European car at the terminal and loaded up, we felt the chill of the English winter. We tried to locate demisters and heaters, to locate all switches as we tried to exit London with its incredible round-abouts and hectic traffic. With a little luck we found our way to Goodworth Clatford, down in Hampshire. My sister Betty had been staying with her son Russell and his wife Sandy. Russell had James and Sandy had a Russell and Caroline from previous marriages. It was a lovely visit and Betty and I had time to catch up on the family and past events. Before we left them, we arranged to meet Betty up in Hull later on after she returned home, then we could visit old haunts together, sort out some of the past.

For us it was off to Wales, across the bridge on the M4. This is where, when entering Wales, the signs are in both Welsh and English. Easy for me but almost impossible for foreigners to read in time before it was too late and they had missed their turn off. Trying to take in everything, even I missed mine and finished up in Caerdydd or Cardiff for you 'furriner' lot. With a little help we headed up the valley, through Tonteg and Treforest, into Pontypridd before we knew it and heading for home territory of Tonypandy.

Dunraven St looked the same as ever as we turned down the lane into Riverview. I can't find the words to describe the feeling of the moment as I held and kissed my Aunty Beryl. Cousins Mick and Angela were there and Uncle Joe of the 'Stick run' story. Beryl is the youngest of the Will and Mam Rees clan, the only one now left.

Angie showed us where we would be staying, it was in the new bungalow at the end of Riverview and where that slaughterhouse had been. It was all guarded by the flock of honking geese and the B.B.D. [Big brown dog]

Aunty Beryl had a royal lunch ready for us in the dining room, cum kitchen that I well remembered. The fire was burning bright, it was so cosy and warm. We talked till both Beryl and I were needing a break for air so I went to unpack ready to meet more family and have another enormous meal in Angie's new kitchen.

The time with Beryl, in the house where so many Rees' were born, was special and I cherish the occasion with her as the representative of all the others. On this trip home I learnt so much from photos that turned up and from many long talks.

43

* Cambrian Terrace *

It was cold and damp as always as Heather and I went to find Cambrian Terrace at Llwynapia. Up the hill passed that old school, no change and there it was! Cambrian, we stood and stared, so much of it came back to me. It was narrow and so old, rather run down and smaller than it seemed back then. The terrace was only a narrow lane, or 'Gooly' as they were called, no room for a car but a Mini may scrape through.

It was difficult to pick out the house we stayed in with the Sparrow's so long a go.

We wound our way down to the old district of Rhondda South to find my Primrose St., we could look out over the valley to Trealaw and back up to Penrhys up passed the still same looking hospital. We counted the numbers till we found No.123. There it was, so neat and tidy, nothing like the grubby, smoky dump I was brought home to in that July of 1924 after my birth in the hospital over 'by there', just another Rees boy, God help him!

In the only photo, as I look at it now, there is my dad and two year old me in front of the unpainted and unfurnished house, just one of the thousands which at the time all looked the same.

Primrose St now was so unbelievably clean and tidy, all the doors and windows painted so spick and span, lovely curtains on the windows and as we had a sticky beak in the window, we could see the old Welsh dresser with silver and glass ware on their lace doilies. There's a bit of affluence now, something never dreamt possible just a few years ago when there was little money for food or sandshoes, let alone all this posh stuff.

Not a lot to say now about Cambrian, it was the wrong end of town, the last place up the back of the urban sprawl. Rough stone paving where we went and played when ordered to "Go out in't Gooly." The stone wall the same where seepage had it as ever, cold and damp. The draughty water closet [W.C.] was still perched atop the wall, the piece of wire or string for pieces of paper there just as ever plus a soggy roll of soft and soluble. In my time there had been no internal plumbing of any kind and as I recall and it can be imagined, it was an ordeal to venture out at night in winter, it was only for urgent big jobs. Even writing this brings back the pong of the potty under the bed, a sickly, warm smell. Mixed in with the smell of the smoky fires, it was rather an off putting atmosphere in those pokey, closed houses with too many people and too little fresh air or ventilation.

Behind the wall there was still the field, the rubbish tip was better but still nostalgically smelt of sardine tins. The Woods we went that day with Dad, looked much the same, thoughts of Uncle Dai and Mam's berry pies, so much flooded back. Archibald Ood's [Hood] big statue, benefactor or scrooge, take your pick, surveyed the now changing Valley scene.

As I had written, 'I shit my pants', so on my own I took a walk passed the school, traced my path home to Cambrian as I had done before, still in drizzling rain.
All the early times came back, election day, Guy Faulkes, the singing in Chapel, especially Moriah, where Mam Rees did the flowers and such for so long. The nostalgic smell of tangerines was there and that Xmas of the 'No present for Derrick', the lovingly made cricket bat that was never appreciated.
One can't help thinking of the amazing amount of presents each child receives today, do they appreciate them as much as one single gift back then?

In the course of putting together all the bits and pieces and having previously mentioned Mrs Sparrow, I received a cutting from the 'Rhondda Leader', our South Wales paper. Cousins Mick and Angie were always finding interesting bits to send me, maps and books for me to be able keep in touch and for which I'm eternally grateful.
This time the full-page article was about a Mr and Mrs Sparrow, formally of Cambrian Terrace. The story went on to say how the Sparrows during the war years [W.W.2] had taken in and cared for children from London, they were given a home in the country in the safety of the Rhondda Valley.
The article went on to mention the terrible mine disaster when the whole valley was so distraught losing so many of its men and boys.
In Llwynapia the Sparrows grief was for their son Clifford who was among those taken. How very strange after all these years to read about this, we were living with them at the time and it all comes back, of Clifford and I sharing our little room, the trauma of that time as a Rhondda boy.

Like so many times we lived or moved in with folk, it is apparent the Sparrows were that sort of people and had taken us in as they had those kids from bombed out London.

Little things do come to mind. Grandfather, as he patted me on the head and said, "So you're Will's boy!"

Mam Rees had a painting done when she was a young and handsome lady. Before we arrived for our visit, they all took a vote and agreed that I, as the now eldest Rees male, with a growing family to follow, should have the painting. It proudly hangs in my son's house in the family gallery at Beecroft.

The family Bible in Welsh was found after going astray for years and was allowed to leave South Wales to a safe place in New South Wales. The old folk still speak Welsh but for years it was almost lost till now it is taught in school, is on the radio and as tourists will vouch for and mispronounce, is on signs all over. As an expatriate, it's great to think our Gymraig is back in strength.

We legitimately claim to have the oldest cultivated language in Europe, the Romans left a Latin influence and some French words have a similarity. In the early days we called ourselves Cymry which means 'fellow countryman', the language was Cymraeg and it was spoken in England and lower Scotland. The Anglo Saxons pushed the Cymry back into the hills so our Welsh is now only heard in Wales. Bishop Morgan, in 1588, translated the Bible into Welsh. Then came the religious revival, changing the Welsh into a pious and God fearing nation after it had been a gay [I shouldn't say that now!] and carefree nation. There are a million books full of fire and brimstone teachings, mostly lying idle nowadays.

44

* William and Margaret *

My Grandma and Grandpa, who for me standing back and viewing the whole scene, are the start of it all. It is always just 'Mam', as these pages will show, and sadly there is little mention of Grandpa, my 'Dadchi', the only one I, of all my siblings, was to get to know.

Intending to say so much about them, the reminiscing keeps coming back to the younger Will, my Dad. How much alike were they? Was Clydach Vale the first pit for both of them? Did Grandpa wish he too was at the gymnasium next to the biscuit factory in the lane training with the boys? The gym Dad, Tommy Farr and the boys built. Joe Louis, the World Champion, beat our Tommy Farr in a rotten 'home town decision' in the U.S.A. but in later years he told Tommy himself that it was the hardest fight of his life and that he still got a bloody nose just thinking about it.

Both Wills revelled in the glory of the times while Mam, like all mums of hard working and harder fighting miners, just tried to ignore it all.

I think Mam may have despaired of her young Will as he was such an enigma. Down the mine as a labourer soon to become a coal hewer, he then took off regular like to become a journeyman and somehow a fulltime carpenter.

His spell in the R.A.F. was a worry to both his parents adding to Mam's troubles when he turned up with his new wife Connie. There was the pleasure of a grandson, Douglas, but in the vague background were two other children. So much happened in a seemingly short time! What would the old folk think of the rest of the events that followed.

Dad held a responsible position in the film industry until he retired and was to mix with and get to know all the stars as they came and went. He collected autographed photos of all the celebrities, mostly signed 'To Dear Taff' and with love etc. To the Beatles, with whom he worked on their first picture, he was Pop or Taff. Even to the locals round his Shepherds Bush he was a bit of a celebrity himself when the four lads from Liverpool went passed in the studio limousine of an afternoon calling out and waving, "Hello Taff."

All the kids in the family want a copy of the photo of Dad and Ringo together as mates which they were, sort of a Dad and Son thing. Strange as I think of it that I, at Ringo's age, had a father figure and it was 12,000 miles away.

It's funny Dad did little for himself, just basked on the borders of others fame and fortune. Margaret and William would have enjoyed his tales of the glamorous world of the new 'Talkies', but it was not to be.
Perhaps only my lovely Aunty Beryl, Dad's youngest and only remaining sister, will have my thoughts on Mam and Dadchi. They deserve a mention in their own right.

45

* Our Brother Bernard (Bugsy) *

Bernard, or as we all call him 'Bugsy', and his wife Patsy Ann have just left after a weekend with us at our Copacabana beach house [Central Coast]. We get together as often as we can for a game of Canasta or just to smell the roses and catch up with things. Married for years with a grown up family, a boy and three girls, it's a nice family unit and a comfortable part of the whole Aussie Rees clan. They have five acres at Kurrajong on the edge of the bush with trees and native bush where birds and wild life abound. Bugs, once mechanic, painter, rabbit breeder then bricklayer, amongst others things, built the huge, comfortable, verandah surrounded home which he finally fly screened to keep out the wogs, thank God. The pool and sauna soon came along to be used on so many family reunions and gatherings.

He didn't last a week as a motor mechanic, just finished his course and got out. As a painting contractor he was feeling his way into the business world of self-employ. Bricklaying was the way to go, so many stories to tell!

He became famous, infamous or is it notorious, for his inimitable style, mainly for the brief work shorts he almost wears with the family jewels, I won't go on about that. As a Cassanova, it was 'lock up your women or girlfriend' [Only joking Bugs] but he was an experience to one and all.

He got away with murder, we had all loved the little fellow back in Treforest, though he and Myrna were at times a menace. We realise how close he was to being lost to us by adoption to that Nurse Llewellyn at Bridgend hospital.

At Glenmore, on the farm, he came into his own with two sisters to mother him and me to keep an eye on things. Yvonne, back at King St, told one and all, "You touch my brother and I'll bash you," which she could and would. Miss Todd said he was her favourite but then, all the littlies were her favourites. She would cuddle them all to her ample and enormous bosom in what must have been such a comfort in a starved for affection situation.

Miss Todd cuddled hundreds of children and cared for thousands in a devoted life time career of care. It was so gratifying in later years to see Her Majesty the Queen personally present Toddy with her O.B.E. and to stop and thank her for the fine work she had done. Knowing about Saints, Miss Todd was one, Miss Scholes too, in her funny way.

Miss Todd was our secretary and bookkeeper, relieving cottage mother, tuckshop lady, general help and whatever. All duties carried out with the boundless love for all which I think was infectious to everyone.

From the farm school, I had left to go to work, Doreen, though young, was able to go into service on the sheep station too. Yvonne eventually had a short stay there too but there was a bit of a riot or something. I was away in the R.A.A.F. and missed what went on.

Bugsy was at the farm school till 1944 when the remaining 44 children were taken to join the sister scheme at Fairbridge Farm School at Molong in N.S.W. Because of the war, no more children were being sent because of the danger, both schemes were short of children. In the post war years they started arriving again but it was never the same. Of the 161 pre-war mob, 117 were at that time, at work or in positions. It must say a lot for the success of the Northcote dream in such a short time.

In 1979, there was the occasion of the 40th Northcote reunion at Glenmore. By now Bugsy owned and drove the biggest car so we all volunteered for him to drive us from Sydney to Bacchus Marsh. It was the first time we had all got together at the old place, though locals often called in there. It was now a Parks and Recreation Centre, the kids all gone but the cottages and buildings were the same as always. The tiny trees we had planted had grown, not all of them without our T.L.C., but the place was well kept and as our first home, we were happy to be back. The centre was only used very occasionally and to us it looked so eerily quiet and lonely without the childish activity.

Though a great success, the weekend was sad in a way. Mum, who never did get out to us in the early days as planned, did eventually get to Perth to Yvonne's outback property. I think it was 1952 before she made the move. She eventually gravitated to Sydney to be with us in her usual vague way and had been there since.

On Saturday midst the activities, the police arrived. They had traced us to Perth in W.A., then to Melbourne, to the Marsh and to here with the news. After all the life of events, it was here we heard that our Mum had died. She had been close to the end when we left Sydney but insisted, actually we all decided as there was nothing we could do, that we should go and not spoil the expectations of the reunion.

We didn't spoil it, just saw the weekend out and went back Sunday night to make the necessary arrangements.

There was a happier reunion in 1988 when we had our 50th anniversary get together. This time there were many of the 117 kids who had gone out to work, there were pre-war and post-war, plus lots of Fairbridge transfers and visitors. There were children and grandchildren, about 800 turned up for the historical and unforgettably happy occasion.

So many faces and names to bring back to mind, all of us a product of the Middlemore machine as we raved on about then and since. Not little kids now, grown-ups with amazing success stories to relate, home here together again. Having lost the senior boy of the first party, I was quite strangely the oldest boy of our scheme. Doreen Tuck, who came out on the 'Largs Bay' with us, was senior girl but only showed up in later years much regretting the happy reunion times she had missed.

It was never intended to go on with all that in the middle of Bugsy's story, so I will go back to the time after the war had finished. I had returned from active service and before they decided what to do with we quickly forgotten veterans, I found myself stationed at the R.A.A.F. station at Parkes, way out west. It was near to Xmas and I was eager to meet Bernard after what seemed a lifetime. Almost like strangers at first, we soon found an easy and lasting understanding, more than brothers now, good mates in fact.

While on leave in Sydney, in a new uniform, a couple of thousand pounds in back pay and from souvenirs made and sold to the rich Yanks in my kick, I wouldn't call the King my uncle.

I picked out the best push bike, a good strong roadster for country work and took it back on the train to Parkes, rode it out to camp like a Gig in my full uniform.

The next leave was just before Xmas, I'd not ridden a bike since Ramsey's when I used to do the 60 miles to the farm school on a weekend, that had been a snack, so I set off from camp at daybreak in regulation service gear to ride to Molong, up to the Fairbridge Farm School and to surprise young Bugsy. About 50 odd miles I think!

It nearly killed me. I stopped for drinks at any tank or mud hole, it was 105 degrees in the water bag, no shade and the roads were bloody awful. So short a distance on the map but I arrived at Fairbridge a staggery kneed grease ball, uniform soaking wet, just making it.

The look on his face, the envy in other boys eyes as he rode it around and showed it off, was worth it. Being the first bike they had there, it was a great success and as a budding businessman he made a profit selling rides to all with something to give in exchange.

Bernard's times at the two schools were happy enough, never enough Donk, as they called bread, because they were always hungry. He may have liked authority a little less than I, we both diplomatically wore it but had to become self employed at the first opportunity. He talked always of 'Pongo' as they called porridge, even today on his visit, we have beaut 'Pongo' for breakfast.

He was able to visit Heather and I in Sydney, on occasions, while still at Molong, we were of course married by then. So when it was time to decide on a future and leave school, it was opportune that Heather's house at Rhodes was a welcome venue. A mechanics course at the Leichardt Bus Depot of the transport department was available if he had somewhere to stay, so being sixteen on December 16, it was all set.

It was not I, but Heather, who suggested he board with us, my old bed on the back verandah was vacant since I moved to the front room and as she said, "there won't be much more to do." I'm sure in retrospect, the extra washing, ironing and cooking on top of two little children, a grubby plumber husband and an ever more dependant mother, was more than she ever really envisaged.

Heather, as an only child, appreciated having a brother who she cared for and mothered. I think she is the only person he ever took notice of and he still thinks of 16 Cavell Ave. as his home.

Despite all his wild ways, his reputation as the great lover, it was Patsy Ann who won out in the end and we got the best sister in law possible.

It was a wild start, a great wedding, a short honeymoon at the Log Cabin at Penrith, till the money ran out and they went home the next day.

How quickly he grew up and sought his independence, he left us to do the round of boarding houses as he moved from place to place, hard to keep track of there for a while till he found his own pad at Ashfield. Alt Street Ashfield was never to be the same again. At seventeen he was into motorbikes and girls, maybe not in that order. The chicks thought he looked spivvy in his leathers, one of the early Bikies but before his time. I have a photo of the girl he was madly in love with but who ditched him or the bike and he was going to ride off into the sunset and kill himself or something. He does admit it was a fantastic time finding independence after his first rather different 18 years and as he let it all take its course.

At Alt Street Ashfield, his house became the venue and home for all and sundry, every homeless kid and anyone in need of company gathered there. Though an absolute shambles, Heather and I, the sort of respectable relatives, visited occasionally. The fireplace where fires like bonfires had been burning, had the walls burnt out to the outside brickwork. There was a panic to find a clean cup for a cuppa for us and the lounge room always had a motor bike in some stage of disrepair in the middle of the floor. It was an experience.

It was while there, he obtained a license to breed rabbits and he had cages of the blighters everywhere. A great idea really, they were the huge white New Zealand rabbits with plenty of good white meat on them and beautiful skins for fur. As we all know, it is illegal to own a pair of rabbits in Australia, having seen the squillions loose on the White Elephant, it's understandable so the license was of great value. More chance of making a fortune than Hubert Harding and my horse ranch caper, so we all thought he'd make a mint.

During the mechanics course which was going OK, in his third year he was allowed to take the big double-decker buses on test runs. He came up to Rhodes, to Cavell Ave. too before we moved and that was alright but we got the shock of our lives when living at 75 Beecroft Rd, Beecroft to see the unbelievable sight of a double-decker stop outside the door. For somewhere different to go and to give the kids a ride, he gave Cheltenham and sleepy Beecroft the first look at a big bus on its, up to then quiet scene.

Besides all that, he was a music freak, loud and continuous, waking the whole district from 5-30 a.m. when he had the first barrow of brickies mud and stacks of bricks ready, till knock off time. He danced with a style which came to be known to all and sundry as 'The Bugsy'. It was eerie and weird that the only person ever with the same inimitable action was our brother Douglas, even stranger still as they had never met in Bugsy's first 40 years and only then in 1969 at the family reunion when so many siblings met for the first time.

It's funny how things work out, the girls having looked out and cared for him before, Bugsy now with a house of his own, was able to come to the rescue of Doreen and her children when Ted lost their house and everything. Doreen moved in with her baby brother and they were good for each other in her time of trauma. It was a good relationship and the first time Bugs felt he was a supportive member of the family.

Somehow all things went well around that time, the new house on his five acres at Kurrajong was completed. More importantly, the sheds were finished and full of busily breeding rabbits, a rapid growth business with orders and contracts coming in and plans already for expansion.

Then, … 'Myxomatosis'. It certainly de-plagued and fixed the rabbit problem but it happened so quickly the rabbits died in millions, including the new breeding stock. Myxo was introduced to solve the problem but the licensed breeders such as Bugsy lost their stock. Though a serum was found, it was too expensive and never readily available, the rabbit breeding business folded up without a hope or final twitch.

All that is left of his dream are a few priceless rugs made from the skins.

At the Leichardt Depot, among the buses, Bugs had completed his apprenticeship and immediately gave the dirty game away. It was too much inside work and no freedom of enterprise.

He did the painting thing with a mate for awhile, house painting and it led to knowing the trades and his becoming a well paid brickies labourer. It seemed no time until he had a licensed partner in a business, with a team of trowels capable of anything involving bricks, anywhere the money was.

He had done fruit picking and itinerant jobs in the early days but haven't we all? Never big on sport, he was never into the joy of cricket or footy, just his music and having a bet, $400 on the toss of a coin, then double or nothing. As it will be seen throughout this tale, it was in his blood because Dad and Doug were inveterate gamblers too. Not me, I was too tinny to throw it away, though in New Guinea I played two up with the wealthy Yanks and finished a long way in front.

Though by retirement, slowing down and a bit of a legend he is still a happy little kid so we'll leave him there for a moment.

46

* Dad and Mum, Early Days

We know about Mum being left on the doorstep of our Aunt, in a basket as a little baby.

The report says, "left on the doorstep of a Yorkshire hotel owned by Mr and Mrs Shaw." Mum's birth certificate shows her as Collinson. Apparently Grandpa Shaw saw the babe and said, "We don't want no Bairns in here." Connie as she became known, smiled at him and, as she did with everyone for her next 80 years, won him over.

Aunt may have been married to a Mathews, a Captain in the cavalry, a bad tempered bugger it appears. Gave Mum a hard time and smashed her bicycle to pieces. Aunt just bought her a new one. There is innuendo he mistreated her sexually and Doreen feels it's possibly so.

It is said that our Aunt always said, "I hope you die with your boots on," which he did as his boat went down with all aboard. Sadly all the beautiful horses were lost.

I may have mentioned that Aunt used to knock around with Edward V11, he gave her the strange present of a pair of red shoes. It was a funny time, the pub catered for the Black Irish dockworkers. Mum, in later years told Doreen she used to peep through the door and watch them play, 'shove halfpenny' with their penises. Also that she used to get locked up in a cupboard so she couldn't go out with her boy friend.

She always did have a fear of the dark, probably too much time in the cupboard.

When we visited Goole in 1972, Mum, by then in Sydney had said, "Look for Mrs English," as they had corresponded over the years. Calling at our old No.20, we asked the lady if Mrs English was at home. She immediately put two and two together and figured out who we were, remembering Mum or Connie, quite well. Heather and Rhondda were amazed how folk over there remembered people and events from so long ago. We got instructions and headed off.

I rang the bell and the lady, my age, who answered the door, got all excited. She was a girl I knew as a playmate back in the thirties. In great excitement, she called out, "Mum, look who's here." Mum came hurrying out, a moments pause and grabbing me in a bear hug said, "Good God, it's Connie's boy Derrick." It was like I'd never been away for those 40 years.

It was party time for the entire street in the excitement, the funny thing, after we left, was that Heather and Rhondda told me why they were so unusually quiet the whole time. They never understood a single word that was said.

We know Doug took off at about age sixteen. Betty always had a thing about being with her family and never went anywhere. When in later years, migration was the big thing, she and her husband Herbert decided to make the move. He even had a job to go to, and of all places, Bathurst. Bathurst, as you know, is the beautiful city of our great early history. It's over the Blue Mountains as you head west past coal mining Lithgow. It would have been wonderful for them, the house and affects were sold, migration papers all in order, then nothing more! Was it a sickness, did Herbert get cold feet! Who knows but our Betty lives in regret at not being with us all out here.

Our Betty and the early days will still remain a mystery. I've just gone through the box of old photos that belonged to Dad, those that Mick and Angela brought out and which Dad had plastered over every wall at Conningham Rd, the 'Bush'. There are photos of family faded into the past, a lovely one of our sister Pat as a girl, one Yvonne must have sent of her and her Johnnie at their wedding and a small two inch by three inch snap of a little boy with family resemblance. On the back is a faded, 'Martin', Betty's youngest. "Is there still an unfinished tale to tell?"

It's so strange that it was Bathurst. My daughter and Alan live there with a thriving business, but that's not all, for in 1989 we only then discovered that Dad's brother after 25 years in the Royal Navy, was to migrate to Australia. Where to? Bathurst. Uncle Dai and Aunty Elsie also got the cold feet thing at the thought of such a major move and they too never made it.

Uncle Dai had passed on by 1989 and Heather and I said to Elsie, while staying in her cottage in Dorset, "Why don't you come for a visit, we'll look after you and you can meet all the family."

We had been back in Copacabana but a few days when we were pleasantly surprised, quite amazed actually, to receive the letter, the date and a time of arrival for a months visit by Aunty Elsie.

The reason I'm telling this is because, besides showing her Sydney and much of the bush, we took her to Bathurst to meet Rhondda and family. She fell in love with the beautiful buildings, all the trees, one with the resident possum and baby in, and all the Australian bush she had dreamed of all that time! She sat and cried in regret for the wrong decision and for not being brave enough to have made the move.

47

* Doreen, My Sister *

When I arrived home on my first leave from overseas, Doreen and I had our reunion and got to know each other again in Melbourne. Having been so involved in the war and my own affairs it was time to come down to earth, to catch up on Bernard and find out what happened to Yvonne after Ramsay's when I lost track. Doreen eventually came to Sydney to live, it was to Rhodes where Heather's Mum, Mrs Gwynne, invited her to stay. She and Heather were to become the best of friends, more like sisters in fact. They shared the front room and slept in the big double bed, as was the way those days. It was good for both of them to go to dances and share the confidences of teenage years. I was of course camped on the back verandah as the star boarder, Heather and I as yet not having decided if we were right for each other. Doreen was to marry from Cavel Ave, Rhodes by which time she had become settled in her own mind and feeling secure.

At Mooleric we saw each other every day, each carrying out our duties. Some not so good times like the time I got my new Malvern Star bike, I took her for a dink on the handle bars in the gravel and threw her off with nasty gravel rash to both knees, loss of ego to me too. She somehow, as she told me later, never ever rode a bike again.

When my call up came and I left the sheep station, Doreen and I sort of lost regular contact, my next twelve months was full of training at camps over the country, she herself was soon restless and deciding her next move. Another boy from the farm took my place and Yvonne took Doreen's place, we were a hard act to follow and neither lasted long. For Doreen, housework as such was a no-no and Melbourne with its bright lights, much greener pastures.

The dairy farm people, the Graham's, in the cottage across the road where we all made ourselves at home, had a relation, Aunty Gert, living in Melbourne. Another softy who couldn't say no, with the consequence her house became the meeting place for all the kids that gravitated to the city. Quite a few lived or boarded there and everyone came to visit or meet each other to compare their progress. It was at Gert's that I was to meet her again.

Waiting for her to come home from work was a new and strange time, our first meeting since my leaving Mooleric. So nice to see her coming happily down the street looking so smart in her jacket and skirt. She had done her transition from child migrant, via the bit of housemaiding Mr Llewellin said was her appointed lot here, to her now settled way of life in suburbia. I had yet to do that and settle down after farm life, service life of four years and knowing not how to behave in a city.

Doreen had become involved with our Bill Wilkes, going steady or tracking square as they say in the bush but it fizzled out. Johnny Bridgwood also came close to being a brother-in-law, either one OK by me. Seeing John many years later, still living around the Marsh, he said he still loved Doreen.

It was so interesting to catch up, to hear the reports of the kids progress, many being accepted and becoming part of a family, even heir to the farm or whatever. Some boys married the boss's daughter and a very versatile and adaptable mob they were turning out to be.

As I have said, Doreen came to us in Sydney, I had dug myself in at the Gwynne's at Rhodes. Bernard came too in due course and as Doreen said, "When the Rees' move in, they all move in," probably well trained in those early days. Both Doreen and I revelled in the social life, house parties and dances from and at Cavell Ave. Just belonging and being a part of a community was great. She and Heather shared the choice of clothes and fashions just getting back into the shops after coupons and rationing. Both thought they were the bees knees in smart tailored suits and Davy Crocket hats of fur so very in style at the time.

It was a nice time and Doreen was infectious, greeting all on her way to the station. It was not surprising the men at Timbrols' factory or the flour mill, asked where she was when she left to get married. They missed her cheery, "Good morning."

Ted came into her life, quite a courtship, quick and, before she knew it, she was Mrs Gardner. As the nearest thing to a patriarch in the family and over protective as I was with Yvonne too, I had my premonitions!!!

There was a lovely wedding with all the family there, and being at Rhodes, it was a hectic time for Heather and I, we being an old married couple by then.

They chose to build their new home at Caringbah across the other side of Sydney, a shame really as we could only visit very occasionally. Ted was always busy with his garden and his goats, a hobby that took up lots of his time. He admitted he was a health nut and when Ian, the first son came along, he needed goats milk. They had two boys and a girl, and though biased, in my opinion it's mostly to Doreen's credit they turned out as well as they did. Ian, a triple certificate sister, Kevin a licensed plumber and lovely Denise, a qualified draughtswoman. There were to be a few traumas, marriage mix-ups and the usual dramas, all eventually resolved or nearly so!

Doreen drifted into her ultimate career to become the best seamstress in Sydney town, in demand by the best firms. Her time at Bookalils was apparently memorable as she still sees Edna, Maggie and other mates of that time. She too is called Taffy or just Reesy. As Doreen is always involved in my peregrinations or story, [Ever since I read that word in a storybook, I've wanted to use it], I'll just let things take their course.

The Ramsay clan was a vital part of my life and I should mention them, the Major and Mrs Ramsay as you will gather, were, with their wealthy way of life, an education! The three elder children went to private school, [Public school], as boarders, while Mary, the youngest, about thirteen at the time, had her own governess. Being the only young ones around, except for Doreen, she and I were good mates.
Ann, a little older than I, was nice to me but very posh. No hope of anything there! Andrew and Robert never could figure me out.
Mary, after lessons, was allowed to saddle her Shetland pony and ride out to meet me wherever I was and we had fun together as just two kids.
Doreen later told me, "Mary was crazy in love with you and told me about her dreams." I learnt how she, Doreen, had 'The hots' for Rob and further more, our Yvonne was in love with Andrew. In those times of don't touch, no one did any good for themselves.
I do admit my love or whatever it was for Mary. By the time I left the temptation was sheer hell, but I held firm.
The four children were always nice to me, as country children they were very free and uninhibited with each other and often asked me to go swimming in the big dam. I couldn't handle it, they all swam in the nude and I was dead scared of my embarrassing them, the mere thought of the girls was enough to set me off.
My singing and yodelling became part of Mooleric and they urged me on saying I should go on the radio. "What will you call yourself ?" they asked.
Perhaps it was the ingrained, 'tip your hat' servant to master of the past or just being embarrassed because of the work clothes I wore, even

though they were neat and tidy as I washed and ironed them myself. I said in answer, "Rags McTaggerty." It said something as I took more care and pride in my appearance from then on.

48

* Yvonne, My Other Sister *

As mum said, "What a looovly baby." We've mentioned that so of course she became a lovely woman and everyone loved our 'Von'. Overcoming a trying and traumatic time of growing up, a few forgettable events before meeting and marrying to have her family of four. The past made her capable of handling them and John who I had those premonitions about.

It was all a challenge, especially when she and John were pioneering their virgin property in West Australia. She needed to be full of life and bubbly and with the loud Rees voice to call across the miles of wheat fields to call the men to dinner.

Just a kid when I suddenly left the farm school, we seemed to lose touch. The years till she married are a little vague with only second hand reports and me being away overseas in problem times. The time at Ramsay's was good for her and Doreen as it gave them time to compare notes and think where they were going at last, out on their own.

Memories of her at Tonteg with the scarlet fever scare when we nearly lost her, then at Treforest and the Alsatian ripping her scalp off thing, otherwise with Doreen at hand, she got through.

There was a rather mysterious time when I visited her in Melbourne, must have been in my Air Force training days while stationed in the Exhibition building. She was in a convent, being rebellious and needing time to settle down I was told and then I was posted north so the turbulent time was lost for me.

It was in Melbourne that Yvonne met Johnny Grave in his Air Force uniform all handsome and smart. As the son of a W.A. grazier, he seemed a good catch. Yvonne, at that very time of her life, was ready for a relationship, desperately needing someone to love and to be loved in return. Thus, when they met it was love at first sight and true romance. John was a pilot but bitterly disappointed in a way, that the war was by then over, his dreams of being an Ace were gone. He did in fact continue his flying and was to have his own plane at the Kalanie property, north of Perth.

For whatever reason we did not attend the wedding, it's only now that Heather reminds me that John and Yvonne came to Sydney to meet us before going home to Perth. Heather remembers because she was in hospital having our son Evan at the time. As she recalls, "Yvonne was so beautiful, so loud and outgoing, I was completely overawed by her."

John took his bride home to the family property where Von fitted in so well to become a true country woman. There were great plans for the future, not knowing the trouble ahead or how the best laid plans were want to go astray.

It's mostly all forgotten now but at that time there was a lot of stupid prejudice against mixed marriages, Catholic to Protestant. It embarrasses me to think of it now but, as I had become involved with the Masonic Lodge and all its workings, perhaps influenced by the family and all the bigotry of the times, feeling big headed and head of our family out here, I advised against the wedding. This caused a breach in the relationship which was soon all over and forgiven. John and I were, over the many visits back and forth over the 3000 mile journey, to become the best of mates.

As it all turned out, in some ways, I am entitled to quietly say a little, "I told you so."

John and his brother worked on the father's property all their years, even after they returned from war service. They never received wages, just a pittance pocket money to go to town on occasions. It was natural they took it as they would inherit the home and property in due course, as there was sufficient to support two families. Mr Grave, their Dad, soon to be referred to only as "The old Bastard", decided to sell up and get out.

For reasons untold, the two boys were not allowed to have the place or find finance to purchase it. Can you believe it, not allowed to have their own property, nor any recompense for all the years of labour, free labour as it now was.

Each had to make a new start, from scratch and John and Von found virgin, untouched land right out in the scrub. Being well known and in sympathy, finance was available and they started the back and heart breaking task of clearing the land to put in a crop. All this while living in a tin shed for ten years and as the kids started to arrive, to rear them.

The rift in the family was never fully resolved and even when the S.O.B. died it went on, little inheritance was forthcoming and indeed only recently in about 1997, those left got peanuts.

By the time Heather and I visited Yvonne in 1977, there was great progress at 'Double Rock', Kalannie. The double rocks being the only elevation [about three feet] on the whole vast expanse spread before you.

Our trip across the Nullarbor Plain, pioneering as it was, had been a nightmare of dirt and gravel, infamous bull dust that could engulf whole cars. In those days before bitumen, it was 1700 miles of potential disaster but a great adventure. By this time, most of the land had been cleared and under cultivation with wheat fields taking shape. Some cattle and a mob of sheep were in evidence and it seemed they were finally on the way to success after all the sweat and tears.

They had lived all this time in that shed, chooks, sheep and the milking cow at the very doorstep. The children seemed none the worse for it all and were growing up fine, sensible people. The only failing or draw back of kids in the bush, they went through cars or vehicles like in a demolition derby. One even ran into the train at Kalannie, that was a clever trick as it only had one train a fortnight.

By now of course, there was a big, real house with plenty of water, the usual problem or worry was the power which came from the noisy smelly diesel generator no one thought to put away from the house, power failures were par for the course.

Yvonne cooked for the shearers or all the men employed at harvest or seeding time. She made pies from her home killed beef or lamb and even delivered them in the ute to the men where they were stopped for lunch. There was a fridge [Big] and a freezer, both always chocker block full with cuts and slabs of meat. John would come in for a beer, no room in the fridge so he'd pop a couple in the freezer and forget them. It was hell to sort out glass from chops or such. Kalannie, up in the sticks of W.A. was hot and dry, the need for grog was vital to survive.

In 1955, our mother finally decided to come to Australia, to join her children, those here at least. It had taken almost 20 years to make the effort. In Sydney we only vaguely knew what was going on, never getting too enthused and with me still sort of unforgiving for the Myrna adoption saga. Mum, psychic as she was, sensed it too and Yvonne being the one to regularly correspond was chosen as the one best to receive her. So Kalannie was the first stop. Von I'm sure, missing her Mum, intended her to stay there permanently.

What a shock it must have been for this English lady when picked up in Fremantle out of Perth, to be whisked out so many miles through what she must have felt was wilderness, to what she thought was a country estate but turned out to be that tin shed with the typical Australian expanse of machinery and rubbish all around. The almost two hundred kilometres with little habitation in sight was nothing, but sharing the shed with kids, cats and dogs, chooks by the dozen, was all too much for the lookalike Queen Mum from up town Goole. I recall Mum's fear of cows from Hayes, Middlesex, she thought if you wore red, they chased you and at Yvonne's place cows were aplenty at the back door.

Mum was a city person, her visit didn't work and she couldn't understand how anyone could live like this, no bread or milk deliveries, no letters and the shop miles in the heat haze distance.

Yvonne said how she had looked forward to her mother's company, bonding as they would call it now, so it was disappointing to take her back to Perth where she would have to stay with the Grave family to acclimatise and settle in. Her stay at Cottesloe was probably the only time she was to experience something of the Aussie beach and surf way of life. Come to think of it, she never even paddled at Barry or owned a swimming cossie. Always with a big flowery English hat, she kept her peaches and cream English complexion till the day she died.

To give you an idea how isolated Double Rock, Kalannie was, I must relate our first visit west by car. After 1700 miles of the grey Bull dust and gravel across the Nullarbor Plains, we had been to historic and fabulous Kalgoorlie, then leaving Coolgardie, we decided to go across country, about 500 miles I believe. There was nothing in sight most of the way, just the lonely clump of trees with a house of sorts tucked in with the big water tank alongside. Dirt all the way and we thought we were lost till after some hours, we met a bloke on a tractor, "G'Day" he said, "Yer lost are yuh mate?"

We told him we were heading for Kalannie and the Grave place. "Y'er nearly there." He said those famous last words, "You can't miss it, it's just down the road." He gave us instructions and as we got back in the car, he said, casual like "Give my regards to John and Vonnie". Off we went with the petrol gauge getting lower and lower, it must have been over a 100 miles before we saw the place, just turned in the gate and she ran out of juice. John's greeting when we told him was, "Bloody city slickers."

There was a most unfortunate hiccup when Mum did arrive in Australia, it was a big occasion and I was happy she finally made it, the past behind us and all so much better in the long run. Unable to meet her, I had arranged through Interflora, to have the largest bouquet of flowers there on her arrival.

Rather peeved they were never ever mentioned, I never knew till the full family reunion in Sydney that she never received them. It was such a shame she never knew that I, her son, had sent his love and greetings, the opportunity of forgiveness she may have wished for was sadly lost.

Yvonne and John, though 3000 miles away, were very close to us. We made it over there on many occasions yet, back home fifty or so miles was apparently too far to visit. On a later visit we found a prosperous property, miles of cultivation and heaps of cattle and sheep, even a milking cow which only Yvonne would milk, if she thought of it. There were pigs for a constant supply of pork chops and bacon. The local butcher used to cure the ham, which with the abundance of free-range eggs, was a breakfast delight.
Mavonney was growing up and the boys helped work the farm. They would work all night in the sowing or harvest season with powerful lights on the massive tractors. The boys said that part was bloody boring but they loved it just the same.
One night we were having a party, Aunty Marge and Rex, our caravanning companions on our round Australia trip, were there and Robert out on the job going round and bloody round. He'd been there partying on for over an hour when John saw him, "What the !|-=#@ hell are you doing here, get out on that,*^+!@ machine." The noise of us all at three a.m. was too much so he stayed till dawn as his machine chugged away to itself till running out of diesel.

It can be seen that our little sister was OK, getting what she had worked for and deserved. John got his aeroplane and they bought a nice brick house in Mt Pleasant, a better class Perth suburb. There was even a 42 foot cruiser, berthed at the Royal Perth Yacht club. They used it to go to Rottnest Island where John had a private mooring at Stark Bay. We spent time there too, a very nice part of this ever more wondrous coast and I think it's a nice place to leave them at this time as we continue.

49

* Myrna, My Youngest Sister *

We did of course receive letters from Mum, vague, not often and from them I never really knew where she was or what she was doing. Being busy as a farmer after just those two weeks at school, it was all 12,000 miles away and really not relative to my new way of life.

By what I can gather from recent talks with Bernard and Myrna, they were soon taken back to Yorkshire and I should have known that from past experiences, Mum always headed back there. From their memories some order takes form of what happened. Bernard thinks he remembers trains going by, he thinks in an orphanage near a railway line but Myrna has no memory of this place. It was not Middlemore in Birmingham, or so they thought. We know that was the staging home for all children going overseas. Both of them say, wherever it was, it was not a nice place. We are to find out they both were in Middlemore in a strange chain of events.

It seems relevant to mention how the lack of a continuous family household, in a community of regular people and with proper parental care, or with the influence of a P&C, 'parent and citizens' membership, or to have teachers who accepted us. This, with the lack of training from regular kindergarten and primary schools as we know them today, would give little hope of our successful absorption into a good social structure. With all this missing, a lack of confidence for most is also affected. Each of us however, being good readers and becoming self educated, were able to bluff our way through to eventually make our mark and catch up with everyone else.

Being involved in my own life which was full and demanding and then not till my return from active war duties in New Guinea and Borneo, did I start to think seriously about what the other children were doing even though we had we kept in touch by writing.

It was the major shock of a lifetime when I heard, hard to believe or comprehend, that our Myrna had been adopted out at age four. It was all over and done with when I heard and too late to do a thing. A man now and though I started it all, I cursed my mother for her bloody stupidity. I couldn't reconcile that she had done such a thing and for reasons only that God knows.

In my mind, even back as we left Treforest, as I realised it, the wisp of a thought was somehow there.

The war had put a stop to children coming out to the farm school but somehow I always took it that Myrna would eventually join us. Many years were to pass before I was able to understand why or forgive Mum, but even when we next met, she never spoke of the time or events leading up to the disaster. Myrna, as it was to turn out, and as I felt, had the worst deal of us all, perhaps not as bad as Doug but that was in many ways self imposed. Myrna lost her own true family for all those important years.

For years we thought she was the lucky one to have a good upbringing, good college schooling and a rich adopted father and mother. It turns out it was a rather unhappy childhood and she was unwittingly rebellious in her maturing years.

It was difficult, she says, trying to be a good daughter and have affection for those who took her in as their own, while missing the brothers and sisters she should have been with. She didn't ever seem to know whether to hate her mother or what, it wasn't till years later she found and got to know her father, and that helped. Both she and Doug suffered the trauma of separation for most of their lives, as these chronicles of events will show.

Our Mum did say she thought the adoption would give Myrna a better chance in life. The girl, who was adopted with her at the same time, would be a sister to her. They both would be brought up as ladies of good standing. Myrna said with a little venom, "What a lot of rot, I just wanted to be with you."

There was a good marriage for Myrna and some happy times. Her husband being a Professor, provided her, the son and three daughters born to her, with a comfortable way of life.

College life with Trevor, he owned the College, in the teaching environment, was not all it seemed to be. His parents were highly involved with the raising of the children and may have caused some friction.

"I love my parents [The adopted ones]," says Myrna, "I love Trevor and the children but my resentment at not being a Rees together with all of you didn't help me to fully accept things and the situation deteriorated."

The meeting with Myrna's girls in 1972 was wonderful, quite strange in one little way, they were grown up by then but knew little or nothing about Myrna's other side. I think it was sort of taboo or not encouraged to be mentioned in their circles. Amelia, had, of her own free will, legally assumed 'Rees' as her middle name. How eerie and strange but that simple event was to enable her in years to come, to emigrate to Australia, using the Rees name instead of Tyler to get back in after being deported from Darwin for working without a work permit. It's another strange passage of events but both Amelia and Angela gravitated to Australia to live.

At that time in '72 when Heather and I were in the U.K., they knew nothing about us and it was an exciting revelation to find there were so many real kinfolk scattered all around.

On that visit, I hadn't notified Myrna of our coming as I couldn't resist the built up of thought and expectation of the reunion. We had our hired car and found our way to Bournemouth, we thought it was Christchurch where they, Myrna and Pat the boy friend, had renovated the old historic building which was the Toll House belonging to Constable, [England's famous painter] and part of his residence. A most perfect part of English scenic and historic magic.

We found the address where Myrna was staying with the mother of the current beau. Simon, her son, was not with them, as it seemed he always stayed protected at the college. It was just Myrna and the three girls there. The marriage had gone sour, she and Trevor, for whatever reasons, had separated and to me it seemed she had copped the short end of the stick and had nothing. Trevor's drinking at the time seemed to have a lot to do with it, in fact later events were to prove alcoholism was the sad and for Myrna a very deprived monetary end result.

In passing, Simon did inherit the college, it and all to do with it dissipated rapidly and our little Myrna, after all that, got nothing.

Any way, we found the place and in trepidation or some such funny feeling, knocked on the door. The old mother answered the door and tersely asked, "Can I help you?" I asked for Myrna. "She's not here." It was not a very friendly start so I told her it was Myrna's brother and his wife from Australia. That caused quite some concern as no one there had heard of us or that part of the family.

A little more helpful, she suggested we call back again when all the family would be home. Deciding there and then, unlike in Australia where there was always room made for visitors, we took off for a nice hotel on the waterfront, to stay the night, shower and freshen up and have good hot meal.

Amelia was the first home that evening, just thirteen years of age but mature and the promising beauty already showing. She was greeted with a, "Your Uncle Derrick and his wife from Australia have been to see you."

Amelia's shocked, "I don't have an Uncle Derrick," said it all. Myrna then arrived with the others and you can just imagine all the explaining that went on. So much to tell, unfold and reveal in a short time.

When Myrna and I met it was … it can't be put into words. She was gorgeous, so little but cuddly as ever. We hugged and kissed till we were able to finally introduce everyone. It was 34 years since we left her in King St and went away rather self-centred on our big adventure. You will just have to try and imagine telling them of so many uncles and aunts, cousins on every side and in places unheard of from here to Australia and even the U.S.A.

So much now came to light, her separation had been difficult, there was a relationship with Pat who owned the Christchurch place but the three girls were hard to accommodate, rear and care for. Pat, I gather, was not too fussy about that part of the relationship. After a life style of comparative good living, brought up not to have to work, Myrna now had to seek employment and fit into a demanding work force. The boy had stayed with grandfather at the college he owned. It was a public school, in England the public schools are private schools. In Australia the schools are what they say they are. Simon was a teacher, hopefully to become a professor and all things being equal, inherit the college.

Simon did get the college and the result from what came to light, he got rid of it for a packet, went into some business or the other, blew it or most of it and that was that. Myrna got practically nothing out of all those years, the girls got peanuts after a bit of pressure and it seemed most of it was a lost cause.

Our Rhondda was with us in '72 and was able to meet Myrna and the cousins. There was a memorable time for us all when grandfather Rees, who we were then staying with in his Shepherds Bush terraced, second floor unit, met us and his grand children. It was a night to remember and the only time that lot got together. More of that later, having found Dad, now with things reconciled and the past forgiven, Dad was a new man and so glad to be back in the fold. The reunion of '72 started a wealth of correspondence between he and every member of the family, to be ongoing to the end.

Myrna was to visit Australia, more of that later and I've told about the girls becoming Aussies.To my knowledge, Betty and Myrna never met except possibly at the time back in Yorkshire after we left and when that awful adoption thing took place. To me, who tried to keep, or get the family back together it is quite weird, incomprehensible in fact, that they both live in England and never made the effort. In Australia, we often go to see Yvonne living in Perth and that's 3,000 miles away. Yvonne and John visit us in Sydney.

I had asked Myrna for her thoughts and memories of the years after we all came to Australia, then just as I completed my first draught, the letter came.

An excerpt is as follows;

"My earliest memory takes me to Goole where I recall sitting on the doorstep dipping rhubarb in sugar on a saucer. It was here I got my head stuck in the palings of a fence at the back of the house, it could be Goole or was it still Wales? I recall the sink where I played with cockroaches. [How strange that those awful creatures were a memorable part of all our lives]. The smell of damp peeling wallpaper, the smell of the settee, which I'm sure, was one of those old chaise lounges. I also remember the big bed, these are memories but fading. [Sounds like Uncle Davy's old sofa and our, all in together bed of so many memories].

The day I left my mother and was put on a train, I had a terrible tantrum. Whoever accompanied me tried to bribe me with a banana. I must have fallen asleep and next remember the excitement of going in a taxi, the big black ones with a little table behind the drivers seat, which I sat on. On arrival at Middlemore, [and there it was, she did go to Middlemore!] and was greeted by Sister Brocklehurst who held out her arms and I ran into them. There are vague memories of the dormitories, the dining room with big chairs and tables, the big white bath, which smelt so clean. [Always a big white bath in the 'Homes' and I pictured her, a tiny babe in those, our dormitories of despair as they were when we just got out in time!

I must have stayed there about six months then all was moved to Wilderhope Manor, a big country house 2 miles from Brockton. I lived there for sometime at the age of four, it was time to go to school. All children of school age were fostered in the villages so they could attend the school at Brockton.

This is where my childhood proper began, having been chosen, [I use this term very loosely], by Aunt Kathie and Uncle Harold and where I stayed until eighteen.

I only discovered about my family by mistake playing in Aunt Kathy's room [absolutely forbidden] while she was away at some village meeting. I discovered a letter searching for me from Doreen, or was it Yvonne? and it was then I was able to write and secretly receive letters, via Aunt Mabel at the post office.

That's the gist of it, the letter and brief remarks spoke volumes of the times I had been trying to discover, there was more to come of course but it answered lots of questions and gives a greater understanding of this little kids trauma. The difficulty to get on with a life of frustration that I'm happy to relate is now resolved.

50

* Douglas, My Brother *

Douglas William was sadly left behind in Yorkshire with Aunt Amelia when he was about 7 years old. For us in Wales the whole set up was very traumatic for him. It made him biased and very bitter in his unrealistic and unforgiving attitude at being unfairly separated from the rest of us. It is difficult now to maintain the correct chain of events that I am trying to recall and relate.

There is a letter from Doug to Doreen and if I include it exactly as it was received it may say something about the times and the end result.

Doreen received the letter after Douglas went back to America. For him then everything went to pieces, resulting in divorce and a complete breakdown of his health. Though he attempted to make a new start time was running out, he was by now unable to cope, both mentally and physically. Inside he was still that same young, energetic and angry man, bitter to the end that he had so little say in the formation of his early days and thus the pattern of his destiny.

The Letter;

> *Dear Doreen,*
>
> *I suppose I should have made the salutation, Doreen and family but then you would have to let anyone who wanted to read it. I think you can tell them whatever you want them to know.*
>
> *I am sorry not to have written sooner, I wrote to Yvonne and telephoned her, she is having a lot of problems, the biggest is perhaps John. I do think she should think of herself for a change, you know there is nothing that will make you ill faster than an emotional trauma. Of that I know of which I speak.*
>
> *I signed myself into the cuckoo's nest a long time ago and once in there I began to realise how much our neighbours and friends can do us in. I really found the people inside the cuckoo's nest were a lot nicer and*

some of them made a lot more sense than everyone on the outside. It was an experience for me and one I will never forget.

I have done a lot of reading on mental problems and also on what the mind and brain can do. Some of it I tossed aside as being useless but in all too many cases I found out that none of us really knows to what extent our mind will go, not only to protect us but to warn us and some times to trick us.

As you know, I have been dead four times, clinically dead, the longest being my heart attack and that was for two and a half minutes.

Each time I had what is known as a veridical hallucination. I saw a picture so clear that it could not be denied, now I have no fear of death and also, I now know that the mind can be manipulated and brought to work for you in many dramatic ways and it is with this knowledge that I tried to make Yvonne listen to me and take care of herself first of all.

I was very upset to hear about Bernard but then I was expecting it.

I know for a fact I am manic-depressive but hopefully I can keep it under fair control. Oh to be sure I do let the lid off now and again and when I do all hell breaks loose.

If you knew our family history you would see there is every reason for all of us to be on the shady side of the street. I have never brought this up as it would upset people and who wants that, my father was one brick short of a load most of his life, he only had one oar in the water and went round in circles most of his life.

Have you ever asked yourself, "Why did Doug have to take care of me so much," and I really did, I had you most of the time and I think you slept in my bed more than you did your own. I can recall oh so plainly how much I love you and needed you. You were the only piece of happiness in my life.

Admittedly mother did go to you later in life and I am happy you two had a good rapport when you found each other but it wasn't always that way and have you wondered why it was at the last, when her time was near, mother recognised me easier than any of you. Perhaps you will argue this point but she and I knew that her time had come and I think in her own way she wanted to go back and change things. I really think she died happy knowing that the next time she came upon this earth she would be a better person.

It has been said that Betty hates me and maybe she does, but then again it is possible that she remembers the past and is trying to be loyal to someone who ruined all our lives, Aunt Athelia as she was called was the fly in the ointment. She was living in the dark ages and we all had to pay for her sorry outlook on life.

I have said it before and say it again. Had we all been together we would have reached the stars or at least we would have reached for them. I know I have thrown away my life and all because of my childhood. It is hard to keep a clear mind when you have so many sorrowful things to remember.

Well at least I shall come back a better man and the next time I will move on for greater things for I truly believe that there is a life ahead for us. There have been too many things happen to me to refute this belief.

Do you remember that night at Derrick's house when I went into a trance to read for Derrick's friends, I had never seen them or Derrick spoken of them but I told them all that came true. I still do this from time to time but now I concentrate more on my own life and what may happen. I still have visions but I all too often waken as the visions are sometimes too upsetting.

When I was little boy I had this awful nightmare, it caused me to walk in my sleep. I would see myself floating up in outer space, I would be lying in a large sewer pipe. It was freezing and all I did was float around in space day after day. Since Ian is into this, ask him about this.

I often think of Kevin, there was a horse over here, Kevin's Delight, I would bet it every time it ran and won a lot of money on it. I always did like Kevin, I know what his problem was and I think he was like me, born fifty years too soon. He does understand this and so can be taken advantage of. Tell him to tell them to kiss his royal backside, go out and do his own thing.

You talk of the troubles our children bring us, no one knows better than I. For example, you know I live by myself right now. I moved away from the woman I was staying with. Well once in a while I visit my children as they are mine and I love them. I visited Le Anne last week and I had Nathan, Cathy's little boy with me. Le Anne's husband was there, Laurie and her two children were there and one of Le Anne's old girl friends. Le Anne asked Sandy, her girl friend if she wanted to stay for dinner as she had too many spare ribs. Sandy agreed to stay.....Now this is my own daughter, she looked right at me when she asked Sandy but did she ask me? Not on your life. I have never been asked to dinner by either Laurie or Le Anne and you know how much I did for them. I fought for them every day of their lives, I pulled headmasters across the table, I made some teachers alter their grades and no one ever dare molest them. I never taught them to be ignorant, for that is the only thing I can say when they completely ignore good taste... I don't have to eat with them, I do not have to be invited but I would never invite someone and not the other. I feel sorry for them. They have so much to learn and I can no longer tell them what it is they need to know.

I talk to Bev now and again but I have to be careful as she has a way of setting me off. She will say something outlandish and so wrong that I blow my top and let off steam

If I were to tell you she is gone and forgotten I would be telling a lie. I lived and loved her twenty five years and you don't chase away time and memories. Perhaps she can forget for perhaps she never did have what she thought was love. I know you can't forget .....sometimes you can't forgive.

You ask about my book, well I put it aside for some time, as I had no heart for it. Then when I went to live with Paula, I found her to be a beautiful person with good thoughts. She was in hospital with me having a nervous breakdown also.

I think I found consolation in having her around and she was so nice I think she wanted to like me more than she knew how.

After a while I got back to writing only it was poetry. I wrote a lot, in fact I have a complete set for publication, all poems by me. So I am writing. Paula was enough to make me want to do this.

She was getting a divorce, a nasty affair. Her husband was a nasty person. He was out to screw her good and she asked me to stand by her which I did but through it all, every once in a while she let it slip out, she still loved him. I told her why she should forget him, her lawyers said the same and tried to show what a scoundrel he was.

We went to court, she begged me to go and hold her hand and be there when she needed me most. In court after talking to her lawyer she came towards me but had to pass her husband. She stopped and smiled at him and fell over him. She started to tell him all she had done and acted like a lovesick schoolgirl,...... I became very angry and called her three times before she came over. I then told her how I had overheard what he had said to his lawyer and how he had instructed his lawyer to get all they could and show no mercy. Then I told her she was acting like a fool and that if she wanted him so bad, then give me the keys to the car and I would leave, he could drive her home.

She was upset and tried to calm me down but I was not to be calmed. She left to go with her lawyer, her husband left with his, all four went to a cafe to talk. She came down, handed me the keys, her lawyer was taking her home and perhaps I should leave as I was upset. I saw her and his lawyers getting in their cars and leaving so I knew where she was and who she was with. She had deliberately lied to me. I felt I had been used for these past months, for I had done all the repairs, I had put in a new *lawn and had pruned and planted and made her house nice again. I repaired all the plumbing and electrical work, in fact I gave her a bill to give to her lawyer to strengthen her case against her husband, it came to over twenty five hundred dollars. I laid into her when she got home and told her she had used me and was a liar and a thief and deserved what she was going to get.*

And so I felt alone and sick at heart for once again I had been used. I needed to be alone and when I was settled down I started to write again. I now have one third of my book written, it is part true and part fiction but it has a lot of family in it. Laurie has read it all so far and she reads a lot, she says it is sure to sell..... so we shall see...that is if I keep going on it.

I am sorry to hear Tony is drawing into his shell, don't let it happen to you Doreen, don't let anyone rule over you, don't let yourself be dragged into the grey world of despair, go out into the sunshine and be warm. I can relate to Denise, she is a beautiful girl and will make some man a wonderful mate, not a wife because wives are passe in this world, what we need is a pal, a mate, some one we can love and enjoy. That is all I ask for but it is too late.

I think as I watch the days slip by that the winter of my life is upon me. I can feel the cold hard days ahead and sooner or later I am going to be covered with a rimey pall and it will be too late to light the fire in the hearth.....it will be too long a wait till Spring and I will have to climb into my sewer pipe, to spin around the earth for all eternity.

The only consolation I can have is that I never once quit, I fought till the last breath and perhaps in the life here after I will find my way into another life, perhaps a better world.

There was a page of trivial ramblings about Cathy and her problems, Doug's thoughts on family, dreams from watching TV and movies and his interpretation of same. Paula, having had similar shock treatment caused him to call her but it was all stupid premonitions. He talks of Myrna the sister he met but once, of Yvonne's John and how he could have straightened him out. Most people, as he said, had only one oar in the water, but to continue;

You know there was Elizabeth, Betty, Derrick, Doreen, Dulcia, Yvonne, Bernard, David, one more boy who was born in Goole and given to the father, a lamplighter, I never did know his name. There were three more, one was adopted by a shipping company owner and I don't think we will ever know who he is so that leaves us with two who are not accounted for. I've tried to dig them up but with no luck. Now I ask you, if you know who they are, how about letting me know.

One thing I would like from you and Derrick, can you relate to me how the four of you got to Australia, when and how, as much as you can remember? Also, if you know, what happened to all of Athelia's stuff? She had money and belongings, a piano worth its weight, such a beautiful piece of furniture. No one wanted to tell me where it all went. Tell me all you can and whatever mother might have told you. I know she was going to tell me the entire story when I was over there....... Then I saw what was going to happen.

It was so eerie, there were so many questions to be answered and once again I hit a dead end. I would like to know it all before I die. I wrote to one of our cousins in London, England and she started to tell me things and then for some reason she stopped writing and I never heard from her again.

I know for a fact our ancestors are Welsh and Scottish, yet none of us know about them or where they are. Only Athelia knew that. Mother knew some of it as she went to live in Scotland for a while, I was born in Edinburgh, in fact I was picked as the most beautiful baby when I was a tiny little thing. I peed all over the new dress of the Mayor's wife.

You've heard the story of how I was lost at the races when my father took me one day. He said it was an accident, I remember what was said, or some of it,.........It was no accident.

If only everything could be told about our past, it would fill several volumes and some of the most amazing things imaginable.

I await the day when I will know who Dr Dooley was and what he meant to us. Why did he turn to drink and lose his license and end up in the poor house, or as we called it, the workhouse. What was his relationship with Athelia. I often caught them in the front room, alone and being very tender with each other. Then again, what did Aunt Athelia do with Morley the man who owned the merry go round at the Fair? There was another deep mystery no one ever talked about.

Doreen, you may not be aware of it but you belong to a family that has more skeletons in the closet than a dozen families, wouldn't you like to hear them all.

This much I will confess to you. From an early age I knew I was different, I felt things and sensed things. I had an uncanny sixth sense. Mother had it and often talked to me about what the two of us knew, yet she would never come out and tell it all............She almost did but too late.

I went out of my way to make life miserable for Athelia, I tried my best to make her become human. I knew she was ashamed of illegitimate children, and I know she didn't like scandal, everything had to be right. I went out of my way to cause a scandal but it was always covered up........ I doubt if anyone to this day knows it was me who painted the fence of the headmaster with fly paper glue just to get revenge for him giving me a caning.

I forged Athelia's signature to get into Naval School and I made Dr Dooley tell me a lot but never all. I think I wasted my life in search of the truth and to get revenge on a woman who messed up all our lives. You may think I'm crazy but I was the only one to listen and find out, with help from you and Derrick, we might get to the bottom of a sad mess.

In the meantime dear sister, try to have a good life, love all who will let you and don't look back but try to put yourself first.

If you think you'll lose you are lost
For out in the world we find,
Success begins with strongest will
It's all in the state of mind.
Life's battles don't always go,
to the strongest and fastest man
for sooner or later the man who wins,
is the man who thinks he can.

I didn't write that but I wish I had. It is true and now since I'm on that kick I want to quote you one more.

Yesterday, this days madness did prepare.
Tomorrows silence, triumph or despair.
Drink, for you know not where you came or why.
Drink, for you know not why you go ...or where.

Did you tackle the trouble that came your way
With a resolute heart and cheerful
Or hide your face from the light of day
With a craven soul and fearful.
Oh troubles a ton, or troubles an ounce
Or a trouble is what you make it.
It isn't a fact that you'r hurt that counts
But only how did you make it.

You are beaten to earth, well, well whats that
Come up with a smiling face
It's nothing against you to fall down flat
But to lie there that's the disgrace.
The harder you're thrown the higher you'll bounce
Be proud of your blackened eye
It isn't the fact that your licked that counts;
It's how did you fight and why.

And though you be done to death what then
If you battled the best you could
If you played your part in the way of men
Why the critic will call it good.
Death comes with it's crawl or comes with it's bounce
But whether he's slow or spry,
It isn't the fact that your dead that counts
But only how did you die.

You know, sometimes we all feel that we have a heavy weight like a millstone around our neck. We alone are not to be pitied for there are others who feel as deeply as we do. We have all read about the savage Indians of America, how ruthless and cruel they were but very few of us ever looked deep enough to see how they thought. This one little verse is taken from an old Iroquois Indian book, oh yes, they could read and write and had their own language........... Think about this.

Oh thous that seest and knows my grief.
Thyself unseen, unknown.
Pity my helpless disbelief,
And take away the stone.

Does that sound like an ignorant savage.... Oh what fools we mortals be, and so I fold my tent and slip away into the shades of night, to dream and perhaps to see or hear, I leave with all my love and affection in the hope your fondest dreams may indeed come true.

As ever,
Douglas,
Your loving brother.

51

* The Letter Continues to the Bitter End *

With reference to Item 11, which you will come to shortly, it is very important for me to point out a bizarre chapter of Doug's life, which was to have such an impact on his future.

He was in the Canadian Police Force at the time. He arrested the Mayor's son for a major felony but due to 'pressure from above' he was forced to release him. From then on the corruption got to him in a 'to hell with them' attitude and became further involved, as Item 11 shows.

The crux of the story was of a very real and genuine threat against his life. He had 48 hours to 'get out of town'.

He headed for the wharves, which he knew so well from his days in the Merchant Marines.

There he met and planned the exchange of passports with another man in a similar need to leave the country. So it was, Douglas William Rees, who wished to get into the U.S.A. and take his chances and a Waldo J. Brayton, hoping to get to England, exchanged identities …. Everything!

From then on, until that letter came from the F.B.I. in L.A., our Douglas William Rees was an 'Alien' in the U.S.A.

Herewith is what was intended as an outline of the book he mentions. Items 1 to 6 are missing and it's a shame to have lost the brief comments about those days but we start with the end of item 7.

Item 7.
Schooling. Escapades, Fatty Thompson, Horse whipping Moody.

Item 8.
Football game, graduation, writing to Naval School. Dooley comes back, now to workhouse, lost license and destitute. Aunt allows him in, he now tells all but I know. I forgive him and swear not to allow myself to be like him.

Norma turns me on, Elsie is upset and while I feel sorry for her I also despise myself for using her as I did. I spent too much time in my bedroom thinking and feeling sorry for myself. I can only see Norma on Saturday nights as I masturbate a lot. Tom and Bob know there is something wrong and I tell them my plans to go to Naval school. They admire me and I'm a hero.

Tippy Gill and the football game, the fight, Aunt Athelia decides I had better go. Dr Dooley had it out with her and it is decided I will go when the new term begins.

Item 9.
First sea voyage. Round the world. Meet with first homosexual, Freddie. Then more travel, Japan and girl dopes me. New Orleans. France and all the girls. Jump ship in Calcutta, food no good and back to sea. Now ready for my papers but my love of sea does not agree with customs of England. I am fast becoming unhappy.

Jump ship in Seattle. On to Canada. Across Canada to join Army. Spent most of my time with Stella in her bordello. She teaches me a lot about women. I go over seas.

Item 10.
Disillusioned by war, all the propaganda. New years in London, girls all over, life on the fast track. Decide to go A.W.O.L. to Canada and we do it.

Brought back, Scotland Yard etc. Detention barracks and fourteen months. Meeting with Goff shortly after discharge.

Sent to intelligence. Most of friends killed out on missions behind enemy lines. Sick and stomach cramps. Will not kill boy. Go to Doctor and am discharged.

Item 11.
Series of shack ups, one girl has a baby, supposed to be mine! Meet Vivian and reservation, several pregnant women. Kicked off reservation. Meet up with Kay who tries to commit suicide. I join police force and meet Rackstraw. Stolen car and I resign, hate the police work and its hypocrisy. Meet up with the safe crackers and earn my ten- percent, as I am now a salesman and a good one.

My new found friends spend thousands of dollars to politicians to get off. C.P.R. railroad yards and Marconi radios.

Inspector tells me forty-eight hours to get out of town. Meet Vivian in Syracuse. Make deal and exchange passports and papers to become Waldo J. Brayton.

Take bus to Syracuse and buy old car. Load up and head for California.

Note;

There is a period in between here and there, later disclosed to me but for whatever reasons, not brought into account but perhaps a most fascinating period in his time.

Item 12.

Con my way into engineers license. Quit this after getting married and go to selling. Instant success. Buy home and start raising family. All is well. Gambling still in the blood, itchy feet, need for women but behave myself. I do con a lot of people. Offered job to run for school board but not registered voter and by now starting to worry about being caught
Meet Dorothy and Clarence.

Item 13.

Really into transcendental meditation etc and try experiments. We do this a lot at beach. Then comes break down and I go nuts. Spend money etc, etc, etc. On security. Wife works as a clerk.

Item 14.

Heart attacks. Operations and time is at a stand still. Our marriage is now on the rocks. Divorce at last. Sell house and split money,............ back together again but won't work. Try up north.

Note;

Though I had read the letter when it arrived so many years ago it passed into dim memory till it again came to light when my current writings were in some semblance of order. So much has come to light to add to or confuse the issue. For instance Doug did live on a reservation with Indians and was revered and respected. However, there it is and it confirms so much, especially what our separation did for he who drew the short straw and got Athelia.
I should add that though an alien in the U.S. for all those years, at the last, wishing to reclaim his true identity, he confessed to the F.B.I. and was given citizenship to enable him to once again become, Douglas William Rees.

52

* Douglas Rediscovered *

As it was in 1972 that we went overseas, it must have been in 1968 that Heather opened the door to find a policeman standing there. He asked, "if there was a Derrick Richard Rees living here? Was he the son of Constance Mary Rees, what was his father's name and had Derrick migrated from Wales?"

To a bemused, "What's it all about," he then told Heather he was making enquiries on behalf of the L.A.P.D., the Los Angeles Police Dept, he could say no more except that we would be contacted later.

What was this all about and who, which family member yet unknown and then the thought, it must be Douglas. Lost to us since we left him on that dismal railway platform, the brief contact while in N.G., seemed a dream I had and I wouldn't have been surprised to have received a, "Killed in action" and then again, who the hell over there knew where I was!

I was intrigued, on coming home, to hear about it but it was several weeks of anxious waiting before we received the long, manilla envelope stamped L.A., U.S.A. Still a mystery because on the back as sender was a Waldo J. Brayton.

It was from brother Doug alright and what a story it was, coming out of the blue after all these years. He first impressed upon us all, he was Waldo Brayton or Scotty. We were never to even mention Douglas Rees at any time and he would explain everything in due course.

Briefly, the gist of the long letter was that he was now living in an outer L.A. suburb, happily married with three daughters. For the last fifteen years he had done many things with success, the most recent as top salesman of California selling Continental or Lincoln cars. The pressure of business, on top of his personal and unusual situation, had brought on a nervous breakdown. Life in the fast, lane selling to and keeping up with movie stars, was all catching up with him.

Whilst resting in bed, the early days, the all going our own ways to God knew where, his thoughts were of an urgent need to find his lost family before it was too late. "The most important thing Derrick," he said, "was don't mention anything about Douglas Rees in your reply."

It seems at this time, his family had not been told about all of us or Doug's past and only after lots of correspondence did he let it all come out. Wasn't it all a shock to them but a relief and a pressure off his mind for Doug, who was now Scotty for a while. The three girls thought it was wonderful to suddenly find there were so many aunties and uncles, cousins by the score as the realisation of it all sank in.

The critical point of all this revelation was of course, Douglas, since his questionable entry into the States, living secured away on the Indian reserve for some time, his spell as a qualified engineer and whatever else, was an 'alien' in America. The 'Sword of Damocles' over his head and that someday, in some way, if he was to sleep at night, he would have to make a clean breast of it all.

Everything to us in Sydney seemed, in a sort of pregnant pause, to indicate action needed. There was also a letter from Dad at Shepherds Bush showing remorse for his past and a desire to see his children, someone, just for a while.
Even Betty, who wrote only once in a blue moon, talked of the missed opportunity she and Herbert had to be in Bathurst, a 'I would love to see you,' sort of letter.
As a result of all this, when all the family got together for a barbie at Bugsy's, we talked it over till Heather and I decided it would be great if we could see Doug and his family, help sort out his dilemma and then go on to England to see Dad, nick up to Aunt Mathews, Goole and Howden to see Betty, visit Wales of course and try to locate long lost Myrna.
What a round of organisation and backward and forward correspondence that caused.
As I have mentioned, we sold our house to get the funds and notified everyone we were coming. The replies by return mail indicated incredible excitement all round, a tingly disbelief that at last so many of us would reunite.

We booked on Pan-Am, packed our bags and left the business for Evan to run, he was fully capable and if disaster struck with builders going bust, we could easily get going again as in the past. Besides all that, this trip was now of more importance.
It was just coincidental that Rhondda's 21st birthday was coming up. I'd love to show her my Rhondda Valley. We were flush with money from the sale of the house and so it was decided she was to come over and join us at Dad's in London. She would visit Doug and Beverly in L.A., have

time with her cousins and for them to show her Disneyland, 'Lost Wages' and the wonders of twenty four hour snacks.

Evan and Robyn were all involved in the kids while at the same time fixing up their new house. Aunty Marge arranged to make the birthday cake for Rhondda to take with her to have with her grandfather or wherever we were on the day. It was in the Aussie colours, green and gold and as it had to get carted half across the world, Evan made a neat wooden frame so not even an icing rosebud was hurt or damaged.
You will just have to picture the scene at L.A. International Airport when customs wanted to cut and inspect it. Rhon cried, ranted and raved, "my Auntie Marge made that to have with my grandad who I've never seen." The actress in her coming out and she was told to stick it back in the bag. She carried it in as hand luggage, and they were glad to see her out of there.

As the first of our group to go off on an extended holiday jaunt, it was a novelty so the farewell at Mascot in the Kingsford Smith room was a riot for the 60 or more family and friends sharing the start of the voyage of re-discovery. The Jumbo 747 travel was so new as was the pleasant day and night in Honolulu before taking off late at night for Los Angeles. Sleep was impossible, not just because of the plane but, with a racing mind and thoughts of the meeting to come after almost 42 years, it was just close the eyes and let it happen.
Arriving at 6 a.m., having gone through customs in Honolulu, we went out through the gate.
Would we know each other, how much true feeling after so long a time, the time he waved the train goodbye in anger? It was almost too much to handle as we hugged and kissed each other. The start of all this says, "Big boys don't cry." Well big men do and it set them all off as the three girls must have wondered what this was all about.

We calmed down and introductions were made, and we met Beverly, Leanne, Laurie and Kathy. On the long trip home to the foot of the California hills it was non-stop talk with so much to cover in two short weeks. The girls had time off from school and were not going to miss a thing.
We took time to unpack the typical Roo and Opal presents from Australia as we talked over coffee till almost 11 a.m. Heather and I thought we were never going to eat or be fed till Scotty, [As he was to be now,] said, "Let's go for breakfast."

It was our first taste of the American way of life where they all seem to go out for breakfast and what a breakfast! It's old hat now and you've all done it, but then it was new, the feast, ice water first and then flap jacks, bacon and eggs, toast and coffee till you can take no more, and for just, 80 cents, Wow!

We actually only ate breakfast at home once in the whole time we were there. It was fun too in pre-diet days.

There was time to talk of Doug leaving Aunt Mathews when just sixteen, about his time in the merchant navy and then the Canadian army. That was the time of Doris who sent the parcels to me in N.G. I twigged that the subject was a bit taboo, the family not knowing much about that part of his life. There was a young lady who called on him once in L.A, they met and she left. It is part of the closed book which is Doris's story, the lady was the little girl. Whether his or not, they had split up and from what I heard, she became a lady of the night, later to die of consumption. Quite sad in a way because she was so nice to me in her writing.

As I read this back it sounds like a made up tearjerker but it's really so true.

As they say, stranger than fiction.

But away from all that, Doug and Bev gave us the most enjoyable and hectic two weeks of our lives. Besides the regular tourist things such as Disneyland, Hollywood and Chinatown etc, we went to Capistrano to see the swallows come back as in the song and right on time on the 27th March, as it is every year.

We did the trip to San Diego and across the border into Mexico where Doug waited this side of the border gates, he informed us that if he went in, he would not get out for years if ever and that's another little story.

They gave us parties to meet their friends, fabulous times, 60 people at a time all talking and asking questions in the fascination of this mysterious brother and beautiful wife from Australia. They were all such nice people but most were married two or three times, every body wanted to knock everybody off and both Heather and I were propositioned to nick out to the campervan for a bit on the side. We gracefully declined.

The big question asked, was why did Scotty and I have different names and they accepted the story of my having to leave Wales in a hurry, the "Wink wink, nudge nudge," made it sound mysterious and satisfied their curiosity. Little did they know of Scotty, who was not Waldo but Doug!

Living as an alien in the States was an on going problem, it meant keeping one step ahead of events all the time. Doug could only go so far in public office or as chairman of the P&C or other groups before he had to resign or answer difficult questions. His friends, in all sincerity said he could have been Governor with his brilliancy and enormous ego but always he moved on. That in itself, with the frustration of not being able to pursue the challenge, would and did add to the breakdown.

He really did have that salesman of the year trophy he boasted about and lots of others too. Mrs Meyer, of the M.G.M. Meyer's, called him her Scotty. She loved his Scot, Welsh, Canadian, cute American accent and bought a new Lincoln every year off him.

The F.B.I. were by all accounts now interested, all these years he had it in his mind a simple inquiry could lead to him being deported back to England where there was nothing for him.

I wonder in the ramifications of it all, the Waldo wanting to be Doug again, if there is a Douglas Rees in the old country trying to get back to being to being a Waldo again?

Part of our visit to California was taken up with a trip, by way of the desert we had seen on film, to Las Vegas, the gambling capital of the world. It was here we saw the side or ghost of Scotty the gambler. We went into Caesars Palace, the Riviera and most of the Casinos but, when we were going into the Golden Horseshoe, Doug backed off saying he was not allowed in there. Beverly told us the story, "He's not allowed in there," she said, "I haven't finished paying them off."

In earlier times he had gone on a gambling spree and blown everything, house, the car, the lot. Bev also told us she didn't know why she put up with him but they had both worked and she had paid off most of the debts. Vegas was off limits unless she was there with him but then, just for fun, she gave him $20 to shoot craps so we could see the performer in action. In no time with his blowing on the dice, shouting out the crap shooting mumbo jumbo none of us understood till the crowd was six folk deep and he on a winning streak.

In his usual dumb form, he wouldn't take out a percentage, in his moment of crowd acclamation, he bet the lot on double or nothing. You guessed it, he blew the lot but it was a sight I wished my Dad or Bugsy could have seen.

Such a pity he and Dad never made it together, both being punters and race enthusiasts. Doug took us to Santa Anita racetrack where we sat in a friend's private box. It was more interesting than the actual races with the recognisable folk of the movie world all around. Santa Anita isn't a patch on our Randwick or Rosehill on Guineas day and Johnny Tapp, or any of our race callers, will leave theirs for dead.

As the holiday in L.A. was coming to an end we resolved the main question. It was Doug and the family's decision to now approach the authorities and make a clean breast of his affairs, that way hopefully, he could claim citizenship so that those future overseas visits could be possible. It was visibly a great relief to now look forward to resuming his true identity and to live a normal life without that fear of deportation.

When we boarded the Greyhound bus, it was a sad but happy 'Au Revoir', sad to be leaving but happy having had the time together. It was such a milestone in our lives.

The next two weeks by Greyhound would make a great travelogue in where we went and in what we saw but I promise not to bore you with it, suffice to say, we did El Paso, Texas and down the old Spanish trail, zig zagging down to New Orleans with its Bourbon St and Jazz out of this world. We took in Memphis, St Louis and Chicago, all the places to Washington and then New York. In New York we stayed in the most 'Posh' Essex House overlooking Central Park with all the cute little squirrels, among other weird and wonderful, decrepit, mind boggling and less than cute things! Courtesy of Pan Am and as their customers, we got a $44 suite for $22 so we could afford to go to Sardi's for drinks and to 42nd St to the theatre. We took in all the tourist bits, even up the Statue of Liberty.

It was great to be there, to see it all but we were ready and anxious to now be off, to get to London for whatever awaited us.

The trip to Kennedy airport with a New York taxi driver in peak hour, was an experience to forget and then the bomb scare with all the Fuzz in riot type gear every which way. Then to make it all worth while, there was a full body search, mine was by a gum chewing but terrific looking dark lady, who checked out my every nook and cranny. It's a dumb thought, but she would have made a good and rather interesting short arm inspection doctor.

There was a thirteen plane stack or queue up and we waited but we finally and wearily got off. Heather had her own tale to tell, she was searched just as thoroughly by an eager and handsome male.

53

* My Mother's Story *

Mum's arrival in Perth in 1955 was heralded by an article in the Women's Weekly that claimed she had 13 children. For we six, as we thought, that was interesting. We know Connie was a peoples person and preferred singing and playing the piano at Butlin's Holiday Camps to rearing her once 'bootiful babies'. Her forte was reading people, which she did quite well with her tea leaf or crystal ball readings. Believe it or not she was brilliant and in great demand at tea parties or lunches as all in and around Beecroft were to find out before Connie was finished with us all. Doug, as we also found out, was even more psychic and with his flamboyance and intriguing accent as he read cups, head bumps, palms or whatever, was always a party winner.

Mum was always tight lipped about the Aunt Mathews relationship, her start with her Will was not too promising but we cannot deny the fortitude in her getting us back from London or her pram pushing days around Treforest. The blackberry selling door to door in a place she didn't want to be recognised, all the little things which perhaps only I remember, might balance out other bad decisions. Not neglect, I suppose, but often taking the easy way out when it all got too much and a bit of freedom was so enticing after years trying to survive in her unprepared early life style. The Myrna adoption bit did not balance out.

Mum did put in my mind, coal mining as such was definitely out. Dad at Clydach Vale was enough for her and things worked out that the pit was not for me.

We never got much out of her about her youth and her parents and origin, never mentioned how she left Doug with our aunt and nothing of Betty or the then unknown of Eileen's beginnings. That took years, and worst of all she never came out and told her side of leaving Wales with Bernard and Myrna or the involved times after that. It was Doreen who first found out about the twins born and gone! In that time it came out about the boy in Yorkshire, not Dad's child, we will call him David and he too was adopted out.

It is relevant and I may miss it in my developing confusion of events so I will tell it as it was. When Heather and I did our 1989 trip, Doreen insisted I try and locate him, our supposed brother, and dragging information from our sister Betty, we found a lead. I eliminated names and located the adopted parents and had a long conversation with a lady who disclosed David was happily married with a family. She implied it was unfair to chance an upset as he knew nothing of all this.

For me, with family so vital, knowing in my heart he should know of the vast family available to him from my experience by that time, I spent a sleepless and decision making time having told the lady I would ring again. Heather and Betty convinced me to let sleeping dogs lie, against my inner desire so I rang back to tell her that I, being the only one to really know, would go back to Australia and she need worry no more. I cry now as I did then at the finality when she simply said, "Thank you and God bless you."

But that's not the end of it because there is another visit back to the old country in 1993 and a time when Heather and I with Doreen, Yvonne and Bugsy were heading for Hull to visit Betty and her family. We stayed the night at Cleethorps on the Humber before heading to Grimsby and the recurring decision time. I stopped the van and explained that our David was right here and went through the ins and outs of it all. Make your decision and for awhile the silence was so deafening I gave up, started the motor and drove off.

At Betty's we told her what we had done, about the shop where we had stood outside, the man serving at the counter, it was probably 'The' shop and the man our David, but that was that. Another Amen.

We won't go into the unanswered question of who dobbed Doug in to the service police when he came to visit them during the war, was it Mum or sister Betty doing what they thought was right but which landed him in the lock-up for all those months before he escaped and went back to Canada.

Doreen, hearing of my writings, told me Mum confessed she was the one. Doreen's comments were interesting as she worked with Mum in later years, what a funny chain of events and was the one to know her best, or at least reasonably well. She reminds me that for all the past, Mum worked seven days a week till quite late in life and then worked for nothing till she died. Doreen says she had a preference for Dad but felt Mum did more for us in the rotten life in early days. It is so interesting to hear each child's so different thought on the family and times. Doreen did say that Mum was a very intelligent person, a talent wasted in misdirection of weird times.

Others appreciated our Mum's attributes more than we did, an example being when she died, at Shore School in North Sydney, the flag was flown at half mast for her, something unthought of before for just kitchen staff.

From the time she came over from Perth, until she died having spent a lifetime at the school. It was the best time of her getting to know us all as we visited her there, children and grandchildren, each of us visited without interfering with her way of life. She was now always happy in her airy-fairy way of life but found time very occasionally to visit our home. 'God', I thought the first time she turned up, it was the vision revisited. The coat, paisley scarf and Queen mother hat and gloves. Ghosts of old times and how she had once looked in the fur coat she hocked to get us back to Goole.

I should say everyone she gathered as friends and acquaintances knew nothing of what had gone before. I don't think Myrna ever came back to a fully resolved love for her Mum. Doug, we found, was desperate for the love he missed so badly and for Doreen it was rekindled through them being together in later years. Yvonne, who loved everyone, always loved her while I did too, though there were times! We all did in fact, at the end, love our Mum. Bugsy's Patsy never got close and those on the perimeter of all the events never understood her letting some of the children go.

Heather, the practical thinker, reminds us that Mum never had a family Xmas with any of us. For whatever reason, she preferred to go to Tumut with friend Joan for her holiday break in the festive season.

The Boarders, boys at Shore where she worked as a live-in maid, all loved her. Like my Dad, she was wonderful with other people's children and I, through personal experience, appreciate how those boys must have felt about her love and attention.

It was Joan, her live in companion with the relations at Tumut, who took Mum with the chance to see a little of our Snowy Mountains, Australia having more snow fields than Switzerland itself. Joan and Mum were snug in an almost rent free flat, a place I later found that Bugsy, in times of unsettled or problem times, went for a little overdue motherly solace.

I'd forgotten that Doreen worked there with Mum every Sunday and gave them both a chance to catch up on lost love.

As a bit of relief or a sideline of events, it's worth a mention that fickle finger of fate thing as when Tony Powell, that pesky neighbour who wrote the best seller joke book, 'Lighten up'. We talked over the fence and the usual questions cropped up, where do you come from, how did that happen, all that repetitious stuff you all know by now so, I gave him the draft to read and each day he'd chat over a section. Then one day, almost at the end as I am now, [Hopefully you may say,] he came rushing out with the amazing revelation! "Your Mum fed me." She did too as the Connie he knew while a boarder from Yass, in his many years at Shore. Tony was loud in praise of Connie's mothering and care for little boarder boys in need of a little T.L.C. Tony said Mum dished out extras if you were still hungry and went up but if Joan was there, just turn round and go back.

It's a long way from that other Mrs Rees in No.6 cottage, Cottage homes but I understood the situation and the occasional feed or barbie Tony now puts on for us is in token appreciation of Mum's care.

My Mum, Connie

Mum, in full regalia, outside the old Headmasters residence at
Shore School, North Sydney.

54

* My Dad *

We know he was William Richard, born third of Mam Rees' thirteen at Riverview in the heart of the old Rhondda. Except for the two Garfields that came to light with the family Bible, the brood were reared in the narrow two storey section of the little terrace. Who of them, Mam, Dadchi and all would have dreamed that every single colliery one day would be closed down, the last to become a Heritage park, or that trees and bushes would be growing in the drab depressing landscape turning it from black to green of regrowth and hope.

There was no plumbing in Riverview till in '72 when Aunty Doris had an inside bathroom installed, it included the inside W.C., the first in the street and a time for celebration. The Loo was always, 'out er back', cold and not even fit for red back spiders or blue tongue lizards like ours.

Uncle David sent me a book in later years after we met in 1972, it was 'Rhondda revisited.' In it were photos of Dunreavan St. about the time of the riots of 1910-11. In it is one he had marked with my Dad as a boy dressed in the not too mix and match dress of the time, it was about where Ebenezer Chapel stands. Not too many nice suits from that, 'Watson the Flannel' of Pandy Square. There was no money for food in those desperate twelve months let alone clothes.

Will, as we know, was the wild one, a bit of a black sheep. At Clydach Vale he handed in his lamp check to do all that moving around till he became a carpenter, his brother David left Aunty Elsie in Dorset to rear their kids while he did a career in the navy. It was there he met Lord Selkirk who was to become Lord of the Admiralty, he owned a large estate in Dorset where in '72 we were to meet them for the first time. Dai and Elsie were caretaking the estate and its many, many dogs, sent back there as poor strays collected by Lady Selkirk from every port of call.

During the war, Uncle David, [Dai], had a ship blown from under him, then while on the Queen Elizabeth in 1931, he received the letter from his Mam saying his Dad had passed away, a sad day and leave from somewhere in the Mediterranean was impossible so, he missed the family funeral.

Uncle Arthur, who I don't recall, finished up a staff sergeant in the Army and Stan went off to somewhere unknown to me. They all left home to do quite well, it was history repeating itself when at thirteen I too set out to make my fortune.

In Dad's case there had been the Yorkshire Aunt Mathews times saga, other bits in between and the cottage homes forgett-a-billia. Perhaps at Tonteg it was the best time for us as a family before King St with Uncle Davy and Aunty Gwen before he took off before the war to take up residence at 125 Conningham Rd, where he was to live out his almost 80 years.

It was there, the same 'Shepherds Bush' of that comedy show, 'Steptoe and Son' that he became known as one of its characters. I have Wilfred Brambles' [Steptoes] autograph, signed, 'To best mate Taffy.' There's also one on a photo to him from Alf Garnet, also of that era. Dad apparently worked with all the stars till he went into his shell on retirement.

It was never dull out the 'Bush' way, the markets and spruikers etc but outer London changed with the invasion of the Pakistanis and West Indians, all with huge families living all around. No.125 became the home of hordes of coffee coloured kids. Ever the same with all kids, always with sweets and biscuits, they all loved him and called him Pop, he was an easy touch, good for a helping hand being a carpenter, had tools could travel and was great as a social and legal adviser to those folk with little legible English.

By 1948, and this all came out much later, Dad had taken a lady as his common law wife, marriage details are vague. Olive Davies bore him a daughter Patricia, [Just call me Pat], who as you may gather he doted on, a little to the others rather unshown and, sorry to have missed out on, envy. On his return from the film making of Christopher Columbus in the Carribean, his son Lloyd was born, a nice pigeon pair. These are the brother and sister so vaguely the whispers were about but who we were to discover were very real on the 1993, mass return, back to Britain trip by about 90 old Northcotians.

It had been so gratifying over all the years to gather in the clan, tie up loose ends, so when we met Pat and family, Lloyd and family, it gave extra strength to the clan to have the three new Rees males. It came as a surprise, when Lloyd got over the impact of having and accepting these new relations, he casually told us of his earlier marriage, then of his two sons about twenty at the time. It was great but the bonus was that only last year, 1998, on a surprise visit, we met a new Mrs Rees, an expectant one and by the time we got home there was another Rees. Further to that, the other son was soon to be married giving us one more Mrs Rees. That, with the most gorgeous bride our grandson Ben had just married made this 75 year old Taffy pretty pleased with the way things were going now.

On our 1989 trip, in Wales and Swansea just down the road, we could have sorted it all out, if we had known, but it had to wait. Out of the blue and like a miracle, Dad's diaries, thought to be lost, turned up with photos and such. A cousin Peter in Hayes, Middlesex of all places, had them, he took them to Tonypandy to Mick and Angela's. They, after our sales pitch on our New South Wales, were, on our return home, to arrive for a month. They brought a token selection of the diaries with them, also lots of photos and letters to create such interest and revelation. The diaries were in about 10 inch by 15 inch hardcover ledgers, from 1955 to 1979, the last entry being just before he died.

It was from these we confirmed the Olive Davies and new half brother and sister part of the story.

The early years up to 1955 were lost or wilfully destroyed, he seemed to want to keep those times to himself. Even in 72 when we stayed with him in the midst of the Bush's amazing mix of folk and coffee-coloured kids, he was a closed book. Like our Mum, for whatever reasons, they were tight as clams about the past. Lloyd had, and still has to a lesser degree, a complex about his and our Dad that could have been eased with more communication.

Will or Taffy, as he was known by friends and all the stars and film folk was to lead a most interesting life as a carpenter or affects man in that Pinewood, Gainsborough and Rank organisation film studio era. He did many small bit parts, he had personally signed photos and letters from the stars of the era. The Beatles were just starting, he made the first film with them and Ringo, whose signed photo I have of he and Dad, were special mates and the others who chatted between takes all called him Pop.

Alan Ladd was his close friend. There's a signed photo of them too but being Welsh, Dad's best friends were Valley or nearby folk such as Stanley Baker, Harry Secombe and Shirley Bassey. Richard Burton and Anthony Hopkins were boys from down his way too.

The industry and its passing parade seemed to make up for missing the events of his own children's lives.

In great demand by directors and producers, a highlight was Rank's 'Christopher Columbus' for Gainsborough. It meant an extended trip to South America and I have a snap of him in native chiefs dress taking a bit part.

The diary of the whole trip and he was big on diaries, was most extensive and came into my hands together with the other collection. It was most gratifying to me, as it will be to the others, especially to young Lloyd who had little time to know his Dad. We all somehow felt let down with his shortcomings but saw him in a new light with the capabilities of the worker he was. Inherently, with 1910 strikes in his blood, he was shop steward in a position of authority and it seemed, respect. At the end of this story, should there be such a thing, I will try and annex some of that diary, there's good stuff in it.

We watched the old 'African Queen' picture the other night with friends, there was Humphrey Bogart and Katherine Hepburn in the boat, in the swamp, rocking about in the storm. It was my Dad in the water out of sight, the one who was rocking the boat. I have a signed photograph of Katherine, which is inscribed, 'To Taffy'.

Dad's sisters kept an eye on him and his goings on, loaned him a fiver when he was short and in return received gifts galore on the occasion he visited flush with overtime money or a win on the Gee Gee's.

He and Uncle David, as we then found out, had had a misunderstanding, one way and another, it was thirty years ago. It was mentioned on the '72 visit and I told him what a silly old goat he was. With a funny cold feeling up the back of my neck. I realise now, why in the last letter to me before he died, he had signed it, 'Bill, the silly old goat.' Still with some apparent regrets, he must have remembered my saying it at that time in 1972.

It was a stupid nonsense so with some directions, Heather and I immediately got in the car and drove to Dorset to locate Selkirk Manor where Elsie and David were caretaking while the Selkirks were overseas. The Manor was doggy from Lady Selkirk's collecting, Elsie being a doggy Dorset lady herself and David and Selkirk being long-term buddies, it was a fine arrangement.

Neither of us could recall meeting in Pandy but it was 1930 something, if and when!

Meeting was a joy, he was so pleased to meet Will's boy, an unexpected pleasure with time running out. Our stay was wonderful, meeting Elsie was to have an undreamed of extension of visiting in years ahead.

David promised to go and meet his brother which he did promptly, a reunion that was lasting till the end so the whole exercise was worth while.

David, after a lifetime of naval service, was a stick in the mud. Aunty Elsie, born around Dorset and as far as I know had been nowhere, was different. We suggested on one visit that she come to see us. Only home a few days, the message came, 'arriving in a month's time'. Aged 78, on her own, first time for everything and there she was, her unmentioned Angina and all.

Elsie stayed a month, she says it was the best time in her whole life, life on the Central Coast with us at Copacabana was magic. We did it all, the Blue Mountains and Bathurst where she cried to think they almost made it there so long ago. Aunty Elsie, a true Dorset lady, met all the family, they had been names only before but as she now says, very dear ones to me. Wasn't that nice?

Back to Dad who had never met any of his grandchildren till in '72 when Rhondda came over with us as part of her 21st birthday present, a time she visited and met family all over England and Wales. It was a memorable and joyful meeting, tears and unbreakable hugs, he just couldn't believe this beautiful young woman, named after the valley of his birth, really belonged to him.

Every room in his house was as immaculate and clean as a man's could be for our visit, over tea and biscuits. We talked into the wee hours of the night. There were so many photos we had brought with us to go through and explain who each one was and belonging to who. This meeting and others to follow started him writing to each and everyone, bridging that long void, seeing and knowing that we were doing so well in Australia. Most importantly that the past he had fretted over, was gone and forgotten. From all the stories that came out, he thought we were all incredibly rich out there.

Having always had to care for himself, his clothes and linen were better than most and even by the few times he turned up in the valley to cook a roast dinner for us, we knew he could cook. The big thing missing in that and most council houses, was a bath so Dad would toddle off once or, twice a week in summer to the council baths down the street. In between times it was a dishpan in front of the gas heater. While there for a few months we made a point of staying at a B&B or pub every few nights. It's hard to believe but it was only twenty two shillings a night then.

He pondered over the photos of our many houses and we alone had built and owned a few. The bungalows he called some, or the four bedroom, two bathroom cottages with all amenities and two or more cars, in the garages too and not on the street like in half of England. The lack of class distinction, so strong in England amazed him and when we talked of Masonry he couldn't believe that I, his son, had been through the chair as Master of a Masonic lodge. "Good God," he said, an exclamation he uttered often.

When we arrived at Conningham Road by taxi from Heathrow, we were met by a wiry grey haired man, so excited I thought he would have a heart attack. As fit as a fiddle, he ran down the stairs to hug and kiss us. He thought my Heather was so beautiful, frighteningly so and not knowing what she would think of him but they got on real champion.

.The table was set with everything, he not knowing our want and we talked till about 10 in the morning when we just had to have a sleep to catch up. We had just had two frenetic weeks in Los Angeles with Doug and family and then two weeks across America by Greyhound bus, on and off as we wished, to the Big Apple as New Yorkers liked to call it. It was four days there as tourists before, in the movie like, hair raising taxi ride to Kennedy Airport to get a plane out of there! There was a real highjacking in progress and my first full body search by a gum chewing, dark skinned lady cop. All that and a thirteen plane bank up had been a bit much.

The dear old fellow, had the seldom used front room all spotless, two single beds made up with fresh linen he had earned from collecting green stamps. "I didn't know if you slept together." he said. We certainly did and pulled them together to make a double. There were blankets, plenty of them, but it was the end of winter and freezing and it was only when we put on pants and woolly socks, put our Kangaroo skin coats over our feet that we could get to sleep.

And sleep we did. Tea that evening had been prepared but on his spot checks, no sign of movement from us as he smoked and watched a night of TV. A breakfast was ready and not needed and then a lunch. How horrible for him, all that wasted effort, because it was evening before we surfaced and came to life.

Each morning he would be up early like a miner did, spring will be here soon and England will be beautiful, he would say. Spring that year in actual fact was a disaster, hardly any sun to bring out the flowers, such a shame as I had boasted how spectacular they were along the embankment of the Thames. London in a real Spring could be breathtaking with its history all around but in the five months in and out of Britain we had only one fine day that year and it was in Edinburgh watching the Highland dancers in Princess St as they entertained the Saturday crowd.

Rhondda didn't arrive till a month after us, she had been to stay with her Uncle Doug, 'Scotty' and Aunty Beverly and to get acquainted with her three cousins. Her flight to the U.K. was delayed and Dad had to wait. There was a wasted trip to Heathrow, where we found her flight had been diverted. Quite an experience Rhondda said, being over the pole with a stop at Anchorage in Alaska. A rather tired and ruffled Rhondda emerged from the terminal to meet her grandfather.

Back at 'Shepherds Bush' he rushed her round to show her off to all the neighbours. I could only watch and wonder at this proud and happy man who was such a fool in a way.

He had a reluctance to use the phone and never rang. We had explained how to call and reverse the charges, so simple but he never did. He was a stick in the mud for never going to David in Dorset, only to his Valley on special occasions.

We took him with us in a car, a thing he never owned or even drove, to see all the tourists things he'd never done, plus Nelson's Column, down the Mall to Buckingham Palace and all that stuff and a lovely trip to 'Her' house at Windsor, with the beautiful gardens of that almost Spring. There was a nostalgic look at Australia House where I explained our visit there to another, "Good God", neither of us knowing in 1938 that he was a stones throw away and not knowing we had gone.

We drove with his instruction to try to find our house from where we left on that big walk with the pram, but all we came up with were 747's taking off, it had all gone to be part of the airport.

A most memorable occasion, very new and a bit posh for us all was a great night out as the result of Rhondda's trip from Australia. Like all the Rees women, they go to tears easily, so at her family farewell and the leaving of the current boyfriend she cried her eyes out on the plane, the nice gentleman sitting next to her thought she had lost a loved one and proceeded to console her. It filled in time and he was fascinated when she told him where she was going, then all the on going family affair and its doings.

He turned out to be Ex-Grenadier guards and was on the board of Lloyds of London. Becoming good friends he insisted that when she was in London, she ring him and as he put it, "Have a spot of lunch."

Rhon did ring him for a good long chat and it was then he said he would like to meet us all, so why not come for morning tea and if we wished, he would give us a tour of Lloyds and its intricate workings.

It turned out to be one of the most interesting days of our visit to Britain, Lloyds, as we all know is the heart centre of the whole worlds shipping insurance. Started before his time, Lord Horatio Nelson had so much to do with its early days, he made it famous in his Armada. The letter, so famous in history hangs in its very special place of honour, the letter we all remember with its, "England expects" message which saved the Royal Navy and England. It was explained to us that every item of insurance business that took place anywhere in the world would be recorded and finalised here at Lloyds before the close of day. We were shown the famous 'Lutine bell', which rang whenever a craft or ship was lost at sea. Can you just imagine the pandemonium during those war years?

Morning tea was served to us on the most elegant silver service as we sat in his office, it and the whole spread was something out of the movies. His office overlooked the business area spread below, about the size of Concord Rugby Park and with all the very pukka, English type businessmen and waiters. The clerks are traditionally called waiters.

The enthusiasm of we mere Colonials and the appreciation of it all against the stuffy circle he was used to, prompted him to suggest another meeting, something special in fact. As an ex guard, he was privileged to take guests to witness the 'Ceremony of the Keys'. This took place each evening in the Tower of London, a most impressive ceremony few got to see, it had so much great tradition and historic significance.

It was a great idea but unfortunately we had arranged for sister Myrna and the girls to come from Bournemouth to London for a too long delayed meeting with Dad. We were all to go out for dinner etc. Being the complete English gentleman and mine host, rather enjoying our outgoing attitude I thought, he said, "Bring them all along." I was embarrassed just the same at the number that fronted up, all of us do-dahed up and just as well as he took us to his private club, 'Rules', where he usually dined and where the nine of us caused a stir and many a raised eyebrow.

The meal was excellent from a menu of which Dad had never seen the like, the prices left him gob stopped for a week and never having got over the, tip your hat, 'yes sir, no sir, threebags full' of a worker, he was amazed that we, his children, took it all in as normal.

After our 9 p.m. visit to the Tower, we loaded into taxis and were taken to the Savoy where Dad with his, "Good God", thought it was all so very posh. It was a memorable night for him with some of his family, all he could say was, "What would the folk in Tonypandy think of me now?"

There was time together at Conningham Rd. to talk about people, the man Rhondda met, the mixed bag moving to Australia and the people moving from every corner of the old Commonwealth with passport entitlement to live in Mother England. There were so many coloured folk around us, 48 in the house next door and God knows how many paying a rental to live in the mile of continuous roof space. Dad said he got on well with them, they did like him but as he said, "I spend half my pension on biscuits and fruit for the children," but then as he thought about it all, "What is happening to poor old England?"

Was he thinking about our visit, the apparent affluence with tales of life back home in Aussie, really thinking of the past and possibly his shortcomings.

After Rhondda arrived, we had hired our car from the usual place at Marble Arch and it was time for the momentous visit back to Wales. Dad jumped at the idea of coming with us, it would be like the two prodigal sons returning. Heather is the better navigator, so I drove and Rhondda and Dad sat in the back taking in the countryside, coming into bud and bloom at last. The Rhododendrons, growing like weeds all through Stains were just incredible, Heather and Rhondda, like most visitors, had preconceived ideas of England or all Britain being coast to coast houses and industry but in the weak struggling sun it was not so, just a perfect picture.

55

* Back to Wales *

We all felt like singing, "Oh to be in England , tra la la," and all that spring time stuff and were just beginning to enjoy the trip when, so soon, we were crossing the border into Wales. It's strange that expatriates, whether Irish, Welsh or Italian, are so proud of their country, it may have done nothing except be the place of birth but, coming home had that intangible something special.

We had stopped for lunch at a Red Lion pub, [We found there was a Red or Black Lion pub in every town or village,] and it was very busy as we found a table and chatted over what to have. All the locals took us in as Americans and I ordered drinks from the half interested barman, I paid and said, "Diolch yn faur i chwi," which is of course, Welsh for thank you. With a good laugh he told them all, "Bloody hell!, a Welsh speaking Yank."

Dad soon let everyone know we were the Rees' from Pandy way and in the course of the lunch embarrassed us, telling them half of our life's history. It was good fun and the service improved no end.

We didn't go into Cardiff, just by-passed it in our hurry, it was 35 years since Porky Harding, Rex and I left to go to Middlemore, such memories but we'd see Cardiff later.

On up through the valley, through towns and villages strange to me as just names on the map, no one owned cars back then and travel was by train or as we say in the bush, 'Shanks' pony', on foot. When we came unexpectedly on the gates of the homes at Church Village, there were feelings too hard to express. You know about our two visits there, now a seemingly deserted place, empty cottages and run down buildings. As we drove round, Heather, as Doreen had once said, voiced her thoughts, "What a bloody awful place."

How the distances had shrunk and we were past the sweet shop and where the Beech trees should have been, we knew our terrace had gone and so was the fish shop and before we knew it we were through Treforest. It didn't matter, it would have taken too much time to stop there and take in the nostalgia of it all. Do that later when we calmed down a bit.

At Pontypridd I thought they were spoiling it all with buildings, new roads and a round-about, the park and the icy swimming pool across the Taff River was hard to see. The river itself, all along the banks was a rubbish dump with the pollution of plastic and take-aways more evident all the time.

Out under the little bridge, I found my way out of town and heading for Tonypandy, the landscape was improved and the slag heaps less dark and dismal. The eyesore of derelict and rusty machinery had partly gone and the buildings after a century of depression and neglect were partly in repair. There were new and modern shopping centres popping up along the straggly way but out of place, I thought, in this world of pitheads and terraced houses.

After a while, a silent looking and thoughtful thinking while, we caught sight of my Valley and still smoky and grey Pandy. Rhondda said, "Is this what I was named after?" No, not really as it was then but as it was 150 years ago and would again return to even in my time.

Aunty Doris and Beryl were so happy to see Will, undreamt it was possible to be there with his son, his son's wife and their daughter. There were so many cousins and relations to welcome us to the No.6 of Mam Rees' days and now also the No.7 next door. The river Rhondda flowed right out the front and across on the hillside, a sight never before seen by me, greenery and the promise of berries and regrowth of Heather. My Heather and my Rhondda! I thought, what an incredible hand the fickle finger of fate chose to play.

Someone was kicked out to make room for us, Rhon and Heather couldn't believe how they all fitted in when all the family was home. As I pointed out, the whole Rees clan lived here even with the front room excluded. They saw it all at its best and as never before with the alterations, indoor bath and W.C. just completed.

Dad, proud as a peacock, took us around to meet those of his old fogies still around. He pointed out places of his boyhood, where the biscuit factory and the gym was, over the hill to where his pit at Clydach Vale was, passed my shitty pants school and to Cambrian where we raved boringly on with, remember this and that! At 123 Primrose St, the good, which were really the bad, old days when his Mam struggled to help everyone out.

Dad and I looked forward to going to and having a look at 49 King St, each with our private thoughts but also to show Heather and Rhondda where so much happened, and where we lived.

Pontypridd seemed so close now and a sort of memory road, the railway station, all the long walks, the hill I rode down standing on the pedal of the big bike escaping from the lady with evil or whatever intent for the innocent boy!

There was the Treforest High School, shades of old Craddock Evans and the soccer field Dad organised and helped move a million tons of soil, everyone on the dole or relief at the time. I tried to pin down Dad about when our Myrna was born, about 35-36? He was no help, he had a forgettery or it was just a blank.

Nearing King St, and driving the girls mad with endless reminiscences, we were quiet, as we stopped outside our old No.49. Dad and I got out together and I knocked on the door, waited, so disappointing no one answered. Being lost as to what to do next and looking up the eerily empty street, we saw this lady coming down with her string bag of groceries.

"That's Gwen." Dad said.

She was putting the key in the door as we approached. She was my cousin. We had been kids together but it was 35 years since we last waved at each other.

She turned at the sound of our footsteps, a micro pause and without hesitation, "Hello Will" and looking me in the eye quietly said, "Hello Derrick." It was as if we had just been to Barry or somewhere for the day.

Then inside, she went to pieces as she realised we had really come to see her, all the excitement meeting my wife and daughter, we needed that cup of tea as we had so many times before. We had to go over our life and times, so very much in a short time. The others had to look at that old room, all the things they had heard and read about. The fireplace and Uncle Davy's chair, my pigeon coop out the back where I had kept my loot and savings, safe from Mum.

Sadly, it was still cold and damp, as was the Loo 'out er back' and I think I saw my old friend, a cockroach or Black Pat.

The grocery shop was gone and across the way, the Chapel looked small, neglected and insignificant. So sad, that those days of singing and services were long gone, and forever it seemed. They, with times of poverty and want, had together slipped away.

As we got into the car, having said goodbye, a rather sad and final goodbye, I thought how wonderful to have got back to see it all but, thank God again for having the pluck or enterprise to get away.

On the way back to London, Dad brought up the 'Nits', how on the return from his travels, he had his fine toothcomb. I'd told the kids about it and now Dad said we all, everyone had nits and he blamed his Connie for not caring for his children. What a strange idea, with him away half the time. There were no nits at the cottage homes, not much hair either with the treatment we got and the Lysol used.

Back at 'Shepherds Bush', we left Dad to recover from all the excitement. I used to slip him ten pounds to keep him in cigarettes, chocolates and biscuits, we tried to pay for everything as his pension was small and didn't go far. We know he was an inveterate punter and gambler but only for small money, a few bob each way and not like Doug or Bugs in their hey-day betting in the hundreds.

He and I enjoyed having a bet together, for him it was a perfect and unexpected father and son thing. I really went up in his estimation when I picked first, second and third in the Grand National, the hardest race in the world to pick a winner and to think I only went along with him and had a measly four bob each way.

Quite casually I mentioned my four years as a bookmaker's clerk, never missing a race meeting in that time. He thought that was great too.

Green stamps were his big thing, pasting them into book after book, so we got them for everything, petrol, trips, major purchases and all. He filled so many that he got a stack of stuff for the house, the garden and for rubbish to sit around on shelves.

While there, we had four trips to the continent, each trip of about fifteen days, he enjoyed the goodies we brought back and in a way shared by our stories, the people we met and the places we had been. He was also having apoplexy over the money we were spending, how could we afford it all.

We told him we had sold our house in Sydney. "What will you do when you get back?" he asked and we had to explain we had bought a block of land before we left and on our return would build on it, better than the last. Such a thing was too much to comprehend for the old stick in the mud but it dawned on him that I really was a plumber and builder, my own business too, and quite unheard of in his comprehension.

His house was tidy but his garden even better with lots of vegies and incredible roses, being on the second floor of the four, the one just up a few stairs and at floor level, he was the only one with a garden. In the season he still went to the scrub to pick blackberries to make into pies and cordials for himself and the kids, blackberry drink too as you might imagine.

Always a smoker and by then it was 40 a day and it finally killed him, though it took till he was almost eighty. In a way we understood the need for a fag as company in difficult times such as in the dilemma or guilt of family.

In the last few entries of his diary he said he had a good innings, born at the turn of the century and almost eighty, he said he was happy and content knowing that after all, as it had turned out, his whole family loved him, all was well. He died with his dark friends and coffee-coloured kids around him. Sadly, everybody else thought everyone else had notified us in Australia and it was month later I got the tidings, too late to attend to his affairs.

Towards the end he also found forgiveness for his Connie, 'The wife'. At one stage he even said, "She was a good wife and mother." This was before November 1979 when he found peace.

I think I've mentioned that Mum passed away about then too, she also saying she always loved him. The great coincidence was of Will and Connie being married in a St Thomas' in Yorkshire and being now in a St Thomas' at Enfield. The brass plaque states that 'Constance Mary and William Richard lie here together'.

I felt gratified if that's the right word, that for better or for worse, like it or not, they were at a final peace. I must admit I cried for ages before being able to drive the ute home the day I set the plaque.

56

* The Family Reunion *

Back in Sydney to pick up the threads and get back into harness, we built the Spanish house like one of the many Heather told Evan Spain was full of. From there we did the 1974 first round Australia trip, we went through a couple more houses and made money before buying our 100 year old farm house in Victoria Rd, West Pennant Hills. It was a run down disaster but we restored it with new corrugated iron roof, wide verandahs and bull nosed iron over them all, privet hedge all round and I planted a peppercorn tree from down on the Murray.

There was lots of room for visitors and for caravans to park, unknowingly then, it was all to be put to good use as a headquarters sooner than we thought.

In L.A. things were slowly hastening along, Douglas had written quite urgently inquiring about Mum's health, he actually always referred to her as, "Mother". He told us (!) that mother was not well and would not be with us very much longer. It was quite uncanny, as she was actually getting a little low and not her usual self but nothing, we thought, to worry about.

It had taken all this time to resolve and sort out the citizenship status, it had become so involved, as you can imagine, now knowing what we do. The F.B.I. had become involved and it now only required their final report, so necessary in this case and all seemed OK.

Even with his premonition and funny 'Fey' feelings, he was most strongly advised not to leave the country at any cost without his clearance.

By now you can see how strong willed and pig headed he was, perhaps he knew more than we did and he insisted he was coming, "Right now." Most adamantly he said he would not see his mother if he put it off.

Heather and I were worried enough to visit the U.S. Embassy where we told them the circumstances and gory details. We were advised that entry would be permitted but, without the re-entry visa and full passport, Waldo, Douglas or whoever? would be sent straight back to England.

Our urgent advice was in vain because the next letter from our brother included the flight times and E.T.A. for Doug, Beverly and daughter Laurie.

Panic is not the word and the excitement was electric, we had to ring Yvonne and John in Perth for them to get their act together. Being retired, they were able to come right away and be in time to meet the plane from the States with us all. Myrna, somewhere over there, was found in Spain and on her arrival back at Heathrow, in something of a confusion, had to re-organise a quick flight and she too was here in time for the welcome. She was to be the biggest surprise as we hadn't, with so little time, told Doug and to think they had never met, hardly a photo or letter, if any to know each other.

The crowd outside the overseas terminal was as if a star or royalty was arriving. Besides Heather, I and family, Doreen and hers, Bugsy and his, Yvonne and John, and little Myrna, all there.
You have to bear in mind the moment, it was more than just a meeting. Doreen was only four when last she saw her big brother. Yvonne and Bernard had not seen Myrna since 1937-8 and most amazing, Douglas had never met Yvonne, Bernard or Myrna. It had taken so many unbelievable years to reach this incredible time of being together, in this fairytale situation, all Dad's six children to our mother were there as one.
The actual meeting when they got through customs is impossible to describe, Heather saw and picked them out first and pointed them out, introductions all round were made with extreme difficulty midst the ocean of tears and back breaking hugging and kissing.

Mum unfortunately was not too well by now so we sent the others off home and only the immediate family set off for North Sydney to Shore, where Joan and Mum shared their school supplied flat. There again it was hugs and tears as I watched Doug and his Mum unable to let each other go. At the airport Doug and Myrna had been quite overcome and now, for Myrna there was the meeting with her Mum after all that had transpired. I don't think with all that went on, Mum took it in that it was her baby girl Myrna. She referred to her as, 'That little girl from Dorset' and I felt so badly for her but Myrna, the whole time, was kind and understanding about it all.
Soon, seeing the emotional scene getting out of hand, I got them together and promising to be back soon, got them off to West Penno to get settled in.
It was to be nine weeks there for everyone except for Myrna who after five weeks had to get back to her lot. It was a trying, happy but demanding time for Heather and I before the long party broke up.

My business never got over it as I only worked two days in the nine weeks and I don't know how Heather lasted the distance feeding and caring for so many for so long.

During the non-stop visits and sight seeing we all had time to get to know each other, each brother and sister going over life's events and filling in gaps or in a way, making up for lost time. Doug and Bugsy, quite uncannily, danced 'The Bugsy', as only Bugs had done before. Evan was amazed that Uncle Doug told jokes that only he could tell and Yvonne and Myrna with the same blonde hair, like peas in a pod, had time to bond as they say nowadays.

To show the visitors a little bit of Australia, ten of us set off in two cars, we motelled at Port Macquarie where it was so good they wanted to stay, then Coffs Harbour likewise, and in fact all the fabulous east coast which they thought was just magic. At Surfers Paradise, a complete revelation, we saw the transformation of a well-dressed Yank to an Aussie Yobbo. Doug had gone off on his own and we all looked up from eating icecreams in Cavel Ave. to see this white-skinned, rabbit-like figure in stubbies and thongs coming towards us, icecream in hand and saying an Americanised "G'Day" to everyone. It was one of those marvellous moments to cherish.

Just like the rest of the family who nearly made it to Australia, he said in some despair, "Why didn't I come here sooner! This is just God's own country." He had shown us the Hoover Dam over there, how big it was etc and Heather, ever the proud and pushy Aussie, told him about our Harbour. Going across on the Manly ferry one day, with the Bridge and the Opera House mothering the craft all around, he said, "This really is the most beautiful harbour in the world." We all knew that.

Everyone loved the trip out to Toowoomba then down to Goondiwindi. I insisted we call at Moree for the hot spa baths, no one was interested till they got in and then I couldn't get them away. The dusty track through emu, rabbit and roo scrub country to Lightening Ridge was a world of wonder that, with the characters of the bush and opal fields, they all never dreamt existed.

We tried to do it all so on the way back we called at Bellata, Phil and Julie Lammie country, where we packed into utes and went for a pig shoot. With it and the rest of it, Doug was in seventh heaven. That night we had a party at the Lammie's where all the town folk turned up. Bellatta! Population? About thirty I think.

Evan, ever the devious one and Robyn too, were somehow there, a phone call home the day before I think it was and it was only six fast hours from Sydney if in a hurry.

It was voted the best party for years with true country hospitality, we told jokes for five hours till no one could speak from laughing. We stayed at the pub, no one else but we ten, as it was seldom that they had a guest. Mine host just left us to it, help yourselves, and that meant brekky too.

Those ten days were the greatest success, for by the end all the past with its good or bad, ups and downs, were happily resolved. The trip itself was so good, it was suggested Heather as the complete conductor, should start guided tours. Over the years we did something like that because with the influx of relations and visitors, that was the sort of thing they seemed to want.

Getting back home it was time to inquire about the F.B.I.'s progress. It had been arranged to be sent to Sydney as it was supposedly almost completed.

The day of departure was getting close and things seemed ominous and a little desperate. Laurie, a little homesick, left for home and we called the Embassy day by day till Beverly said she would have to go and leave Doug sit and wait. On top of all the excitement of the past weeks, the thought of him not getting back, or worse still, being p----d off to bloody England was getting to us all.

There was a call to the Embassy and such relief, citizenship granted, the stipulation being that he stayed in the States for two years. It was over and he was home free.

Enough said about the farewell, it was quiet and sad not knowing when we would meet again but the last weeks could not be taken away.

Our psychic brother was right again and must have known something to have treated the visit with such urgency. Our Mum's health deteriorated rapidly and she passed away soon after, such a chain of events, such a life! She died content, having seen the family together as never before dreamed of as remotely possible.

There was no happy ending for Doug and Beverly as we now know.

57

* Settled in Australia *

In Australia, Heather and I seemed to have become something like the heads of the large and ever growing family. Patriarch! Uncle Dai in Dorset had told me he was then the Rees Patriarch. Who would have thought that the shitty pants boy from Cambrian Terrace in Llwynapia would now take that title. Heather, of course was the one to always look after us, come up with ideas and keep us all together. In Tonypandy I was given the Welsh family Bible, photographs and family history, my lovely Aunty Beryl gave me the painting of Mam Rees and it now hangs in Evans house. Only in 1972 did Beryl find out how I had written to Mr Llewellyn to find out about the English lady's scheme on migration.

When I said to Heather at the dance at Katoomba, "May I have this jazz waltz," little did we dream of all the events to come in the 50+ years together as of this date.

It is worth while and should be mentioned that George Gwynne, Heather's Dad, was one of eleven children born to Evan Gwynne of Gawler, South Australia. Evan Gwynne was one of seven born to Robert Gwynne. Evan died age 76, he was a blacksmith by trade but became a nurseryman and florist. The 'Bunyip', a Gawler newspaper, 3-5-1935, paid tribute to him as the 'Father of Willaston'. A plaque to his father Robert reads, 'Robert Gwynne, 1822-1868, arrived in South Australia on the 'Ramillies' in 1853.'

He too was a farmer and another of those Welshmen who had to migrate to get away from the coalfields of the Rhondda.

By now, having almost completed my ramblings and what I had to say, Heather, being around to check and advise, tells me I haven't said anything about the grandchildren. It was deliberate, why impose all this on them, 'my epic' as Alan laughingly calls it and it is mainly for them to read in the future. It could be so embarrassing and I can see Rhian even now, saying, "Oh, Taff!"

The 1993 trip when about 90 old Northcotians and some others went back to their roots in Great Britain en masse, all together on one plane. It was an occasion of joy, tears, reunions, renewed heartbreak, and everything 55 years away could create. We all had a civic reception at Australia House attended by the Lord Mayor and more Lords and Ladies than you could poke a stick at. Quite a few Fairbridge representatives toasted us as the success story we now believed we were. They presented each one with a beautiful pair of Scottish crystal tumblers with our name engraved on each.

It's too much to go into here but our visit coincided with the series, 'The Leaving of Liverpool', all that 'stolen children' media madness. Coincidently, our busload of former kids, a couple actually from Liverpool were in town the night it was broadcast. Don Coleshill, Bugsy and I had eight minutes on the B.B.C. prime time radio before sneaking out in our bus to avoid the media madness when it found we had been in town, in person.

Don, on that trip, met a brother and sister he never knew he had, [Others were to come later as well] and all through the good work of Margaret Humphries of the Child Migrants Trust. Margaret was to write her, 'Empty Cradles' about Britons most shameful secret, as she calls it, and though not fully and deservedly recognised for her work in Britain, in Australia there was a more than well deserved award in the Honours list.

It was on that visit we met our sister Pat and family, and our brother Lloyd and family, for the first time ever. In addition we got to know every relation scattered far and wide but as you know, we left David alone.

A marvellous time, a time that we all put ghosts to rest on the visit to the homes at Church Village. There was myself, Doreen, Yvonne, Bernard and Heather, cousin Angie too.

My cousin, living in Tonteg, gave my niece the book Rhondda Boy to take for Mrs Tomlinson to read as she was researching the old homes and their history. [Long gone by then] In the book was so much she wished to know.

Quite briefly, she wrote before we left to ask us to call and see her, so we did, to a reception by the whole school as if we were royalty. The school choir were gathered in assembly to sing for us as only a Welsh choir can and we sat on little kindy chairs, in the school, in the homes, the once horrid homes you now know all about, and cried. It was actually a most wondrous visit and all was put right.

We were to be inundated with visits over the years, Mick and Angie, Julie and Richard, Russell and Sandy, he is Betty's boy. They were here this year and last year too and perhaps best of all Lloyd and Carol with the three children finally made it too. On the recent '98 visit we stayed with sister Pat, she and I had time to really do our bonding. That's my last trip and I don't think she will ever visit. Auntie Elsie you have heard about. We have been over four times, even last year we went to L.A. again to see Doug's girls, meet their men and the children. What a lovely visit that was and after a few days with each of the others in England and Wales, we did the only bit we hadn't done and had a holiday round the entire coast of Scotland.

Just a little sidelight was at the meeting of Nathan Rees, Doug's grandchild and that may come as a total surprise to everyone. We met Doug's three girls on our recent visit to L.A. We also had the wonderful pleasure of seeing all his grandchildren. Nathan being the eldest, the first and by the letters we received, the one he loved and had time to get to know. There were difficult early years of the lad not knowing who he was and it was with inexpressible feelings we found on our visit that he had, of his own free will, changed his name to Rees.

Many of the grandchildren, Yvonne's, Doreen's, Bugsy's and mine have travelled to visit the relatives, as has Rhondda and Alan, so I really started something writing away to 'The People' as I did.

There was, of course, our 50th wedding anniversary where Ben acted as our M.C. In return, and soon after, I was able to be M.C. for Emma and Ben at the event of the era, their wedding.

My beautiful Copacabana on the Central Coast of N.S.W.

58

* Copacabana *

Not the South American one, but the one on the beautiful Central Coast of New South Wales.

Our Central Coast is really the flavour of the decade, as is the city of Gosford with its modern amenities and centres set in an abundance of parks and reserves and with beaches to equal that other Paradise place. The waterways are magnificent and as a fisherman I vouch for them as real beaut.

With the new freeway eliminating that old horror, the winding Mooney Mooney section of the Pacific Highway, the coast here is only an hour away from Pennant Hills and Beecroft where Evan and family still live. It's great to visit Sydney [The big smoke] and be home in just over an hour to the greatest spot to retire to and where everything is beautiful.

It has taken me six busy years of retirement after 53 years of hard work, to learn to relax and enjoy the scene from the top deck of the Pole House Heather and I built. We did it all in just five months, every single thing except the electrical wiring, so it's all our own work.

The reason I'm sitting here is my need to write. It is difficult as I watch the blue Pacific Ocean breaking over the headland of Copacabana to the north and Macmasters to the south. From here I can see the top of the monument to Captain Cook. The brass plaque shows the navigational lines of his journey and tells how 200 years ago he passed, paused and said, "I'll call this place, 'Cape Three Points'." Just over 200 years ago and I've been in this country over a quarter of that time.

It is all so different now looking out at a surfeit of surfies on their boards waiting to catch one of a perfect set of the waves Copa 'Point' is famous for. When we have a Southerly Buster and the breakers are monstrous, the world champion wind-surfer, who is a local boy, comes and trains. Words cannot describe his magic in those conditions.

There are dolphins or porpoises all along this coast but not as close as they come to play here as they share the fun of catching a wave with the locals. From here we can watch the classic yacht races such as the Sydney to Mooloolaba each year. The best I can recall was the day the

Southerly blew up. It was a bright sunny day to make it even more perfect and nearly all the fleet, about seventy to our count, were spread between Mac's and Copa's headlands. They were scattered and all going flat chat, every spinnaker was out straining at the rigging, the colour were just magnificent and the overall scene beyond description.
All this and at my front door, so to speak.

That's not all, for we had a birthday party on the 21st July and the first guests arrived to witness the sighting of whales just there offshore. Those who later arrived were sad to have missed them but after lunch the next Pod arrived and it was just magic, as if on cue. We saw many that year but the best was yet to come as we watched the lone whale come into the safe waters off Tudibaring Point and I went for my glasses. There was a dark shape, seemingly attached and about six or eight feet long. With the glasses it turned out to be a mother and calf. It was a treat and so beautiful to see the calf playing around like any child with its mother.
Albert the newsagent rang the local radio station and the mother kindly stayed around while the helicopter took video for the news that night before she flipped her last goodbye and headed north.

After we came to Australia, Dad lived in Shepherds Bush and there he met and married Olive Davies. They had a boy and a girl, our new, unknown brother and sister. We had tried to find out about them from second hand information. Pat had heard a little about us but Lloyd was almost thirty before he discovered he may have a large family somewhere. Neither of them knew or had a clue where to start to look and it was a stalemate but I was so happy to find they wished to find out about us.
Everything started to fall into place when Dad's diaries, thought to be lost, came to light. Peter, my cousin, had cared for them and probably read them. He would have been in a quandary with what to do with them. When I finally received them so much fell into place and I felt I had to write another draft of the story. Then brother Bugsy's daughters, Donna and Sue, while in Britain, armed with some information went to Swansea and made enquiries. With perseverance an address was found and a telephone number. Everything matched. It really was Lloyd Rees. There was a sister Pat, the mother was Olive Davies and the father had lived in London. We could now contact them being almost certain our enquiries wouldn't hurt anyone.
We have since corresponded and exchanged a few photos and Lloyd and I have spoken on the phone.

Both Lloyd and Pat are happily married with lovely families. Both are teachers and doing well. It now just remains for us to fill in the gaps for them to learn about us, the new found family.

By now I'm 75 and stopped counting, having built our Copacabana beach house to fish and swim and to entertain the procession of visitors and family. I have had time to write. There is a book, "Taff's Tales and Trivia" plus several volumes of short stories, anecdotes and humour, many as an extension of times and events stemming from Rhondda Boy. Someday I may publish them as a bit of a laugh or perhaps to remind the kids of bygone times.

That's about it except for an update on the kids.

Evan is now a master everything, a coxswain and ships master to boot. Robyn, the one to thank for what she is and what she does.

Rhondda is a dynamo, Rees like loud and bossy but also a star on the Bathurst stage.
 Alan; What can a father in law say about his best mate?

Adam is a workaholic, Evan says he still has his first dollar. I thought he took on shoplifting, but it turned out to be, shopfitting. He and our Angela, [Not cousin Angie] are a steady item with house, a dog and a rabbit but no grandkids in sight there!

Sebastian is the success I had predicted, at work, at play and with the gorgeous birds he brings home all the time.

Benjamin, little Ben goes from good to better and then some. What a joy after a long school romance which they said wouldn't last, to marry our lovely Emma. Her family and ours in a wedding so great for others but to a couple of oldies it was heaven. For family continuity, for me 'The Patriarch', it was another Mrs Rees.

Nathan is still on a learning curve, still mad on sport but also able to manage the family business at Bathurst where Rhondda is king and Alan gets on with his rugby.

Rhian, other than attending Bachelor and Spinster balls all over N.S.W is in her second year of nursing. She can do no wrong as she is my little Welsh Princess. Actually in Welsh, Rhian or Rhianon is 'Witch.' As such, she will do many magic things.

And to finish, Rikki, the tall, beautiful, inches taller than me blonde is in second year at Uni doing some fancy new name degree and that's it.

59

* Farewell and Thank-you *

So at long last it's back to where I left off. In closing I would like to refer to an article used by Lynne Clough in a copy of the 'Old Northcotian'. I should explain that Lynne and Ken came to visit Northcote in the early days, they fell in love with the whole concept even to adopting one of the lucky boys.

Northcote was formed on the lines of Fairbridge. It was Kingsley Fairbridge who started the homes in Pinjara, Western Australia and then at Molong, out of Orange. Kingsley Fairbridge was the most dedicated man with that splendid vision.

He wrote these words and I believe they bear thinking about.

> **Some men, they say**
> **strew rags about the shrine**
> **where at they pray,**
> **Having nought else to give.**
> **Thus, all of mine-**
> **Each hope wherein I live**
> **I bring at last to you**
> **Dear, on my knees**
>   **I bring another failure;**
>   **In your hands**
>   **I lay this gift.**
> K.F. 14th April 1910.

Northcote School Prayer

O God, who by the inspiration of Thy Servant, Lady Northcote, hast so wonderfully made this school, and has set us here to learn and to do Thy will, teach us to live together in love, joy and peace, to check all bitterness, to disown discouragement, to practise thanksgiving, and to leap with joy to any task for others. Strengthen the good thing thus begun, that with gallant and high-hearted happiness we may strive to build according to Thy will. Direct the paths of those who have gone forth from this place. Inspire the hearts and minds of those in authority, and fill us all with love towards Thee. To Thy honour and glory, through Jesus Christ, Our Lord, Amen.

Finally to Miss Scholes, for her love and care. Most of all for her teachings, part of which was Rudyard Kipling's timeless, 'If'.

The Last verse;

> **If you can fill the unforgiven minute**
> **With sixty seconds worth of distance run**
> **Yours is the earth and everything that's in it**
> **And which is more, you'll be a man my son.**

End

Derrick (Taffy) Rees

BIBLEOGRAPH

Athelia, Aunt Mathews;
What relationship? Who was she? We all wonder but she was such an influence, good, bad or indifferent on all our lives.

Archibald Hood;
He of the big statue in Llwynapia and his row of terraces, especially our Cambrian with the toilet and tip up the back.

Alfie Philips;
Of the pig swill, of the cadged tickets to the Flicks and shared ice creams and sweets. I thought I never liked him but truly and really!! he was my friend.

Aunty Gwen;
Who was there, just simply always there to be taken advantage of when most needed. Was she glad to see us go?

Bernard Oswald;
The one who was almost adopted out, [Nurse Llewellin]. He of the, "Too long on the potty," our little brother and favourite of everyone.

'Boyo';
He of the back lane stick or wood run production.

Craddock Evans, *!=#|\/&*;
So much I could say but to quote a crude quotation and simply put it to him, "Get fluffed."

Cousin Gwen;
Of the train trip and picnic at Taffs Well, the one I loved for unwittingly sharing her joy of first discovery with me.

Doreen Constance;
My sister of the long pram trip and all the others we shared then, and in the years ahead.

David;
This one is hush, hush, Doug did ask about him but for reasons untold here, it's never to be brought up.

Dai, [David],
With Arthur, Stan, Doris, Betty and Lal, brothers and sisters of our Dad.

Douglas William;
My brother, [For such a short time], the pal we reluctantly left behind with our notorious and overpowering Aunt.

Dr Buck Ruxton;
He murdered his wife, then the maid and gave us all something to talk and sing about.

Betty, Elizabeth?
The sister we left in Yorkshire, we never knew her as Elizabeth till Doug called her that.

Evans the Shoe;
I think he was in shoes but it's he of that Xmas party and that cricket bat, non present time.

Evans the Sweeper;
Of the marbles collected from the drains and of the kind word and cheeriness to every man and boy.

Edward, Prince of Wales;
Teddy, Our 'lost to Mrs Simpson Prince', the sad looking almost King of Wales. England too I suppose.

Guy Faulkes;
Made of straw and raggedy old clothes and ready to go up in spectacular flames with big bangs on Nov 5th.

'God.'
Of the many expressions, "God knows who, why or when". Never really taking his name in vain but with due Chapel reverence.

Mrs Cadbury;
We drank her Bourneville cocoa on so many cold nights in so many places and then not knowing she was a benefactor, ate the chocolates she brought to Middlemore and had in abundance for us at her home near by.

Mr Paul Cadbury;
Another unpraised and unsung benefactor.

Middlemore, John;
He really set it all off in 1872 when he took in the first of the 8,000 children to pass through the homes in the 100 years ahead. None will forget Middlemore.

Mr Price;
Old Pricy of next door in King St and my two sisters very dear friend.

Malcolm, long for Mal;
He of the Dad in full work and the giving out of regular pocket money for sweets and stuff to share with his friend! "Me."

Mrs Simpson;
She who stole our Prince.

Nurses;
My two Florence Nightingales, the two loves and highlights of my life at times of the need for a little love and attention.

Nurse or Sister Llewellin;
She who wished to take away our Bernard.

Hubert Harding and Rex Chamberlain;
Two bits of Wales to leave with and then share a life in Australia with.

Sparrow, Raymond;
A real Rhondda Boy, lost to me and taken by the mine.

St David, Dewi Sant;
The only real Welsh Saint.

Tosser Evans.
Come, come, that's enough of that back lane talk.

Her, *-@&=1\, *?!
That cottage mother at the Cottage homes, the dislike of her from all the boys is the closest thing to hatred.

Ilene;
A sister but we know her just as a name.

Jenkins the shop;
My boss, the flirt with all the ladies, expert butter and sugar packer upper and a time for me of experience and fun.

Lady Alice Northcote;
She with the similar to Kingsley Fairbridge vision, she who left her residual estate so that kids such as I could go out for a new start in life. "God Bless."

Llewellin the Chemist;
He, the father of the son who played Rugby for Wales, this simple fact saved his shop from any damage in the riots of 1910-11. The only shop in the town untouched!!

Mr Llewellin;
No relation to the other Llewellins. This is the one who mercifully answered that letter I wrote and who ultimately put us on the train to catch a boat to get to Bacchus Marsh.

Myrna Loy;
A pretty name of the star of Dad's fancy but the unlucky sister left behind to slip away,--- lost for so many years.

Mam Rees;
A Saint and Matriarch out of necessity, dearly loved by all who came within her orbit.

Her Will, William Richard;
Our Dadchi, grandfather of the front parlour or bedroom, his sickroom for all those years.

Uncle Joe;
He of the stick run, even as I was for a while. I'm glad he and our Beryl got together.

Uncle Davy Jones;
Of the permanent pipe and the paper quills to light it while living in the land of the big 'Black Pats'.

William Richard;
Our Dad on occasions. One of Mam Rees' who left the Valley, as did so many countless thousands. He is an enigma of our time is our Dad. A bit of a mystery I mean.

Watkins the Flannel;
For all your clothing requirements in Tonypandy. No ???% off or any of those endless modern-day sales.

Yvonne Arnold;
Our sister of the Scarlet fever and the dog scalping times but she of the happy, happy nature.

Northcote Children's Farm,
"Glenmore," Bacchus Marsh, Victoria.

Report for the half-year ended 30th June 1939 on Derrick Rees
of the   'Largs Bay' party April   1938'

Full name; Derrick Richard Rees.
Date of birth; 21-7-24.   Date of leaving England; 9-4-38.
Date of arriving in Australia; 17-5-38.

Health Report.
A very strong boy.   No medical attention.

Cottage Mothers report.
One of the best boys in the cottage, as far as conduct and aptitude
generally are concerned. Is always cheerful and ready to help. Takes little
interest in indoor games but likes reading. Inclined to be forgetful, and
at times careless but never shows resentment when spoken to. He is a
good worker and a very likeable boy.

School report.   Nil Two weeks only.

Farm Managers report.
This is a particularly bright and willing lad, fond of work. Without doubt
this chap will be a big success. His make up is a decided advantage for
the avenues of occupation that he could be trained for.

Principals Report.
A splendid boy in every way. Enjoys every moment of his life at
Glenmore--- he is popular with all--- a fine product of the old country, a
promising young citizen. A good pal to his brother and sisters.

That is a sample of the half-yearly reports on all the children and which
we all received on request. Typing out the copy and reading it, perhaps
the first time I've really read it, I feel,-----?--------and perhaps should let
it go at that though in the report, Colonel Heath's words were so very
kind to me.